CULTURES MERGING

THE PRINCETON ECONOMIC HISTORY

OF THE WESTERN WORLD

Joel Mokyr, editor

CULTURES MERGING

A HISTORICAL AND ECONOMIC CRITIQUE OF CULTURE

ERIC L. JONES

PRINCETON UNIVERSITY PRESS
OCM 62118245
PRINCETON AND OXFORD

Published by Princeton University Press, 41 William Street,
Princeton, New Jersey 08540
In the United Kingdom: Princeton University Press,
3 Market Place, Woodstock, Oxfordshire OX20 1SY

Library of Congress Cataloging-in-Publication Data

Jones, Eric L.

Cultures merging : a historical and economic critique of culture / Eric L. Jones.

p. cm. — (Princeton economic history of the Western world)

Includes bibliographical references and index.

ISBN-13: 978-0-691-11737-9 (hardcover : alk. paper)

ISBN-10: 0-691-11737-3 (hardcover : alk. paper)

1. Economics—Sociological aspects.   2. Culture—Economic aspects.

3. Social change—Economic aspects.   I. Title.   II. Series.

HM548.J66 2006

306.301—dc22

2005029493

British Library Cataloging-in-Publication Data is available

This book has been composed in Goudy and Blearex

Printed on acid-free paper. ∞

pup.princeton.edu

Printed in the United States of America

10 9 8 7 6 5 4 3 2 1

Contents

Preface

As early as 1879 Frederick Amasa Walker, first president of the American Economic Association, asked why economics was "in bad odor among real people."[1] He answered his own question by saying that economists found their predictions became inconclusive if they took account of every particular law, custom, or institution. But "real people" still insisted that their own eyes showed them how customs and beliefs led to behavior that market rationality did not predict. A century later, anthropologist Clifford Geertz declared that culture is "as observable as agriculture."[2] It is observable, no doubt, but what effect does it have? There is a real need to establish the origin, nature, and limits of culture's influence.

References to cultural phenomena are so matter-of-fact and culture is taken as so obviously fundamental to social life that this alone would seem to ensure its relevance.

[1] Quoted in Robert H. Frank, *Passions within Reasons: The Strategic Role of the Emotions* (New York: W. W. Norton, 1988), p. 227.
[2] Clifford Geertz, *The Interpretation of Culture* (New York: Basic Books, 1973), p. 91.

The importance of cultures is plain to the eyes of ordinary people, and cultural explanation is congenial to noneconomists, including historians and other social scientists. Yet most economists seem not to be of this mind. The professions differ over whether cultures are so basic and stable that they decide how production and consumption take place or whether the imperatives of the market ultimately determine cultural life. How far or in what sense may it be true that culture underpins world history and the global economy? Are differences among cultures unbridgeable in principle? And to what extent is culture used as an excuse for protectionism in the modern world?

The current literature is seldom directly helpful in addressing the conceptual questions, although I do draw attention in the first chapter to a promising handful of recent works. More often writers declare or merely imply their own position without engaging one another outright; few step forward toward the ranks of the opposing army. In assessing cultures it helps to take a historical view, which is what I shall do here. This exposes the shallowness of the convention which assumes that, simply because at any one time we can observe them in full blossom, cultures are tangible and lasting phenomena.

Must we therefore swing to the opposite extreme and think that culture is so labile that it has little significance in itself? This alternative is also unconvincing. Although economic interpretations that make culture depend on current incentives are more satisfactory than the fixity view, we cannot suppose that culture is no more than a mask for materialism. For economists to assume culture away is to abandon the topic before fully investigating the possibilities. As I say later in this book, while culture makes only a ghostly transit through history and has far less independent effect than many noneconomists propose, it does in some measure color behavior, sway choices, and influence decisions.

Culture is like class: it has no generally accepted, operational definition. Insofar as the many literatures that allude to it do offer a common meaning, culture is the pattern of beliefs, habits, and expectations, of values, ideals, and preferences, shared by groups of people, large and small. In this respect we can speak, however, only of central tendencies; even at a single moment behavior may vary widely about the mean of any group. Habits and values are always changing incrementally, yet they may sometimes alter kaleidoscopically. Cultural characteristics are learned at one's mother's knee, or they are more or less unconscious imitations of family norms, or they are instilled by the surrounding society. Early influences are vital. By and large, later influences have less effect and may even be resisted or rejected. In other words not every shift in relative prices elicits the fluent response that economists are trained to expect. "By and large" says it all—there are no hard and fast rules.

Unless we are totally convinced by a definition, we should not let ourselves be bound by it. There is little point to inserting a break in a continuum if none is present. Culture is in any case an unstable amalgam. Most of the proposed rules about it are vague enough for even academic treatments to slither among the criteria. If, however, we do not permit ourselves some latitude, it will not be easy to extract insights, or at any rate gain sidelights, from works that approach culture from so many angles. Culture, custom, and civilization are often used almost, although not quite, interchangeably, and it would be a shame not to be able to mention each of them in its place. There are thus constructive as well as evasive reasons for a degree of looseness in definition.

Some of the inconclusiveness about culture stems from lumping it with institutions. I am inclined to separate out organizations and formal types of institution from culture, because they derive from conscious political choice and have routine methods of operating, while culture consists of unconsciously assimilated beliefs with consequences that are more dimly perceived. This is a tricky area; no doubt there was originally an element of power relations in the formation of many social patterns, however obscure those origins may now appear. Each culture may be disposed to create institutions of a particular character; in other words, part of the causation may flow from some mistily encompassing cultural feature to the prevailing set of institutions, which as a result stays congruent with the community's values. This possibility is sometimes introduced in an attempt to rescue cultural arguments, especially by attributing the formative role in the rise of the West to Christianity in general. Yet Christian societies whiled away innumerable centuries without achieving consistent economic growth. More plausible arguments along this particular line refer to innovations in church policy and institutions during the Middle Ages. They rely on the effects of historically specific synergies of culture and institutions rather than a pure, unaided cultural impress.

Despite the doubtful role of religion in the rise of the West, debate continues. For example, in *Understanding the Process of Economic Change*,[3] Douglass North attributes di-

---

[3] Douglass C. North, *Understanding the Process of Economic Change* (Princeton: Princeton University Press, 2005).

vergent economic and political performance to different sets of institutions, correctly in my view, and asserts that the intentions of the actors are crucial to institution building and hence to economic change. It is human intention, he says, more than genetic inheritance that accounts for cultural variation and, one might say, a fortiori for variation in institutions. His emphasis on intentionality also leads him to dismiss as false the superficial analogy between biology and culture, between genes and so-called memes.

But North continues to reserve a role for culture. He implies that culture and religion distort the rational maximizing behavior on which most reasoning in economics depends. He cites research by anthropologists on small groups to the effect that notions of self-interested maximizing actors were violated *in all societies studied*.[4] This surely means that deeper human propensities than culture drive behavior (nor does the finding as reported seem to invalidate the possibility that maximizing behavior may still explain more behavioral variance than any other single factor). Pure culture, despite his claim that it is "central" to economic performance, does not emerge from this discussion as particularly influential. It remains a live possibility, nevertheless, that particular mixtures of myths, superstitions, and religions did give rise to different institutions for establishing order and conformity, thereby imposing different levels of transaction cost on different societies. This is consonant with my own willingness, noted above, to accept that cultural features, in a very broad sense, may underpin economic organization. But, as North himself notes, the topic remains a frontier for future research.

[4] Ibid., p. 46.

Dogmatic assertions that every culture is unique and can be studied only in a self-referring way have hitherto been de rigueur among students of this field. For instance, it has been the view of French and American sociologists that Indian society (or indeed the society of one's choice) is so special that it can be treated only in its own terms. Yet during the last decade or so, as is observed by Dipankar Gupta, a sociologist at Jawaharlal Nehru University in Delhi, Indian sociology has taken a more comparative and "less obscurantist" view.[5] As North's work demonstrates, economists and economic historians, after having long been put off by the prevailing relativism, are beginning to renew their interest in cultural explanation.

This may be the point at which to state that, notwithstanding the abstract musings above, it is none of my purpose to engage in academic combat with high-flown schools of thought, though the analysis of culture cannot easily be understood without some reference to existing strands of opinion. I have tried to write at the level of my MBA students, who usually bring much intelligence but little prior reading to subjects like this. Furthermore, when I refer to economists, other social scientists, and historians, I do not imply that every individual who might be included in these and other professional categories shares the views attributed to his or her profession. What is meant are the mainstream opinions of each profession as they appear in the writings I have examined. Those works can be sampled in the footnotes and bibliography. To make more individual attributions would be to turn the book into a literature review.

These points perhaps need to be labored because such

[5] Quoted in *Financial Times Magazine*, 8 Jan 2005.

strong opinions are held about aspects of cultural studies. There are too many ideology hunters in the social science and arts departments of universities nowadays, seeking to pigeonhole one another as political enemies. Coming to the subject from the less familiar disciplinary perspectives of economics and economic history, I have nothing much to add to their disputes, which seem to relate mainly to domestic doctrinal antagonisms in the United States. Nor, despite my location in a business school, have I much directly to say about attempts to introduce cultural issues into commercial studies. The works I have read along those lines seldom appear compelling. The characteristics of individual businesspeople, or of categories of people so finely tuned that we know almost nothing about them, seem to me more relevant to their economic performance than their national cultures or ethnicity, as is now starting to be recognized.[6]

The insistence that culture is fundamental continues to spill over into demands for the protection of languages and the arts, usually as represented in national cultures. In objecting to the idea that cultures are sacred as well as fixed, my views may seem radical. They are certainly not conservative. One of the tactics of protectionists and rent-seekers—and ideology hunters—is to label market liberal positions as conservative, which is quite wrong. It is protectionism that is conservative and hurts the poor. At any rate, I favor contestable markets, rather than subsidies and quotas, as the way to give people choice and inspire creativity.

[6] Sunkyu Jun and James W. Gentry, "An Exploratory Investigation of the Relative Importance of Cultural Similarity and Personal Fit in the Selection and Performance of Expatriates," *Journal of World Business* 40 (2005): 1–8.

Complacent people often state that their own culture is superior to all others: the "dogmatism of the untravelled," Bertrand Russell called it. Anti-Americanism is a special case of this, although Americans are prone to a similar chauvinism in reverse. Americans "simply can't relate to other cultures. They have no sense that other kinds of experience are valuable or interesting" is the generalization made by Margaret Wertheim, an author who lives in Los Angeles, though since she is an Australian this rather takes the biscuit![7] Everywhere one goes one hears, "This is the best country in the world," from people who seldom have more than holiday experience, if that, of anywhere else. They cannot all be right. The hidden assumption is telling: that one can inhabit only a single culture.

The expression "roots and wings" denotes that it is perfectly possible to come from one place and remain attached to it for life, yet settle happily somewhere else. The principle is illustrated by a remark of Daraius Ardeshir, managing director of Nestlé India: "Indians are capable of living in several centuries at once. When I visit my father's home, I still kiss his feet."[8] An integrated world economy requires large-scale international labor mobility. Fortunately, modern technologies mean that going home is easier than ever before and keeping in touch, by telephone, e-mail, and even video, immensely easier. Watching home-country television by means of satellite is nowadays common, though whether this is desirable depends on circumstances.

Just as individuals cannot help but simultaneously occupy different social roles—in the family, in the workplace,

[7] *Daily Telegraph*, 16 Jun 2003.
[8] *Far Eastern Economic Review*, 31 Oct 1996.

in clubs and voluntary organizations—international labor mobility requires many workers to hold more than one passport or visa. Two percent of the world's population live outside the land of their birth, and there is a growing number of children of mixed marriages. These people operate in more than one culture, in most cases well enough.[9] There is scope for conflict, yet when individuals are unhappy it may be less through their own failings than because of the prejudices around them. It takes time for cultures to merge.

Acknowledgments

I have long toyed with the idea of writing a book on culture, something my former colleagues at the University of Reading, Mark Casson, Ken Dark, and Andrew Godley, encouraged by their own publications and by our conversations. Intensive talks, over many years in several countries, with Kate Burridge, Lou Cain, David Ch'ng, Murat Cizakca, Grace Davie, Kent Deng, Patrick Dillon, Colleen Downs, Mike Foss, John Frearson, John Gatt-Rutter, Joop Goudsblom, Ian Harper, David Henderson, Michael James, Kunio Katayama, Shaun Kenaelly, Marvin McInnis, Stephen Mennell, Frank Milne, Joel Mokyr, Jeremy Mulholland, Geoff Raby, Vernon Reynolds, David Robertson, Ekkehart Schlicht, Michael Tarrant, John Webb, Minoru Yasumoto, and the late Yasukichi Yasuba have also been very stimulating. Visits to universities and research institutes in Europe (especially Germany), Canada, and Japan, together with the task of teaching students of many nationalities at Melbourne Business School (University of Melbourne), and the University of Reading,

[9] Alex Soojung-Kim Pang, "Mongrel Capitalism," *Atlantic Monthly*, Nov 2000, pp. 118–20.

sharpened my observation of cultural differences and how people interpret them. All the librarians in the McClennan Library at Melbourne Business School were invariably helpful. As to the assistance I have received from people other than those mentioned, the breadth of the topic and the fact that I have been dipping into it for years means that the list of incidental acknowledgments could be almost as long as the book itself. I am no less grateful to everyone involved, whether or not they are listed here or have even known they were helping.

My intention to write was turned into reality when Joel Mokyr invited me to contribute to the series he edits, The Princeton Economic History of the Western World. A request by Razeen Sally to contribute an article on culture to a special issue of *Economic Affairs* that he was editing led me to put pen to paper sooner than I might otherwise have done and resulted in an early version of the first chapter. Versions of chapter 5, "Institutions as Cryptogams," were presented as papers at Queen's University, Ontario, University College, Dublin, and La Trobe University, Australia, in 2002–3. The bulk of the book was written at my new home in the English countryside, out of convenient reach of university libraries. This obliged me to be a *bricoleur*, using such materials as I had already collected. But a restricted palette was not a great disadvantage. I already had far too many notes, clippings, and reprints; the task lay in summarizing them within the intended word length.

During part of the period of research and writing I was fortunate enough to be appointed as a Distinguished Fellow in the Institute for Advanced Study at La Trobe University. The Borchardt Library at La Trobe was particularly useful for my purposes because, when I was employed by the university,

I had been responsible for ordering many of the relevant works— presciently, as it turned out. Thanks are due to Greg O'Brien, Gilah Leder, and Julia Anderson for making this visit possible and to my friend and former colleague John Anderson for his companionship and invariably astute comments. John commented on the draft, as did my son, Christopher, and my wife, Sylvia. The last-named contributed mightily at every stage; I could not have written the book without her skillful editorial help and business management.

PART I

CULTURAL ANALYSIS

Chapter 1

The Revival of Cultural Explanation

Economists agree about many things—contrary to popular opinion—but the majority agree about culture only in the sense that they no longer give it much thought. The hope that a strong relationship would be found between economic and cultural change mostly faded during the 1960s and 1970s. Those who still believe that culture is formative, whether they are "real people" or the culturally inclined minority of economists, take culture as primary and the economy as secondary, seldom considering that it could be culture which is secondary. On the other hand, the majority of economists, who are trained to expect substitution among variables, find the notion of culture as fixed for all time an arbitrary idea. They see no reason to believe that culture is primordial and impervious to economic inducements. After reviewing numerous propositions about the influence of values on Indian economic development, Dasgupta remarked that "no theorems follow from such intangible associations."[1]

Thus, no major schools of thought in recent years locate the explanation of economic development in culture, with a couple of exceptions. The first of these consists of some institutional economists, exemplified perhaps by Anne Mayhew's presidential address to the Annual Meeting of the Association for Evolutionary Economics in 1986. It was called "Culture: Core Concept under Attack" and opened, "I begin with the proposition that the concepts of culture and instrumental valuation are the concepts from which all the rest of institutional economics flow."[2] Mayhew argued that analysis must start from the position that we are bound by our cultural patterns. All that need be said for the moment about positions of this type is that they have not been generally or even widely adopted within economics.

The second exception consists of economists in the tradition of Max Weber, who are interested in the nexus between East Asian beliefs, business practices, and economic growth. An example from this school is the historical work of Michio Morishima. Although he is a leading technical economist, his explanation of the Japanese Miracle is Weberian.[3] Yet even he eventually temporizes and relies on the reciprocity between culture and economics, saying on the one hand that ideologies given by Japan's history "constrained" (directed?) economic activity but on the other that ideology can

[1] Ajit Dasgupta, "India's Cultural Values and Economic Development: A Comment," *Economic Development and Cultural Change* 13 (1964): 102.
[2] Anne Mayhew, "Culture: Core Concept under Attack," *Journal of Economic Issues* 21/1 (1987): 587–603.
[3] Michio Morishima, *Why Has Japan "Succeeded"? Western Technology and the Japanese Ethos* (Cambridge: Cambridge University Press, 1982).

be altered by the economy. This throws us back on a historical analysis to trace the actual direction of influence.

Most economists adopt the position I have called elsewhere "cultural nullity."[4] Strictly speaking, this can take more than one form and is often adopted unconsciously. One version is vague about whether cultures really exist but assumes that, even if they do, they are so marginal to economic concerns that they may be safely ignored. Another version accepts that cultures do exist but hypothesizes that they are creatures of the economy, able to adjust so painlessly to changing incentives that in this case, too, they may be ignored. The latter position fails, however, to grapple with one of the main difficulties encountered in completely dismissing culture: the fact that markets are not self-enforcing and depend on customary rules for creating trust.

As Mark Casson has observed, the professional culture of economists prevents most of them from seeing that culture matters at all.[5] The topic has been left to other disciplines, together with journalists, travelers, expatriates, and business commentators, all of whom are prone to note that "in reality," as it were, there are important local or traditional peculiarities of dress, diet, and social habits, plus influential beliefs and values. A type of nonmarket fundamentalism prevails among sociologists and anthropologists, which can be illustrated by an exchange between the philosopher Roger Scruton and the sociologist Brigitte Berger.[6] Speaking of Russia

[4] Eric L. Jones, "Culture and Its Relationship to Economic Change," *Journal of Institutional and Theoretical Economics* 151/2 (1995): 269–85.
[5] Mark C. Casson, *Economics of Business Culture: Game Theory, Transaction Costs and Economic Performance* (Oxford: Clarendon Press, 1991), p. 22.
[6] "Symposium: The New World of the Gothic Fox: Culture and Economy in English and Spanish America," *Partisan Review* 62/2 (1995): 179–233.

and Eastern Europe, Scruton urged that law should be established before any attempt to introduce the market economy. Berger interjected that for law to be accepted, culture must first be transformed. The sociologist Claudio Veliz lent support to her approach by asserting that the free market is itself a cultural artifact: witness its failure to take hold in Latin America despite prolonged experimentation in the nineteenth century. This is essentially a substantivist opinion.

Those economists who are still aware of the dispute in the 1960s between formalism and substantivism assume that it was decided in favor of formalism, whereas noneconomists believe the opposite.[7] Formalism implies that economic theory has universal scope. A careful economist has made the point that introducing cultural difference is a form of relativism which disrupts the universal character of analysis.[8] The burden of substantivism is that each culture maximizes its own values and therefore cannot be analyzed by the modes of economics. These are portrayed as spuriously universal and crassly Western in their individualism and market orientation. A more reasonable position might be that, since economics is the analysis of an abstract category of behavior—choice—its techniques are culturally neutral and universal by definition. If some economists neglect to allow for the legal, religious, and social impediments to full-blown market behavior outside Western society, that is a weakness on their part, not on the part of the science.

[7] The locus classicus of this dispute was the even earlier exchange between the economist Frank Knight and the anthropologist Melville Herskovits in 1941, reprinted as an appendix to M. J. Herskovits, *Economic Anthropology* (New York: W. W. Norton, 1963).
[8] William Oliver Coleman, *Economics and Its Enemies* (Basingstoke, U.K.: Palgrave, 2002), especially pp. 65–66, 84, and 250.

In the substantivist canon a specific type of economy is embedded in each and every culture. The extreme holders of this view stigmatize any attempt to extend market economics beyond the West as disrupting other cultures for profit (they scarcely admit the role of profit in encouraging the taking of socially desirable risk). All cultures embody the inalienable rights of those born into them and deserve protection for that reason. Trying to integrate other cultures with the international economy (globalization) is wrong, and any hint that each culture may not be distinct is "racist," a term which is too often used as mere abuse. This syndrome amounts to cultural relativism in holding that every culture is unique, and desirably unique.

One of the most eloquent voices raised against this position is that of a retired anthropologist, Roger Sandall, who claims that when he was a university teacher he would have been unable to publish what he has since written, so far was it contrary to the culturally relativist mood of the times.[9] Sandall documents how ludicrous was the indiscriminate praise for non-Western cultures, pointing instead to the horrors of corruption and even massacre that occurred in them, the absence of much contribution to world economic or scientific advance, and the ecological destruction readily wrought by primitive agriculture long before European colonists hove onto the scene.[10] Lest Sandall's publication seem the work of an isolated contrarian, a wider shift in opinion is indicated by the fact that indigenous African

[9] Roger Sandall, *The Culture Cult: Designer Tribalism and Other Essays* (Boulder, Col.: Westview Press, 2001).

[10] The last point accords with my own findings. See Eric L. Jones, "The History of Natural Resource Exploitation in the Western World," *Research in Economic History*, Suppl. 6 (1991): 235–52.

writers have started to discard the view that the ills of their continent can be sheeted home to colonialism. Some of them may now be found criticizing what they represent as internal defects of apathy, fatalism, convivial excess, conflict avoidance, reliance on superstitious explanations, and lack of a notion of personal merit. This litany would have been unthinkable during the last third of the twentieth century and would probably still be unacceptable had it originated with non-African writers. The new self-critical approach is epitomised by Daniel Etounga-Manguelle, who recommends learning from other civilizations the way East Asia did and not hankering after an "African way."[11]

Cultural relativism takes little account of its own economic implications—the costs that ensue (and fall most heavily on the poor) from insisting on cultural separateness and hence segregated markets. Cultural relativism is thus congruent with what is discussed below as "cultural fixity." No attempt is made to face up to the reality that cultures are artifacts, created and recreated, and that most of them have borrowed from hither and yon. No anxiety is expressed that protecting cultures as they stand favors the current holders of power and suppresses other people's freedom to choose. We can submit this to the test of revealed preference, which means asking what people do rather than what they say. Revealed preference suggests that people from all around the world are happy to adopt elements from alien cultures, especially so-called global or Western culture. Many even strive

---

[11] Daniel Etounga-Manguelle, "Does Africa Need a Cultural Adjustment Program?" in Lawrence E. Harrison and Samuel P. Huntington, eds., *Culture Matters: How Values Shape Human Progress* (New York: Basic Books, 2000), pp. 65–77.

to migrate to the West, where they can share not only its material success but also other features such as independent law and a free press.

I

Surprisingly, many historians, who might be expected to emphasize cultural change, likewise write as though cultures are fixed and dominate other aspects of life, including economic life. One reason for this may be that historians tend to be period specialists and seldom write about the long reaches of time during which change becomes most evident. Like other people, historians also witness cultural diversity at the present day, and this may reinforce their supposition that economies are adapted to a particular repertoire of cultural preferences, abilities, and taboos rather than the other way round.

Where academics from fields other than economics are involved, claims that "culture matters" are insistent. Such assertions are not infrequently coupled with attacks on neoclassical economics. These rarely mean what they say, since few commentators distinguish between neoclassical and other branches of economics, just as they fail to distinguish between market liberalism and conservatism. This suggests that "neoclassical" is code for an antipathy toward market competition, aversion to the economist's professional supposition that all actions have costs, and hostility toward businesses and governments supposed to be implicated in maintaining capitalism. Economists have largely responded with a disdainful silence.[12] Faced with all the prejudices of economists and noneconomists, it is tempting to call down

[12] Coleman, *Economics and Its Enemies*, p. 7.

a plague on both their houses. But that would be to evade the issue of culture.

Sometimes culture really does seem so routine and invariant with respect to price as to warrant a closer look by economists—though we should be careful: Alfred Marshall thought it was easy to overlook creeping changes and strikingly observed that "short-lived man has little better means of ascertaining whether custom is quietly changing, than the fly, born to-day and dead to-morrow, has of watching the growth of the plant on which it rests."[13] Yet at other times behavior touching on the most intimate human concerns can change almost overnight. What accounts for the periods of stability, and what brings about the transitions?

The instincts of a leading development economist, Peter Bauer, were probably correct ones. During his career he seems largely to have avoided cultural relativism but near its close he moved toward acknowledging the importance of culture by criticizing his fellow economists for virtually failing to consider the subject at all. I take *From Subsistence to Exchange and Other Essays* to be representative of his mature views.[14] At various points he alludes to culture and moral ideas as deep influences on human affairs. He does so in asides which indicate that however much others may wish to ignore it, he takes the point to be obvious: indeed, he ends one essay with a quotation from George Orwell to the effect that restating the obvious has become our first duty.

---

[13] Alfred Marshall, *Principles of Economics* (London: Macmillan, 1961), p. 532.

[14] Peter Bauer, *From Subsistence to Exchange* (Princeton: Princeton University Press, 2000).

Perhaps what Bauer recognized as culture's obvious-ness explains why he developed no explicit model of cultural change. Nevertheless, though his observations were studiedly casual, they demonstrate a refusal to be diverted from seeing the world whole. If his observations contradict other economists or are politically incorrect, bad cess to his critics, or so he implies: it is simply a fact that ethnic groups differ in their economic performance and that the original idea of material progress was the West's, and the West's alone. The decline of traditional religious belief has eroded a coherent worldview, and into the vacuum created by the consequent diminution of personal responsibility has poured collective guilt. He protests that guilt has malign consequences for policy, spawning aid programs that sap the will and are ready sources of corruption.

Bauer's sentiments were surely right on two counts. On the one hand, it was well to avoid the cultural relativists, because theirs had become an intolerant dogma, convinced a priori that market economics cannot have universal application and destructive of efforts to discern general propositions: every culture is unique. On the other hand, Bauer felt that to follow the bulk of the economics profession in ignoring or even denying the existence of cultural features capable of resisting price incentives—or, alternatively, straining to explain away every apparent anomaly in neoclassical vein—would have been doctrinaire. Defining culture away in the face of the descriptive evidence, he thought, adds nothing to understanding and prima facie subtracts from it. But in practice Bauer does not seem to have traveled far down the middle road that his views indicate, in search of the precise impact that culture may have. We should ourselves take the matter further. As Marc Bloch said, it is by criticizing their work that we keep faith with our intellectual forebears.

II

Only during the 1990s did cracks appear in the relativist facade. We may mention three of them. The first was the result of tensions over practices engaged in by some Muslim immigrants to Europe, such as the wearing of headscarves, halal modes of killing animals for meat, and female genital mutilation.[15] These practices placed liberals and feminists in a dilemma. They had either to defend them as the cultural rights of immigrants or swing round to condemning them as violations of the rule of the secular state, the autonomy of women, and so forth. The problem was felt most acutely in France, where immigration was large and the secular state particularly cherished. The outcome was a hardening of secularist opinion in line with the long-standing position of French intellectuals.

A second blow to relativism was struck within the non-Western world itself. This was the appearance of spokesmen for so-called Asian Values, who turned relativism back on the West by finding Western culture wanting. What they urged, especially about 1994, was that the economic miracle of East Asia had been built on neo-Confucian cultural values, notably thrift, hard work, education, and concern for the community rather than the individual.[16] The corollary of

[15] In Britain, official condemnation of the practices of slaughtering animals in halal and kosher fashion was long delayed, until a report in 2003 by a government advisory body, the Farm Animals Welfare Council (BBC Radio 4, 10 Jun).

[16] Eric L. Jones, "Asia's Fate: A Response to the Singapore School," *National Interest* 35 (Spring 1994): 18–28.

Asia's value-based economic success was to be the crumbling of Western competitiveness as Westerners abandoned puritanical values in favor of self-indulgence and reliance on the welfare state.[17]

What was not brought out in the Asian Values debate was the historically selective, not to say anachronistic, nature of the argument. The dynamics of the situation were missed. Thrift, hard work, and so forth had characterized the Western world during and long after industrialization. They constituted the Protestant Ethic. Its values had begun to melt in the warmth of high incomes in the West and through the accompanying decline of churchgoing in Europe, though not in the United States. But by sleight of hand, Asian countries were expected to remain immune from a similar value shift, a rosy expectation that was actually being undermined by Asia's prosperity just when the Asian Values School was most loudly touting its wares.

The sheer speed of economic growth in East Asia accordingly meant that its version of cultural relativism was soon seen to be inadequate. Ironically, Singapore, some of whose top people had been most vociferous and gloating about Western decline, was the first to lament the spread of "affluenza" that threatened the work ethic among its own newly prosperous young people. In a double irony, affluenza outlasted the Asian Crisis of 1997, yet the shock of the crisis did curb excessive enthusiasm for Asian Values. At the time of the Enron and other American business scandals, there was a brief revival of gloating, which only discloses the antago-

[17] Deepak Lal, *Unintended Consequences: The Impact of Factor Endowments, Culture, and Politics on Long-Run Economic Performance* (Cambridge, Mass.: MIT Press, 1998).

13

nism toward the West behind what had been passed off as serious analysis. The revival does not seem to have lasted.

A third blow to relativism was that the study of development economics had been languishing. Economic growth had taken place successfully in many less-developed countries, and this expelled some of the motivational steam from the field. Furthermore the mechanistic nostrums offered by development economists had seldom succeeded in curing poverty on a wide scale. There was an embarrassing gap between the market-related successes of East Asia and the failure of the interventionist policies recommended to unfortunate regions like sub-Saharan Africa. This began to turn certain economists back toward thinking that culture might after all provide deeper clues to growth than the engineering variables of technology, investment, and so forth. Whether culture was a sufficient explanation remained to be seen; acknowledging that it may have been at least a necessary component of the explanation was the intellectual volte-face of the 1990s.

III

A bold, symbolic announcement that cultural relativism really could be dispensed with came first in the field of international relations, with the publication by the political scientist Samuel Huntington of an article entitled, "The Clash of Civilizations" (*Foreign Affairs* 1993). Foreign policy, at any rate American foreign policy, had by then ceased to pay attention to culture or religion.[18] The story is told that when Hillary Clinton was to visit Pakistan, her advisors were in-

---

[18] This was noted from time to time, e.g., in James Finn, ed., *Global Economics and Religion* (New Brunswick, N.J.: Transaction Books, 1982), but

formed that the president's wife would be in purdah. "How far away is that?" one of them asked, getting the sardonic answer, "about four centuries." Besides being no way to make friends or influence people, this anecdote points up the cultural isolation in which some of the American elite lived, at a time when one-third of the members of Congress did not, it is said, hold a valid passport.

One might not expect religion to have been discounted in this way, given that the United States is more wedded to moralistic religion than other developed regions, like Europe or Japan. Yet social scientists in the United States, and indeed the West generally, embraced secularization theory and ignored religion as a form of fading, irrelevant superstition. Predominantly atheistic or agnostic television executives in the United States "mirror-imaged" and behaved as though audiences shared their own attitudes. They failed to acknowledge the significance that religion has for a majority of their own compatriots, let alone for many foreigners. They were like Stalin asking contemptuously how many divisions the pope has. There can be little doubt that this pervasive inattention to the role of religion helped to disarm decision makers when it came to understanding, to cite the most obvious example, the Islamic world.

Religious values are intrinsic to culture: they are far more important than matters of dress and deportment. The gap between the cultural relativist view that culture does not merely matter but is fundamental and the dominance of secularization theory is therefore paradoxical. We might have

---

became more widely remarked on in the 1990s; see, for example, Douglas Johnston and Cynthia Sampson, eds., *Religion, the Missing Dimension of Statecraft* (New York: Oxford University Press, 1994).

anticipated that religion would be seen as part of culture, with great influence attributed to it. Instead, during the second half of the twentieth century, conventional thought about the social world became compartmentalized: religion was regarded as of negligible and declining significance, whereas cultures as a whole, or at any rate certain ill-defined aspects of them, were taken as determining economic differences around the world. In the political rather than the economic sphere, nation-state politics and the interaction of states on the world stage were assumed to be what mattered, and both cultural and religious issues were sidelined.

Huntington therefore upset standard "realist" political analysis when he predicted that future conflicts would be between groups of states united by their supposedly indelible cultures rather than groups united only by opportunistic political alliances. He described political groupings of that type as shallower and less stable than civilizations. The idea seemed to presage ethnic or racial war, but his typology of civilizations was really based on religious adherence (or in the case of the Sinitic world on the moralistic philosophy of Confucianism). Huntington's thesis was bitterly resisted, not least because he toppled the nation-state from the throne of international politics, threatening a whole generation of political scientists who had invested their careers in the study of the state.

As a result of the dispute stirred up by Huntington, it was beginning to dawn on policymakers even before 11 September 2001 that the goals of some Islamic regimes might not be readily aligned with those of American democracy. When in 1996 Huntington elaborated his ideas, in a book called *The Clash of Civilizations and the Remaking of World Order*, dissent continued, but by then a debate in his terms

16

had become, though hardly acceptable in all quarters, at least somewhat routine.[19] Events, however, conspired, if not to validate his interpretation, at least to lend it support. The prominence of this very public and only partly academic debate helped to prepare economists as well as political scientists and foreign affairs personnel for a swing back toward cultural explanations.

A seal of respectability was bestowed on the reversal by the MIT economist Peter Temin, in his presidential address to the Economic History Association, published in 1997 under the teasing title, "Is It Kosher to Talk about Culture?"[20] Temin's answer to his own question was in the affirmative. He argued that while so-called Anglo-Saxon culture was important for the start and spread of industrialism, it is not the wave of the future. That, he thought, is Japan's collective culture, which will have the economic edge in coming years despite its current difficulties. Temin was aware that many analysts traced the dynamism of America's knowledge-based industries to the diversity and individualism of American culture. He chose to think, nevertheless, that problems in producing software would come to resemble those of manufacturing production and would be solved better after the Japanese fashion, not by implicit contracts with individualistic employees but by stock options that aligned their interests with those of the company. The degree to which Temin's discussion is really about institutions, and therefore about political or power-based choices, rather than about culture

[19] Samuel Huntington, *The Clash of Civilizations and the Remaking of World Order* (New York: Simon & Schuster, 1996).
[20] Peter Temin, "Is It Kosher to Talk about Culture?" *Journal of Economic History* 57/2 (1997): 267–87.

in the sense of inherited and slower-moving patterns, is moot. That distinction will need to be discussed.

A much larger audience was reached by David Landes in a 1998 book called *The Wealth and Poverty of Nations*, a scholarly work that, like Huntington's, entered the public arena.[21] Landes went so far as to say that the postwar economic success of only one in each of two pairs of countries, South Korea and Turkey, Indonesia and Nigeria, could have been predicted from their respective cultures. He is extensively cited as claiming that culture "makes all the difference." The number of academics who began to reiterate this suggests that they were already nursing similar views but had been engaging in preference falsification and only in the late 1990s felt emboldened to come out of the closet. It became reputable, one might say fashionable, for leading American social scientists to urge culture's role. The 180-degree turn was confirmed by a work jointly edited in 2000 by Lawrence Harrison and Samuel Huntington, based on a Harvard symposium and unashamedly entitled *Culture Matters: How Values Shape Human Progress*.[22]

A few younger economists and economic historians had already begun to take culture seriously. I will list five whose analytical contributions have been outstanding. Gregory Clark contributed an article on culture to a symposium in *Historical Methods* as early as 1988.[23] Clark's interest in the Western world's rise in per capita output led him to

---

[21] David Landes, *The Wealth and Poverty of Nations* (New York: W. W. Norton, 1998).

[22] Lawrence Harrison and Samuel Huntington, eds., *Culture Matters: How Values Shape Human Progress* (New York: Basic Books, 2000).

[23] Gregory Clark, "Economists in Search of Culture: The Unspeakable in Pursuit of the Inedible?" *Historical Methods* 21 (Fall 1988): 161–64.

consider conventional economic variables only to eliminate them as explanations, obliging him to conclude, "albeit reluctantly" (p. 161), that culture must have been playing a part. He pointed out, as Frederick Amasa Walker had done, that economists believe that anything, meaning nothing, can be explained by postulating different preferences or values among different populations. They assume instead uniform preferences. Yet Clark's findings included the discovery that people do not necessarily work harder where material conditions are poor, implying that cultural norms reverse the usual expectations of the economic calculus. At least, they reverse them in the workers' home territories—the low-productivity norms did not travel with them when workers migrated to areas of higher productivity.

Clark admitted that if people really did work harder in some societies than in others, regardless of material incentives, economists were going to find it hard to accommodate what he called "'such a startling fact" (p. 163). Startling to economists, that is—whether the fact was really startling is another matter: men have always been willing to respond to nonmaterial incentives, witness the way they sacrifice themselves for their religious beliefs or in war. Recall that Clark was writing in 1988, and, as might have been expected at that date, his work was not much taken up. He supposed that other economists thought the anomaly would not so much be explained as (some day, somehow) explained away.

Nevertheless, at much the same time others were coming to the conclusion that "culture matters," but they did not use this label and did not seek a wide public audience for their work. One was Avner Greif, whose work dealt chiefly with the differential effect of institutions, though he extended it to differences in the actual beliefs of collectivist and individualist societies around the medieval Mediterranean.[24] Greif brought a game-theoretic approach to the topic. Another writer was Timur Kuran, a specialist on Islamic economics.[25] Kuran considered the explanations proposed for the poverty of Muslim countries over many centuries, including the illegitimate use of Islam to prop up the worldviews of power holders, religious obstacles to innovation, and communalist norms that reduced the incentives to create capitalist institutions. None of these sufficed, he said, to account for the failure of out-groups to bring about major reform, since they would have had so much to gain by this. His solution was a cultural one: the role of stylized public discourse in keeping individuals from questioning, or even noticing, chronic social inefficiencies.

A fourth contributor to the new discussion of cultural influences on economic life was Ekkehart Schlicht, author of On Custom in the Economy (1998).[26] Custom is very like, if not exactly like, what is usually meant by culture. This is the most profound work I have read on the subject and the one most deeply concerned with methodological issues. Schlicht shows that market processes depend on and are affected by custom, and that while custom probably adapts to economic change in the covert way noted by Marshall, psychological rigidities always act as some restriction on the

[24] Avner Greif, "Cultural Beliefs and the Organization of Society: A Historical and Theoretical Reflection on Collectivist and Individualist Societies," Journal of Political Economy 102/5 (1994): 912–50.

[25] See especially Timur Kuran, "Islam and Underdevelopment: An Old Puzzle Revisited," Journal of Institutional and Theoretical Economics 153/1 (1997): 41–79.

[26] Ekkehart Schlicht, On Custom in the Economy (Oxford: Clarendon Press, 1998).

scope of economic activities. Despite the prolonged failure of the economics profession to take these matters fully into account, it is not difficult to suppose that a mixture of individual conditioning and network incentives and restraints, describable altogether as culture, might resist economic forces such as changing price incentives in the short- or even the medium run.

A final example is a thorough, cautious, empirical book by Andrew Godley on Jewish entrepreneurship in late nineteenth- and early twentieth-century London and New York.[27] In both cities Jewish immigrants from Russia came to dominate the segment of the textile industry halfway between mass production and bespoke production. Godley saw that the experience of two such closely matched groups offered a controlled experiment capable of revealing how far the larger culture of each city affected the level of entrepreneurship. To carry out the experiment, he undertook laborious data collection on the occupational structures of London and found that entrepreneurship was weaker there than in New York. His explanation was that the craft culture of London was stronger than New York's and impeded the full emergence of individual entrepreneurs.

The work of scholars like Clark, Greif, Kuran, Schlicht, and Godley indicates the stage recently attained in the investigation of culture. It inclines one to take culture as a determinant of economic life seriously, despite the objections that have been mentioned and despite the somewhat off-putting rhetoric of the better-known revivalists. These five scholars have not solved every problem. They do not work

---

[27] Andrew Godley, *Jewish Immigrant Entrepreneurship in New York and London 1880–1914: Enterprise and Culture* (Basingstoke, U.K.: Palgrave, 2001).

to a single definition, though it is evident what each is trying to explain; they wander a little between discussing values and institutions, though again it is clear which category each of them has under review at any given moment; and they do not fully elucidate the mechanics of cultural change. But they and some others who started to enter the fray in the early years of the twenty-first century have begun to cast light on what is an undeniably murky area.

IV

There are several possibilities for interpreting the relationship between culture and economy. Among these are that culture is primary, the interpretation that I have termed "cultural fixity"; another is that it does not exist or does not matter ("cultural nullity"). These may be found in the literature, though it may be necessary to hunt around to find any view stated clearly and frankly. The "nullity" position was, however, openly adopted by the economist and demographer Julian Simon, always a bold reasoner. He asserted the following strong proposition: "in the context of long-run analysis, culture and values do not have independent lives . . . [but] serve as intermediate variables between economic conditions and fertility, serving only to transmit the effect of income onto fertility behavior."[28] The causality runs only one way. Simon went further and stated that the lag before values respond to fresh economic circumstances is about twenty-five or thirty years.

The catch in this is the implicit admission that culture does exist after all, if only for a generation at a time. Simon is

[28] Julian Simon, *The Effects of Income on Fertility* (Chapel Hill, N. C.: Carolina Population Center, 1974), p. 105.

so determined to conceive culture as an epiphenomenon of the economy that he does not recognize the anomaly, but it is impossible to get away from the fact that he is acknowledging the persistence for two or three decades of values different from those appropriate to economic conditions. On the basis of his assertion, culture and the economy are probably always out of step. Just when values catch up with the economic situation, circumstances alter again. Values—say, the desired size of a family—are once more left wallowing in their wake. This is a game of tag in which no one is ever caught.

Accordingly, culture is a creature of the economy but a creature of the economic life of a former generation rather than of the present one. It does have independent meaning, but this is always detached from prevailing economic conditions. Simon lets in by the back door what he is eager to push out at the front. Stated abstractly, at the start of each period of analysis relative prices are already distorted, and it may take a generation to amend the distortion, requiring values to be readjusted, perhaps through cognitive dissonance. No one can seriously believe that values are instantaneously bid away or that they have no effect on economic behavior, any more than, say, do other historical legacies or the initial endowment of natural resources. The economy does not start as a featureless tabula rasa. It has a prior topography.

A case against cultural explanation has been made in terms of income inequality. The argument is that poor young men engage in competitive risk taking or lethal violence because they have little to lose. This is held to be superior to traditional explanations of lethal violence as the product of unexplained cultural differences.[29] But surely it would pay

[29] Report of a workshop presentation by Martin Daly and Margo Wilson

people whose human capital constitutes almost all their resources to husband it? Moreover, a universalist explanation merely in terms of income distribution cannot account for regional, temporal, and group variations in levels of risk taking and lethal violence. For instance, young male farm workers in nineteenth-century England played very high-risk sports. Nevertheless, their backswording and shin-kicking did finally die out, and in any event a proportion of such people, equally poor, shunned such sports and became Primitive Methodists or, later on, members of the far-from-martial Salvation Army.[30] Low incomes cannot be held to explain both great risk taking and extremely cautious lifestyles. By the nineteenth century, violent crime was lower than it had been in earlier times, and despite worsening rural poverty it was still decreasing. A generalized interpretation cannot account for these variations. And the fact that pertinent cultural differences may not yet have been identified does not warrant emptying out the analysis by denying in advance that they can have mattered.

Let me give another example where the existence of a long-standing culture is taken by anthropologically minded Western scholars as sufficient to account for the observed behavior: the business behavior of the Chinese and the special structure of their firms. A considerable literature describes the "Chinese characteristics" of Overseas Chinese businesses,

---

at the Wissenschaftskolleg zu Berlin, May 2002, in Alex Kacelnik, "The Sciences of Risk," *Wissenschaftskolleg zu Berlin Jahrbuch*, 2001/2002, pp. 363–64.

[30] Compare the opposite reactions to poaching of the game-dealing blacksmith and the "Ranter" shepherd in Richard Jefferies, *The Amateur Poacher* (Oxford: Oxford University Press, 1978), p. 194.

meaning such features as an extreme dispersal of family members and assets among industries and countries, reliance on personal contacts rather than open markets, and a deliberate opacity with respect to deals and accounts. Mainstream economists will retort that these are adjustments to risk, as in terms of function they are. Others will disagree, citing the extreme nature of the behavior and its tendency to persist even in developed countries where the ambient risk level is much lower than in Southeast Asia.

In reality, Chinese business behavior is not a timeless phenomenon. Functioning courts and customary law were quite widespread in Qing times. Business actually retreated from using them because of the uncertainties and depredations of the state toward the end of the Qing dynasty, again under the Republic, and once more under wartime Japanese occupation.[31] Shareholder power was sidelined, and corporations became personal fiefdoms. At each stage, entrepreneurs intensified their use of practices considered inherently "Chinese" in attempts to evade untrustworthy and intrusive governments, despite the obvious disadvantage of relinquishing the ability to raise capital from the market. Businessmen who fled China in 1949 carried the element of secrecy with them. They brought it back to the emergent private sector under Deng Xiao-ping in the 1970s. Hence, there is no need to depend on ageless culture as an explanation of Chinese business methods. The phenomenon can be adequately explained in historical and economic terms.

The foregoing examples show how perilous is the tightrope that we have to walk and how it continues to sway

[31] Parks M. Coble, *Chinese Capitalists in Japan's New Order: The Occupied Lower Yangzi, 1937–1945* (Berkeley: University of California Press, 2003).

dizzily from side to side. Culture does not explain everything, nor does economics. Cultural practices may be explicable in economic terms, yet they also persist as a residue that is not explained by *current* forces. Ways of behaving are capable of being transmitted from one age cohort to another, learned early, and replicated in inappropriate circumstances. To that extent, culture resembles neurosis. To suppose otherwise is to think that selection environments are always severe enough to "correct" behavior and bring it instantly into line with fresh circumstances.

V

What about demonstrations that culture makes a difference in fact? Every society has its superstitions: my son lived on a street in Melbourne that had no number 13, and in Illinois I found the buyers of my house exceedingly reluctant to accept the thirteenth of the month as the date for closing the transaction. A skeptic might argue that this is nugatory and few resources are expended as a result of superstitions, which often differ (and cancel out) among societies. Beliefs about, say, black cats or magpies hold them lucky or unlucky according to country or locality. Proverbs often contradict one another, perhaps because they are hangovers from random connections asserted in different places when there was no large and unified market in which ideas could be tested.

There are, however, reports in the demographic literature of traditional behavior in Asia that surely does have economic significance. The most striking cases relate to son preference and markedly skewed sex ratios in China, India, and elsewhere.[32] Other cases involve the timing of concep-

[32] Amartya Sen, "More Than 100 Million Women Are Missing," *New*

tions to accord with zodiacal criteria.[33] As to further effects, I need refer only to Charles Horioka's survey of the high personal savings rate of the Japanese, in which he canvasses many purported explanations, including "tradition," which is akin to conventional notions of culture. The most rigorous test that Horioka reports is a 1986 study which found the savings rate among ethnic Japanese in the United States to be five percentage points higher than for other ethnic groups. Since the institutional setting was the same for all groups, he suggests that culture is one explanation.[34] Another study, this time of savings behavior in Japanese prefectures defined as traditional or nontraditional according to their consumption of traditional foods, also suggested that "tradition is one explanation (albeit a secondary one) of Japan's high household saving rate" (p. 272). Leaving aside the question of the rather small size of the effect, these studies seem to confirm a minimalist position that culture does exert an influence on economic behavior.

We also know that culture can change—think of the adaptation of many (though not all) immigrants to the mores

York Review of Books, 20 Dec 1990. Nicholas Eberhart ("Some Strategic Implications of Asian/Eurasian Demographic Trends," [Harvard Center for Population and Development Studies Working Paper 14 # 8, Nov 2004]) considers unbalanced sex ratios at birth a serious threat to China's future stability.

[33] Daniel M. Goodkind, "Creating New Traditions in Modern Chinese Populations: Aiming for Birth in the Year of the Dragon," Population & Development Review 17/4 (1991): 663–86.

[34] Charles Yuji Horioka, "Why Is Japan's Household Saving Rate So High?" Journal of the Japanese and International Economies 4 (1990): 49–92, reprinted in H. Smith, ed., The Economic Development of Northeast Asia (Cheltenham, U.K.: Edward Elgar, 2002), pp. 265–308.

of new societies. Let us assume that individuals internalize the culture surrounding them in their home countries when they are young and ask under what circumstances they may change. Immigrants may find that a new host culture is alien to their upbringing but simply cannot avoid adjusting their behavior to it. Adopting its unfamiliar habits will produce cognitive dissonance that can best be quelled by adjusting their personal values to suit. Whole societies may change as a result of the totality of such responses. On the other hand, some minorities may hold out and preserve old norms within societies that they perceive as alien. Why most people adapt while other groups and individuals cling to their original ways, uncomfortable though these may be in the new situation, is not so obvious and presumably requires fine-grained analysis of their circumstances or psychology.

Young people find it easier to change than old ones, who have had longer to internalize some prior set of values. On the other hand, there may be an early imprinting period, and young people subject to propaganda may find themselves trapped by allegiance to norms inculcated early in their lives. German prisoners of war who had been teenagers when Hitler came to power were hard for the Allies to decondition; older men could be returned more easily to their former beliefs.[35] This complicates the issue by introducing the possibility that cultural values may be subject to age-cohort effects and be contingent on events at the time when imprinting actually took place. Generalizations about group mores may therefore be risky, unless they are qualified to allow for variations induced by the group's composition and

[35] Henry Faulk, *Group Captives: The Re-Education of German Prisoners-of-War in Britain, 1945–48* (London: Chatto & Windus, 1977).

history. National stereotyping is particularly called into doubt, because nations are far from uniform.

All told, we may consider an evolutionary mechanism. When there is no strong incentive to change, or rather no strong disincentive against sticking with established habits, change is likely to be slow. Older immigrant women confined to the house may change little, whereas their children may alter with astonishing speed at school, though switching back at home to manners their parents find acceptable. Truly ancient cultural features may survive as relics when there is no special reason to dispense with them: dialects, for example, illustrate the persistence of sluggishly changing forms when markets for modes of speech remain isolated. On the other hand, the young and upwardly mobile make plastic adaptations to their speech. Even very young immigrant children may act as translators for their parents in the doctor's surgery and, with embarrassment, while their mothers try to haggle in the supermarket. Another example of the paradox of change and stasis is the suggestion that traditional Chinese culture did not persist through the innate conservatism of the Chinese peasant, whatever "innate conservatism" may mean, but was a sign that over long periods there was little change in incentives.[36] There is no doubt that when circumstances permit the Chinese people can change their behavior astonishingly fast. The sensational shift from Maoism to Dengism during the late 1970s is hard to overlook.

More often, cultural change hides from view. Marshall's caution about the problems we have in detecting slow,

[36] Richard Wilhelm, *Chinese Economic Psychology* (New York: Garland, 1982), p. 45.

creeping development should always be borne in mind. Participants may delude themselves that it is not happening, having no more sense of change than the fly on the wall. Forms of behavior present at the same time may in truth be out of phase. Practices are likely to persist if there is no reason to change them, but the outward appearance of survivals may be masking real changes. Old names outlive the functions for which they were invented; labeling errors, translation errors, and poor recording can all disguise change. One reason why the economics profession neglected cultural change for so long was the difficulty of observing it.

Chapter 2

Cultures Fluid and Sticky

Culture beckons our attention for at least two reasons. Firstly, although few economists now make much of it, the topic looms uninvestigated in the background of a surprising number of scholarly discussions. Secondly, in both developed and less-developed countries assertions about it are used to justify restricting individual freedom. Right-thinking people are expected to agree about how to live, how to worship, with whom to associate, what to watch and what to read, as if the powers that be and the cultural pundits are merely reminding us of our inheritance and duty. Both uses of culture deserve to be recognized more explicitly and examined more skeptically than they usually are.

The subject matter is sprawling and diverse. Almost anything may be included, from the world religions to the codes of behavior, manners, and dress of whichever subgroup one chooses: entire nations, regional communities, occupational groups like scientists or artists, and on down to the fam-

ily next door, even as far as the great apes. All this is part of
the fascination, though it does not make for tractability. It is
odiously misleading when culture is extended to include race.

How, then, should we approach the topic? We need
first to explore its nature, above all the extent to which it is
fixed as opposed to malleable. An ample literature treats culture as hard and fast, and it is difficult for authors to portray
nuance and shadow where others see distinct categories. Being
a "splitter" means introducing endless ifs and buts. On the
other hand, being a "lumper" risks accepting cultural labels as
if they always mean what they say and creates unfounded impressions of permanence and uniformity. To give instances, we
commonly speak about the Arabic language and about Islam.
But there are twenty or more Arabic languages, while, despite
the fact that, as religions go, Islam is *relatively* homogeneous,
it includes at its extremes the puritanism of the Wahabi sect
in Saudi Arabia and the more relaxed admixture of Hinduism
and folk religion in Java. Although it would be tedious to insist on the point at every tick and turn, we can seldom speak
of more than the mainstream tendencies of any culture,
around which there is continual flux. The vocabulary of cultural studies is a repetitive one. To compensate for "lumping"
we should try to keep in the backs of our minds that there is
variation within any culture and flux is always occurring.

Direct observation is chancy and less useful than it
seems, especially without guiding concepts. Historians may
not agree, but as Rodney Stark says in an outstanding book,
they are not trained in distinguishing between concepts and
instances.[1] They seldom work with explicitly stated networks

[1] Rodney Stark, *The Rise of Christianity: A Sociologist Reconsiders History*
(Princeton: Princeton University Press, 1996), p. 22.

of concepts and think that a single counterinstance is enough to invalidate a theory. Anthropologists and others, who do know about concepts, seem to have a lot of trouble using those from economics: there is market resistance to market conceptualization. At any rate, with raw observational data there is often a sampling problem. What one comes across in the field may overshadow and distort statistical reality. As a case in point, knowing that Japan is an aging society I looked for evidence on the street but could never spot it. Crocodiles of kindergarten pupils were far more conspicuous than the elderly, who doubtless stay in their homes. Japan's twenty thousand centenarians are not likely to be out and about.

Personal observation may be helpful, at least to the prepared mind, and ordinarily I am all for drawing on one's own experience and studying the natural history of society. But observation is better at supplying examples than creating generalizations. Straining for street cred can lead to the "eyewitness fallacy," in which foreign travel substitutes for deeper inquiry. Hidden features may be more important than what is on the surface, and verisimilitude may trump verity. Plenty of people who never visited a given country themselves or were never present at a particular event have written accounts that have seemed engrossingly realistic to people who actually were there: Stephen Crane's "masterpiece of psychological realism," *The Red Badge of Courage*, is an outstanding example.[2] Crane did not fight in the American Civil War, but after they had read his book veterans swore they had served with him. Arthur Waley, who is credited with the best translations of Chinese poetry, declined to go

[2] For this and other examples, see Eric L. Jones, "Through the Garbage Can, Darkly," *National Interest*, Fall 1996, pp. 100–101.

there; he wanted to protect his personal image of the scene. It may be best to stand back from the subject matter, as Waley did. I agree with Sid Smith, who has written two well-received novels on China, that one can learn more about it in the British Library than by visiting the country.[3] The best ticket is a library ticket, because things may be found in books that are not apparent on the ground, and books offer more ideas than most of us can dream up for ourselves.

My first inclination was to take the economists' side in the debate about the cultural variable. This meant arguing that culture is seldom, if ever, more than a creature of the economy. My leaning in this direction was the greater because almost every fixed assumption about society alters if one takes a long enough perspective. People in some societies or periods have responded to incentives in ways that would as yet be unthinkable elsewhere or at different times. How did Kipling put it?—The crimes of Clapham chaste at Martaban. Sir Henry Maine noted that the Spartan and the Venetian aristocracies, far apart in time, both responded to the taxation of separate households (legally deemed to be created on marriage) by turning to polyandry: brothers could save on tax by sharing a wife. How much more responsive can custom become?[4]

I

Cultures seem sticky but can be fluid. The stresses and strains affecting religion in the modern world make this domain an

[3] *BBC Radio 4 Books Programme*, 12 Jan 2003.
[4] Cited in Johan Goudsblom, Eric Jones, and Stephen Mennell, *The Course of Human History: Economic Growth, Social Process, and Civilization* (Armonk, N.Y.: M. E. Sharpe, 1996), p. 95.

exceptionally good indicator of how things may change or stay the same, or change while seeming to stay the same. Admittedly, it is hard to maintain the distinction between belief systems (cultures) and related institutions (churches). The conscious choices of priesthoods are seldom the same as the drift of popular opinion. Both alter over time and may diverge markedly.

The conservative Anglicanism of a generation ago has given way to acrid disputes over women priests, homosexual priests, divorce services, and political activism which must have the clergy of my youth spinning in their graves. The lives of divorcees were once made miserable by preventing them from remarrying in church, but now that competition for church members has become intense, the eternal truths that were invoked prove to be negotiable. Flux and dissension must be painful to many who once found the order and sonority of Anglican services comforting, and it is perhaps not surprising that the church has driven away most of its working-class members. On the other hand, the sonorities and complex language of Christian worship are blamed for driving away the young: two specialists in religion at Lancaster University are projecting trends that seem to show that by about 2025 the number of Christians in England will be exceeded by those professing only a diffuse spirituality.[5]

In Western countries it is possible to spot a drift toward behavior by Christians that would once have been regarded as unseemly or worse. The personal and sexual practices of churchgoers, however, change more slowly than

---

[5] *Times*, 4 Nov 2004, referring to Linda Woodhead and Paul Heelas, *The Spiritual Revolution: Why Religion Is Giving Way to Spirituality* (Oxford: Blackwell, 2004).

those of the community at large, and acceptance by the various hierarchies typically lags still further behind. One of the social purposes, or at any rate latent functions, of churches may be to slow down potentially disruptive change. Yet although authoritarian churches may succeed for a time in holding their adherents and prescribing their behavior, practice eventually conforms to popular taste. Cognitive dissonance sees to this, since to ease the tension of doing something one has been schooled to think is wrong, values are adapted to fit the new behavior. In some circumstances novel interpretations of the gospel by the clergy may make the running and forge ahead of anything their congregations, or at any rate the older members, will accept, but community norms prompted by younger people predominantly influence how congregations behave and which beliefs will emerge.

On the other hand, traditional Anglicanism is being reinforced by the growing congregations in less-developed countries. These oppose the appointment of homosexual bishops, which American Episcopalians endorsed and which English Anglicans only narrowly rejected. Traditionalists assert that Christianity will lose its drawing power vis à vis Islam if it does not repudiate homosexuality. Against this, reformers urge that the church has a duty to remake itself in the image of modern, progressive social attitudes and scrutinize the Bible for fresh justifications of their stance, just as their opponents doggedly rely on older interpretations of the same text. The struggle between these groups reveals that social context does remodel attitudes that in former days were held to be the revealed truth. The turmoil within Christianity helps us to perceive culture as adaptive, responding to shifts in the social, economic, and political norms of the larger society. Such degrees of malleability seem to validate the generalizing power of economics. Whenever fresh incentives alter an outcome, the economic calculus is in the ascendant and notions of social permanence are undermined.

Roman Catholicism has been particularly challenged by African conditions. It is asked to accommodate leviratic marriage, that is, to permit a man to sleep with his brother's widow. Failing to sanction this would contravene the church's stated position that all peoples have the right to convert to Christianity without abandoning their own customs.[6] Perhaps we may coin the term "African widows' syndrome" for the tendency to modify supposedly eternal belief systems in accordance with current realities. Yet the contradictions affecting culture are apparent, because some groups respond to challenges of this type in other ways. The success of charismatic Pentecostals in the less-developed world is in part a vote against customs like leviratic marriage. Pentecostalism reinforces the more adamantine and supernatural forms of Christianity from which churches in

[6] Michael C. Kirwen, *African Widows* (Maryknoll, N.Y.: Orbis Books, 1979). East African societies enjoin a duty of care on the brother of a deceased husband in return for sexual access to his widow, which is, however, represented as her substitute union with the deceased. (It is not clear who is to care for widows who lack brothers-in-law.) Kirwen's deprecation of individualistic Western theology and impersonal, but universal, state welfare schemes neatly illustrates the strains of cultural change—but change, nevertheless—first, in the loaded wording of his subtitle ("An Empirical Study of the Problems of Adapting Western Christian Teachings on Marriage to the Leviratic Custom for the Care of Widows in Four Rural African Societies") and, second, in a note on the verso of the title page in which the Catholic Foreign Mission Society of America claims to be publishing the book in order to promote "international dialogue" yet puts responsibility for its contents onto the author.

the developed countries have moved away.[7] African and Asian churches as a whole may sense the latent merit in strictness, perceiving monogamous marriage as a safeguard against the spread of HIV/AIDS, to which customary practices unhappily contribute.[8]

Are there, then, nonnegotiable attributes of Christianity and its churches? With the occasional Anglican bishop given to doubting the divinity of Christ, one might suspect not. Some Nonconformist sects may remain unyielding, but in Anglicanism, at least, Christianity has tended to display an intermittent, contested but nevertheless real, tolerance of the personal views of clergymen and patrons of livings. Anglicanism has prided itself on being a broad church, fudging issues to keep the peace, encompassing opinions so much at variance that outsiders may think it hypocritical or confused. How else to explain the nude and lewd imagery in some parish churches or the posting nowadays of prayers from a range of scarcely compatible faiths?

Faced with contradictions like these, it is scarcely enough to invoke a general veneration of the Bible story; clever men have often enough reinterpreted the meaning of that. For any religion or sect to remain independent it must presumably possess beliefs, attitudes, rituals, and ethical practices that are internally consistent and distinct from

[7] Peter Schwartz, *Inevitable Surprises* (London: Simon & Schuster/Free Press, 2003), pp. 144–45.

[8] Hugh Russell, writing from Zambia in The *Spectator* (1 Mar 2003), describes three highly risky heterosexual practices designed to increase male pleasure and points out that male homosexuals are rare. This crossover of attitudes clearly sets African society at odds with "advanced" Western countries and renders contentious the adjustment or nonadjustment of Christian policy.

those of its rivals. But locating these central propositions becomes difficult because of the variability that may exist at any one time. This situation serves our purpose by reinforcing the point that belief systems do alter with the times and that, for all the fury of short-term resistance, something akin to the "African widows' syndrome" typically brings change in the end. Nevertheless, favoring malleability in this way should not lead us to think that culture is merely the grin of the Cheshire cat, because at each specific moment cultural relationships do have force. Perhaps "conservatism" never means more than lagged responsiveness. The methodological point is that lags in the adjustment of cultures to new norms require us to treat the subject historically. The subject cries out for a movie rather than a set of still pictures. Snapshots of culture conceal the mutability that appears in the long run.

The official situation in Islam is less equivocal. The range of legitimate disagreement was limited, some would say abolished, by the slamming of the Gate of Interpretation in what was, in Christian terms, the tenth century. Even so, closure seems to be contradicted by all the continued Sunni-Shia and other internal dissensions, and the Hindu elements later incorporated into Javanese Islam. Hinduism itself approaches the problem of consistency from the opposite direction, because it readily assimilates a variety of practices. If we extend our examples to animist religions, they seem to be far more, indeed intrinsically, arbitrary in their forms of worship. They designate many types of natural phenomena as sacred: mountains, streams, trees, and animals. But here we reach a check. Animism may be arbitrary overall, yet in any one society or place or time the objects of worship are firmly understood and fiercely guarded. Worship is not so plastic or fungible that everything is immediately substitutable for everything else. We are obliged to acknowledge that at any one time cultural features are real.

II

Nevertheless, a categorical fixity position is as unsatisfactory as one of total malleability. Any proposition that cultures are permanent must imply that they have descended unaltered from some zero point in time. Almost no authority who implies as much does actually go on to describe the history of culture in these terms, and of course it cannot be done. The mark is quite overstepped if it is further held that cultures embody the inalienable rights of the people who share them. Fixity slices the population of the world too sharply into groups, as if the array of modern nations and ethnicities has always existed. Some nations are merely concoctions created by the setting down of colonial boundaries and other strictly historical events. The notion of fixity overlooks the evidence of adaptability and the shifts in seemingly ancient practices that can be found the minute one digs beneath the surface. Ultimately there is nothing permanent about any behavior that derives from human construction. Religious fundamentalists, of course, believe that divine agency is at the root of their beliefs and founding texts. Other people think of such claims as foundation myths, wherein lies the nub of many a bitter conflict.

Some old patterns really have persisted or (an important caveat) have remained distinct from one another, despite the political power, religious intolerance, or corrosive commercialism of the societies surrounding them—think of the way the Amish have resisted so many American fashions. The Amish exemplify the capricious nature of the entire topic of culture. An Amish cultural *pattern*, like many more widespread *patterns*, has indeed survived for a long time. What is easy to overlook is that a pattern may have been hollowed out and its constituent features replaced by others, so that what remains may be, though more than the grin of the Cheshire cat, substantially altered within. It does not help much to say that the Amish are maximizing something other than material outcomes or something in addition to material outcomes or even that they are sticking to peculiar folkways because these offer competitive advantages over the larger society or are insurance against the risks it entails. None of this would account for the survival of so many Amish forms and beliefs; after all, they could have adopted a more comfortable lifestyle and resorted to the insurance markets for protection.

Archaic though the Amish may seem to be in the stability of their values, old-fashioned dress, continued use of the horse and buggy, and reluctance to adopt the materialism of those around them, whom they please to call gentiles, they have not remained categorically faithful to the lifestyle their forebears brought from the eighteenth-century Rhineland. They differ among themselves in the extent to which they have adopted modern equipment, but their overall tendency has been to accept a good deal of what is on offer. The only difference is that they have done so much later than their "gentile" neighbors. They have found ways round their own prohibitions, taking up forbidden devices by proxy. Because electricity is banned, they adapt pneumatic and hydraulic tools to run off propane gas; because cars are banned, they arrange for their non-Amish neighbors to drive their produce to market; because telephones are banned in

41

their houses, they install them in their barns; and because using e-mail is banned, they ask their neighbors to send their messages.[9] The Amish community as a whole is a hangover from the past but is characterized by lagged adoptions, not fixity. This brings it at least partly within the scope of ordinary diffusion models of change.[10] Yet the fact that Amish sluggishness is underpinned by religious beliefs and community consensus rather than unaided patriarchal power allows the influence of what might, indeed must, be called culture to reenter the picture.

Acceptance of the automobile in one Amish community first needed a few young men to transgress community norms by buying cars. Without the issue being raised head-on like this, there was no formal means of getting a determination as to whether it would be allowable in future. Significantly, and as social conservatives among the Amish might mournfully have predicted, the seed had already been sown for the acceptance of the automobile by the gradual easing of other rules, sometimes well before the present generation. Moreover, the development of communications in the community surrounding the Amish increased the social distance from their gentile neighbors and intensified the pressure to conform in outward respects in order to reduce the dissonance. A narrower cultural distance would have been easier to live with, though it should be added that no

[9] *Financial Times*, 4 Oct 1999. The employment of a Shabbas goy to perform otherwise forbidden household work on the Jewish Sabbath is another example.

[10] Details of the decision making that surrounded the acceptance of the automobile in one Amish community are given by John A. Hostetler, *Amish Society* (Baltimore: Johns Hopkins University Press, 1980), pp. 356–60.

general pressure was actually exerted on the Amish by the surrounding community, some of whom (like the taxi drivers who had previously driven them about) stood to lose from their adoption of cars. Others, like the car salesmen, who were reportedly ecstatic at the change, stood to gain. It was certain younger Amish men who most felt the cultural gap as dissonance and they who, so to speak, kicked over the traces.

Whatever forces prompt cultural change, all the values of a society do not respond instantaneously. The unconformity between maximizing behavior and historic values must distort behavior; otherwise the Amish would have adopted automobiles at the same rate as their neighbors. Social behavior is not a bland jelly but a pudding with fruit in it. Economic reasoning can probably digest this fact but not necessarily all at once. A little time has to be allowed for the logic—the digestive juices of economics—to operate. History is made up of a stream of hesitations. Cultural differences, which translate into whole spectra of lag times, accordingly do influence transaction costs and the allocation of resources. In short, culture does have a measure of economic significance.

III

Groups of people have distinctive behavior patterns, and there are adjustment costs when they mingle. This is evident in the classroom. Some students are accustomed to rote learning and uncomfortable with intellectual challenge. This is not merely an Asian phenomenon. Right across Eurasia, from southern Europe to Japan, many students think they are getting their money's worth only if they leave the lecture room with notebooks full of facts, preferably facts that seem to have a current market value. They do not enjoy being asked for argument or analysis, which they confuse with subjective opinion. Procedures have been worked out for overcoming their dislike of participating in class discussion, but these take time that ought to be devoted to getting the course material across.[11]

Chinese students in particular do not like unstructured class discussion, though, much more interestingly, many of them are starting to engage in it. Formerly, the lack of participation used to be palpable—see, for instance, P. J. Kavanagh's "nightmare" experience of teaching Indonesian Chinese students in the 1950s.[12] Yet, in a way that undermines simple cultural attributions, Kavanagh explains the failure of both Indonesians and Indonesian Chinese to ask questions in class by saying that "their conception of a University derived from some eighteenth-century Dutch pattern in which the teacher played the role of God, they took down his words in silence and then went away and learned them by heart" (p. 167). Methods inculcated by Dutch colonists in Indonesia cannot, of course, explain why the preference for rote learning is widespread among East Asians, while the fact that Dutch professors once taught in that fashion may suggest that even in Western classrooms independent-minded approaches to learning are often recent in origin.

China itself is now gradually becoming what the Japanese call a "normal country," starting to open like a flower-

[11] E.g., Alvin Hwang et al., "The Silent Chinese: The Influence of Face and *Kiasuism* on Student Feedback-Seeking Behaviors," *Journal of Management Education* 28/1 (Feb 2002): 70–98.
[12] P. J. Kavanagh, *The Perfect Stranger* (London: HarperCollins, 1991), pp. 167–68.

ing bud and in some ways coming to resemble other societies. Of course, there are limits to convergence. Styles of classroom debate differ even within the West; some American students are positively garrulous. They have been socialized from kindergarten in a special way. The upshot is that we see change and convergence but also discord and the persistence, or re-creation, of national and other differences.

What would be more fruitful than encouraging Asians to feel self-conscious in class, thereby slowing their adjustment to new methods, would be to investigate why some students do have little trouble adapting when they are away from home. Very little is known about the causes of these different responses. Looking for the reasons and capitalizing on them would be more helpful than stripping one's talk of color and cultural references or any mention of contentious issues. In my experience, intrinsic ability, prior familiarity with the language of instruction, and a positive attitude go far to explain the different responses. As to making unfamiliar cultural allusions, central issues rarely hinge on them. They are often used for what might be called reinforcement by garnishing, or just for a change of pace. Alert students can usually tell what is being referred to from the context, and it does not take long for the teacher to mug up a few references in order to touch base with class members from other cultures. In any case the problem is not solely one of different national cultures. Engineers from English-language backgrounds, for example, can be just as fixated on structure as Asian students, just as intolerant of the ambiguity which the world provides so plentifully, and just as uncomprehending of references to Shakespeare, the Bible, great painters, or classical composers. Yet, once again, by no means every individual exhibits these weaknesses, and the intriguing issue

45

is why some individuals are so much more responsive than others.

Nowadays there are consultancies devoted to acclimatizing expatriates in foreign environments; English business travelers can even buy advice about how to cope with thin-skinned Australians. Business school libraries are crammed with books instructing Westerners how not to offend the cultural sensitivities of non-Westerners, sometimes across a wide range of countries, sometimes with respect to a single land (frequently Japan). Extravagant sums of money are spent on such advice by governments that think they are promoting export drives and that do not even grasp that exporting is not always the best use of resources.

The acclimatization advice industry adopts a sort of "don't mention the war" approach; much of the advice deals with secondary matters such as the dos and don'ts of etiquette or how to handle negotiations with foreigners. Guidebooks can be laughably out of date. Very seldom do they invert the message and recommend that non-Westerners abandon their own shibboleths, though that is what foreigners often end up doing when they are obliged to operate in a Western environment. The assumption is that non-Westerners are unadaptable and ignorant of the West. I am reminded of the stories of the New Guinea accountant who said, "I suppose they think we are all cannibals up here. Well, tell them to get stuffed," and the Western woman in New Guinea who thought a local believed she was a spirit from the dead but who was told a week later, "I remember now who it was you remind me of. Dolly Parton."[13]

---

[13] Edward Marriott, *The Lost Tribe: A Search through the Jungles of Papua New Guinea* (London: Picador, 1997), pp. 19, 53.

Reminders about etiquette are not undesirable, because offending people of different persuasions without knowing one is doing so is easy enough. Businesspeople are even likelier than others to find themselves accused of giving offense, because the accusations can be bargaining ploys. The question is, how much does culture, in the sense of etiquette really matter? It is surely more useful to investigate what influences shifts in underlying values and behavior.

IV

Despite recurrent evidence of malleability, some degree of fixity—but *transient* fixity—does remain. Economists will not be surprised that fixity is only conditional. However settled a culture may appear, it is really in permanent disequilibrium. Cultures are never as rock-solid as they seem; a sort of continental drift is always at work. If that analogy suggests an interminable geological timescale, remember that earthquakes reveal how abruptly the most sluggish system can be transformed.

Many pragmatic noneconomists will object to treating fixity as conditional because they view cultures as historic, eroding so slowly that change is immaterial and may even be reversed in phases of puritanical reaction. They will say that cultures are what they appear to be: too antique, sticky, and intractable to be anything but the prime force in the decisions of individuals or societies. For all practical purposes, they will claim, we should take cultures as fixed. But even realists like these cannot seriously believe that culture does not sometimes alter dramatically. The extent to which Kemal Atatürk succeeded in converting the former Ottoman Empire into a secular regime is a conspicuous example. To appreciate the forces acting in given situations, how far culture adapts to them, or what success it may have in blunting their pressures, we need dynamic models.

The task is to analyze a system that, as Walter Bagehot said of Lombard Street, is mostly dull but sometimes agitated. Few available generalizations are guides to which aspects of culture are most likely to alter and which are likely to persist, what causes change and what accounts for stasis, which individuals will readily adapt and which will not. Some of the difficulty arises from the lack of tight definitions, as can be seen from the multiple, overlapping use of expressions like culture, civilization, and custom, besides the additional confusing use of culture to mean the arts. There is little help for this. Choosing a single usage sounds more scientific than working with a range of meanings, but if one imposes a finite definition, whole swathes of the literature that do not conform to it will have to be abandoned and along with them the very history of the subject, plus a host of potentially interesting observations. In thought, flexibility is better than sterility.

This book discusses cultural fusion when markets coalesce and competition starts between behavior and symbols that seldom came into contact before; it also deals with consequences of the cultural fragmentation when markets remain separated. This use of the term "market" may need to be elucidated for some readers. Noneconomists associate markets with specific institutions of which, often enough, they think they ought to disapprove, like stock markets or any transaction involving dollars and cents. Instead of merely (market) places where goods or services are sold or exchanged, what is meant here by "market" is any state of competition between beliefs and ideas and forms of behavior, or the arena in which interaction takes place between the peoples who hold or practice them. It is essential to grasp this more general meaning of "market."

Many cultural differences that are held in esteem appear little more than the elaboration of trivial initial choices: they survive or are recreated because people are easily persuaded to favor the known over the unknown and find comfort from huddling together as teams. Innocent bystanders are often treated as opponents, though I would interpret this as arising more from social tension than innate psychology: competition between street gangs is of this type. To give another example, English country folk used literally to fight people from the next village and try to expel strangers. This is well documented and was still going on in the Hampshire chalklands—flints were being hurled—as late as the childhood of my father and uncles just before the First World War. But it is telling to note that it had become habitual only during the harsh competition for resources during Napoleonic times.[14] Sometimes differences between populations are maintained to safeguard the interests of political leaders and cultural producers. Differences maintain themselves—they are "negatively" maintained—whenever there is no strong reason to deviate from established habits. And very often differences are preserved simply by the weakness or absence of competition when markets have not yet been brought together.

Given free choice, a majority of people might acquiesce to living in a modern market economy with a relatively (but never fully) uniform consumer culture of the type some-

[14] See K.D.M. Snell, "The Culture of Local Xenophobia," *Social History* 28/1 (2003): 1–30.

what carelessly described as American. They might be happy communicating with as many people as possible by sharing a common language and thus, if the implication were made clear to them, having access to the largest possible stock of human knowledge. In the developed world, where the English language reigns, they already behave in this cosmopolitan way, despite the anti-Americanism and cultural protectionism embraced by the media. In the less-developed world, revealed preference—the consumption of manufactured products and pop culture, the choice of English as a second language, the flow of migrants and would-be migrants—shows how many others would like to join in. Intergenerational conflict is often exacerbated by the fact that the young seize on these possibilities, though there are cases where even the young in their desperation accept antimodernization ideologies instead. At any rate, this version of modernity should not really be identified with Americanization: modernization is wider than that.

Although the reduction of poverty, disease, and suffering would make the price of a uniform culture and single lingua franca worth paying, centrifugal forces mean that in reality no pallid uniformity need be feared. People have a propensity to manufacture differences, create strangers, and raise up enemies just when they are embracing global norms in other respects. The resultant diversity is not as desirable as it is fashionable to declare. I am pleased to find a professor of English at Oxford commenting, "if cultural diversity is part of what makes life worth living, it has also brought a great many lives to a bloody conclusion. The call to celebrate such diversity is nowadays the merest cliché in the mouths of theorists and politicians; but it is only when cultural difference can be taken for granted, rather than defiantly affirmed, that it will have ceased to be a source of conflict."[15]

There is no real likelihood that an undifferentiated world culture will emerge. A few manufactured goods may have been standardized by the relevant international agencies, but only with difficulty. And everyone who has lived and worked in more than one country will have suffered the failure of national and international bureaucrats, not to mention university administrators, to bring about any real standardization of services. As usual, those responsible for such tasks are too well paid to suffer the consequences of their own inaction. Fresh cultural attitudes and institutional practices are more likely to spread via personal contact or the general diffusion of information than through official channels. Thinking of the world as becoming a single market and culture is little more than a hypothetical device for drawing attention to the long, slow, and only vaguely unifying processes beneath the profusion and confusion of human behavior. It does not depict any currently feasible prospect. There are important tendencies toward unification, but alarm that human society will become featureless displays a failure of the imagination. In society as in nature, to quote Gilbert White, "that district produces the most variety that is the most examined."

[15] Terry Eagleton, *The Gatekeeper: A Memoir* (London: Allen Lane/Penguin Press, 2001), p. 34.

Chapter 3

Culture as Mediocrity

The anthropological record contains astonishing sets of customs, many likely to strike outsiders as bizarre. It is as if there is nothing that has not been practiced somewhere by some group. Yet however strange other people's customs may appear, they are usually interpreted as purposeful. They are assumed to meet real needs or at least to have done so in the past. The question is whispered, "who are we to set ourselves above our ancestors, tribal peoples, and so forth?"—which presupposes that people in other places and at other times were no sillier or more whimsical than we are, had access to equivalent information, and acted with comparable motives that were merely disguised by unfamiliar dress. Foreigners and our own forebears operated under different constraints, it may be granted. But whether we really would have acted in the same way in similar circumstances is uncertain. It may be so, but there is seldom an obvious way of telling.

Often it is hard, too, to tell how practices began. With few means of documenting the oral reports of their informants, early European explorers may have come to believe that customs really were as old as the locals professed. Chiefs and shamans wanted to represent the practices over which they presided as right, proper, and sanctified by age; their own status was bolstered if they were seen as the repositories of society's essential lore. As Sack says, the aim of oral history is "to maintain the illusion of stability in the face of change."[1] Just how time-tested most "traditional" practices really were or are is thus uncertain. Being venerated does not make them venerable. Some may have sprung from the dislocation caused by the arrival of colonists, though colonization is not the only way societies have been shocked into disharmony.[2] Supposedly antique practices may have altered over the years, some of them switching on and off as the inducements varied.

"Age-old" Western traditions in their present form sometimes date only from the nineteenth century and, like the maypole, morris dances, and mummers' plays in England, were revived in fits of nostalgia. An interesting earlier example of a practice almost instantly accepted as hoary with age comes from Mere, Wiltshire. In 1565 the villagers arranged for a "Cuckoo King" to preside over their annual parish feast.[3] This lapsed in 1573, and was revived in 1576,

[1] P. L. Sack, "The Triumph of Colonialism" in P. L. Sack, ed., *Problems of Choice: Land in Papua New Guinea's Future* (Canberra, Australia: ANU Press, 1974), p. 201.

[2] Robert B. Edgerton, *Sick Societies: Challenging the Myth of Primitive Harmony* (New York: Free Press, 1992), p. 3.

[3] Ronald Hutton, *The Pagan Religions of the Ancient British Isles* (Oxford: Blackwell, 1991), p. 325.

yet the very next year was described as being performed according to "old custom." Twelve years and nine performances had been sufficient to cover the Cuckoo King with a patina of age. Only the fact that sixteenth-century Wiltshire was a passably literate society in which the churchwardens kept accounts exposes how novel the practice really was.

Of more general significance is the artificiality of the timing of Christian festivals.[4] The example of Christmas is striking. There is no historical warrant for celebrating the birth of Christ on any particular day, and the twenty-fifth of December was not selected until three or four centuries of the Christian era had already passed. The fact that different days over the Christmas season are imbued with significance in different countries is well known, but what is less familiar is the way the original choice was made. The church saw that pagans celebrated the birth of the sun on 25 December by lighting candles in a festive manner, and that "the Christians had a leaning to this festival." But although it was built on the practice of a much older Syrian cult, the pagan ceremony on 25 December was not old, the date having been decreed by the emperor Aurelian only in A.D. 274. It was transferred to Christianity throughout the Roman empire by Constantine in A.D. 323, and even after that Christians had sometimes to be warned that it was Christ's nativity they were supposed to be celebrating, not the birth of the sun.

Calendar customs are often assumed to be rural in origin and to be readily eroded by urban-industrial society. They are thought of as survivals of practices unchanged for cen-

---

[4] Ronald Hutton, *The Stations of the Sun: A History of the Ritual Year in Britain* (Oxford: Oxford University Press, 1996), p. 1. I am indebted to this work for most of what follows about calendar customs.

turies. In reality many flourished best around industrial towns and have been altered several times in response to changing circumstances. By the late eighteenth century, Christmas had become a quite insignificant festival in England; for working people it was no more than a humdrum day of rest. The *Times* did not mention Christmas in twenty of the years between 1790–1835. Soon afterward the importance of Christmas as a holy day and holiday was reemphasized by authors like Dickens, who professed themselves alarmed at the harm done to the family unit by industrialization. Other appurtenances of modern Christmases were adoptions or inventions, often devised by the commercial world; for example, a London businessman invented the Christmas cracker in 1846. The secular figure of Father Christmas was imported to England in 1854 in the guise of Santa Claus, who had been developed in America from Saint Nicholas, a figure imported in turn to America by the Dutch settlers of New Amsterdam in the seventeenth century. As Ronald Hutton tells us in his rich compendium *The Stations of the Sun* (p. 118), in 1879 the new Folk-Lore Society in England, unaware of practices in the United States, was, "excitedly trying to discover the source of the new belief."

While the natural rhythms of the British year impose some patterns on calendar customs and prompt symbolic observances at seasonal turning points, the forms have continually altered. They have risen or fallen according to the needs of changing social groups. In early modern times, the church gave way to the local community as the most important unit involved and over the past 150 years the community has given way to the family. Only a vague case can be made for thinking that the observances of any one phase have persisted for a very long time.

Cultural practices and beliefs are commonly rooted in the natural world. They use, abuse, or make reference to animals, plants, or topographical features. They have inconsequential origins arising out of the profusion of nature. Throughout the world innumerable species and natural formations have been chosen as objects of worship, sources of medicine, or ritual adornments. With almost infinite pieces of ecological jigsaw to choose from, it is not surprising that different peoples selected different totemic species. The mind turns readily enough to the idea that the customs of people close to the soil were adapted to the environment and must have been useful in some way. When markets were small and segregated and there was little communication among communities, the efficacy of an item of worship or a particular type of behavior was seldom systematically tested. Beliefs may have prevailed because they originally offered some material advantage rather than because they were better at explaining life's phenomena.[5] When belief systems came into contact, they competed on political rather than scientific turf and skeptics went to the stake.

During recent decades it has not been fashionable to question the appropriateness, justice, or salubriousness of other people's choices. At the extreme this leads to accepting, say, honor killings or female genital mutilation on the grounds that they are the inheritance and right of other tribes. There is more than a touch of the noble-savage myth about this cruel and condescending nonsense—static nonsense, too, since it does not envisage the people involved as

[5] As is persuasively described by Rodney Stark in *The Rise of Christianity* (Princeton: Princeton University Press, 1996).

ever being capable of graduating to less harmful practices. They stand condemned to the frozen choices of their ancestors.

The power and status of elites, including shamans or the priestly caste, accreted around motifs, totems, and rituals chosen in earlier times. Customs were elaborated to the point where their origin and even their purpose vanished in obscurity. Peter Conrad notes that Portuguese explorers wondered at the amulets around the necks of West Africans, which were bestowed by magicians supposedly to fend off evil. They coined the word fetish, which means "a made thing." "If the symbols were so patently invented, manufactured like toys, how could they be believed in? And the very immanence of the indwelling spirit underlined the fictitiousness of it all. . . . The fetish was, by definition, an idol unworthy of worship."[6]

Local strong men and shamans retained their authority by reference to the supposed wishes of the ancestors, which gives the anthropological past its air of permanence. Yet private innovations—though there may have been few of them in face-to-face villages—can enter rapidly at times. Tom Harrisson, a field observer with close experience of Borneo, was unusual among anthropologists in his insistence on the mutability of remote cultures. Harrisson noted the quick spread of the *palang* or penis bolt and slyly remarked, "It implies, as so many new ideas here do, that often the pattern everyone has grown to regard as essential, and almost im-

---

[6] Peter Conrad, *Where I Fell to Earth* (London: Chatto & Windus, 1990), p. 194. For the Portuguese, their own Christian symbols deputed for the Christian God but did not pretend to contain Him.

mutable, is in truth readily changeable. Change can come very swiftly, even almost unseen, in the dark."[7]

Harrisson's further comments on Borneo are especially worth quoting. He observed that it is always possible to persuade animist peoples that necessity overrides considerations like omens and taboos. Going through the motions of respect for such things is little more than lip service, less a matter of ineradicable belief than a means for animists to safeguard their relationships with others in their tiny communities. This implies an openness to amendment when opportunities present themselves. Rather than being stuck in their ways, animist communities were just not often challenged. "Many observers," wrote Harrisson, "even highly trained anthropologists, have been more than somewhat deceived as to the [shallow] extent and depth to which this type of religious or socio-theological feeling penetrates *inside* the minds and real actions of the people, as compared with its superficial and of course extremely important influences in ritual, agricultural observances, long-house organization, and so on."[8] Since the Second World War entire tribes "have demonstrated the point . . . by abandoning the whole framework of old and supposedly deep-seated beliefs within a few years, to become Roman Catholics, Methodists and Seventh Day Adventists on a mass conversion scale over huge areas both of Sarawak and of what is now Indonesian territory."

The fearfulness surrounding the choices of poor communities is reminiscent of that staple of economic development theory which states that farmers whose margin of sub-

[7] Tom Harrisson, *World Within: A Borneo Story* (Singapore: Oxford University Press, 1984), p. 62.
[8] Ibid., p. 252.

sistence is slim and who have few buffers against crop failure will be reluctant to try even the most promising new methods. Faced with uncertainty they will not hazard the scant quantities their existing techniques yield. Yet this assumption of constrained optimality barely holds in the face of the suboptimal nature of many folk practices and beliefs.[9] As C. R. Hallpike states, "almost everything will work in small groups and subsistence technologies in conditions of limited expectations and absence of effective competition."[10] He adds that "a limited number of institutions, based on such ascriptive principles as kinship and affinity, gender, age, and ritual status perform all those 'functions' which, in more complex societies, are differentiated."

|

Hallpike's view is heterodox. Generations of economists and Darwinians have treated customary practices as if they were purposeful. To do so accords with the rationalist methodol-

---

[9] It is believable that witchcraft's function is to reduce chronic uncertainty. See Patrick Chabal and Jean Pascal Daloz, *Africa Works: Disorder as Political Instrument* (Oxford: International African Institute/James Currey, 1999), which points out that even some Africans educated in the West resort to witchcraft. Under uncertainty extra insurance implies being safe rather than sorry. It would, however, be interesting to learn, a la Harrisson, how much of this belief is deep and how much a mere reversion to group norms. Superstition is prevalent in the developed world too but is more readily set aside when important decisions are at stake. This suggests that superstitions are also increasingly likely to be ignored in less-developed countries by the pragmatic and the educated, for very shame, when they are with their modern-minded fellows. See also on optimality Kaushik Basu et al., "The Growth and Decay of Custom," *Explorations in Economic History* 24 (1987): pp. 1–21.

[10] C. R. Hallpike, *The Principles of Social Evolution* (Oxford: Clarendon Press, 1986), p. 122.

ogy of economics and evolutionary biology, two subjects with a common rootstock that can be traced back through Charles Darwin and Karl Marx to Thomas Malthus. Rational actors are assumed to be led by an invisible hand toward maximizing material outcomes. The harsh environment in which early and tribal peoples lived is thought certain to have eliminated dysfunctional strategies. This approach at least has the merit of going beyond instructionism, which holds that behavior is adopted because its advantages are recognized. Under selectionist or adaptationist theories, behavior need not be conscious; whether or not its merits are understood, it will persist if it avoids being selected out by competition. It has only to escape rejection by environmental pressures.

In Hallpike's opinion, selectionist and adaptationist theories do not explain much behavior where there is little competition. The common assumption, carried over from biology and economics, that rigorous selection environments are almost universal, is wrong. In similar vein, and contrary to the bias of a literature that glorifies cumulative progress, superior technological practices have often been abandoned in favor of inferior ones.[11] The concept of "lock in" proposes that even today inferior initial choices may block the adoption of better technologies. The supposed contest between the QWERTY and DVORZAK keyboards is the cockpit of this debate. Whatever the merits of the example, the preponderant view has become that superior technologies are by no means guaranteed to prevail.[12]

---

[11] Gary Bryan Magee, *A Study of the Abandonment of Superior Technologies and the Reversibility of Technological Change* (B.Ec. honors dissertation, Department of Economic History, La Trobe University, 1990).

[12] Paul A. David, "Understanding the Economics of QWERTY: The Ne-

A Darwinian style of explanation is common in other spheres. Scholars seek to find some purpose to behavior that their peers have missed. Searching in cultural materialism for a purpose in unfamiliar behavior is a scholarly hunt with the bonus that a quarry can always be caught. A catch does not confirm the finding; all that is indicated is how many explanations are possible.[13] Functionalist arguments tend to be neat and revealing, suddenly making everything fit. But they refer to latent functions and are merely beautiful hypotheses. They cannot demonstrate that any particular solution is the only conceivable one.

The idea that dysfunctional behavior would have been eliminated in the past seems reasonable until we try to explain human sacrifice, honor killings, or the circumcision of women. In such cases, the slightest renegotiation could have increased the sum of human welfare. Inferior practices—mediocre ones—are most readily perpetuated where markets are small and isolated. Where little comparative information is available, news about viable alternatives may never see the light of day, and the social inefficiencies of the existing practices may never be debated. We have to conclude that folk practices have not typically been exposed to strong competitive selection, hence the persistence of what Hallpike calls "the survival of the mediocre."[14]

---

cessity of History," in William N. Parker, ed., *Economic History and the Modern Economist* (Oxford: Blackwell, 1986), pp. 30–49; and S. J. Liebowitz and Stephen E. Margolis, "The Fable of the Keys," *Journal of Law and Economics* 33/1 (1990): pp. 1–25.

[13] Ekkehart Schlicht, *On Custom in the Economy* (Oxford: Clarendon Press, 1998), p. 68: "for any function that may be imagined, there are less costly ways to take care of it."

[14] C. R. Hallpike, *Principles*, p. 142.

Obviously, if the position of the elite or the viability of the community were genuinely threatened, one might expect the offending customs to be abandoned—to be selected out. Yet isolated populations have gone on inflicting drastic wounds not merely on one another but on their habitat. They have persisted in activities for which "mediocre" would be a courteous term and shown few signs of correcting the damage they were doing.[15] Pre-European occupation of tropical Pacific islands brought about the extinction of over two thousand species of birds before A.D. 1000, reducing the number of avian species in the entire world by approximately 20 per cent.[16] In Tahiti, which European seamen were seduced into thinking was a paradise, large fish and turtles were scarce enough to be reserved for the elite and human infanticide was practiced—indeed, it was mandatory for the large priestly-entertainer class.[17] Nor can the assumption that

[15] Eric L. Jones, "The History of Natural Resource Exploitation in the Western World," *Research in Economic History*, Suppl. 6 (1991): 235–52; and Eric L. Jones, "Environment: Historical Overview," in Joel Mokyr, ed., *The Oxford Encyclopedia of Economic History* (New York: Oxford University Press, 2003), pp. 215–19.

[16] Jones, "Environment," p. 216. Diamond argues that environmental damage is a frontier phenomenon, a function of the rapid colonization of unfamiliar environments or of disequilibria when people acquire a destructive new technology. Jared Diamond, *The Rise and Fall of the Third Chimpanzee* (London: Vintage, 1992), p. 301). Small, long-established, egalitarian societies will, he says, recognize their self-interest in conserving their environment. But there seems little evidence either that destructiveness waned in the Pacific or that small-scale societies are egalitarian: consider the condition of their women.

[17] G. R. Lewthwaite, "Man and the Sea in Early Tahiti: A Maritime Economy through European Eyes," *Pacific Viewpoint* 7 (1966): 33; David Howarth, *Tahiti: A Paradise Lost* (New York: Viking Press, 1984), p. 35.

harmful customs will be reversed in the face of ecological reality survive the example of Easter Island, where the population failed to mend its ways before it had inflicted almost terminal ecological damage.

II

Other domains may be explored to see if the practices in them have resulted from competitive pressures. Is competition strong enough to explain the pattern of food taboos? Contrary to common opinion, the answer is no; their distribution is almost incoherent, as the second edition of Frederick Simoons's classic work shows, starting with the best-known food taboo of all, the banning of pork from tables in the Middle East.[18] Simoons considers various explanations of Hebraic food laws: they are arbitrary and can be understood only by Jehovah; they arise from a desire for hygiene; the banned animal (here, the pig) symbolizes sinful behavior; or they originated in the Hebraic rejection of cultic practices among alien peoples. Clearly, explanations that refer to Jehovah, symbolism, and the rejection of other cults would need to be tortured to contort them into functionalist reasons for avoiding pork. The explanations derive from different logics altogether. This leaves the matter of hygiene, which is the suggestion that springs to mind for most people.

Simoons points out that, on the contrary, there is no biblical support for such a hygienic rationale, nor are temperatures and hence the risk of food poisoning higher in Israel than in many pork-eating regions. He adds that, rationally speaking, the threat to health might have been dealt

[18] Frederick J. Simoons, *Eat Not This Flesh: Food Avoidances from Prehistory to the Present*, 2d ed. (Madison: University of Wisconsin Press, 1994).

with in other ways, such as banning pork in the summer only, eating it up quickly in feasts, or preserving it.[19] Moreover, besides banning the pig, the Hebrews banned the hare, which is a notably clean animal.

Working through beef, chicken, and eggs, horses, camel flesh, dog meat, and even fish, Simoons has little difficulty in showing how confused and manifold the purposes of food avoidances seem. With respect to horseflesh, he offers as a partial explanation the fact that Christianity rejected the sacrificing and eating of horses in pagan cults. Committed Christians today, at least in England, still disdain horsemeat like the remainder of the population, but this is not a reason they are likely to cite. I would be surprised if 5 percent of them remember hearing of the horse skulls in prehistoric burials and would be astonished if they made the link that Simoons suggests. They say instead that it is tough and yellow, that eating it indicates poverty, and that it is an undesirable habit of the French.

The last piece of chauvinism is ironic given the awe in which the English hold French cooking. An association with poverty or hard times is more understandable.[20] My father encountered horsemeat at the end of the First World War, and I was fed it once or twice during the most severe period of rationing in England in the late 1940s. It was

[19] The English rubric with which I grew up was that one should eat pork only when there is an "r" in the month.
[20] This is presumably why, during the 1930s depression, there was a Horse Meat Shop in tumbledown premises near the market in Leeds. The front was painted by law a vivid red to distinguish it from ordinary butchers' shops. Keith Waterhouse, *City Lights* (London: Hodder & Stoughton, 1994), p. 59. Yet even in the notorious early nineteenth-century Andover workhouse, the paupers had disdained horsemeat.

tough, and I associate it with other miseries of the period, such as having to eat whale meat and snoek. Nevertheless, an aversion to horsemeat would probably not survive a well-judged effort to introduce it as a speciality in expensive restaurants.[21] It could be cooked and served attractively— the reverse of "meals out" in 1940s England, where food was atrociously prepared and presented. Resistance to eating horsemeat must be lower now because few people can remember the era of rationing. Besides, horsemeat does not figure among modern culinary possibilities because it is no longer available.

Objections there would be, but less on grounds of taste than cruelty to horses. animal lovers tend to make scientifically unsupported distinctions between species, just as the antihunting lobby privileges foxes above pheasants and fish. Nor do the taboos in Western countries against eating cats, dogs, and other supposedly cuddly species primarily reflect the merits of the food. They are prejudices of a different kind, witness the pressure brought by activists on Australian supermarkets not to sell kangaroo meat, despite the nutritional and agricultural advantages (it is a low-fat meat and kangaroos are a major farm pest that needs to be culled).

No one could explain the Australian situation in terms of high prices for protein: that cornucopia, Victoria Market in Melbourne, sells crocodile steaks, kangaroo, emu, and witchity grubs, but these things supplement the abundant mutton and beef that Australians have always enjoyed. Australian cuisine, rightly described as "Mediterrasian," is

---

[21] Michael Green, who ate horsemeat in London in the early 1950s, describes it as "quite palatable and rather sweet in taste, except for the fat." *Nobody Hurt in Small Earthquake* (London: Bantam Books, 1991), p. 166.

replete with fusion foods. In this respect, Australia is out-standingly awash with creativity and, like immigrant soci-eties elsewhere, lavish with ingredients. It illustrates per-fectly that the introduction of fresh tastes into novel cuisines is possible when peoples and markets merge—more than possible, probable. In an integrated world, food taboos are challenged by the purveyors of the new experiences always sought by people with high disposable incomes. The inter-mingling of cuisines that globalization has now produced is turning one-time food avoidances into "foodie" experiences. This reveals how shallow older conventions really were, how little they were based in untrammeled human preferences, and how readily they can be uprooted when choice is no longer confined to customary products.

The conclusion Simoons reaches is that there are complicated and interacting food ideologies that "present difficult and even insoluble problems to the culture his-torian" (p. 322). His material suggests that many of these problems relate to gaps in the evidence about the history of dietary habits and the difficulty of knowing just how repre-sentative many reports actually are. But it is plain that food avoidances have a habit of fading when fresh opportunities come to hand.

III

Now consider wider categories of custom and belief in an-cient and small-scale societies. Here the locus classicus is Robert Edgerton, *Sick Societies: Challenging the Myth of Prim-itive Harmony*.[22] Edgerton decries romanticizing small soci-

[22] See note 2, above. A work in a similar spirit is Lawrence H. Keeley, *War before Civilization: The Myth of the Peaceful Savage* (New York: Oxford Uni-

eties and assuming they are particularly rational. "Populations the world over have not been well served by their beliefs," he writes on his first page. He lists beliefs in witchcraft, the taste for revenge, male supremacy, traditional practices involving nutrition, health care, and the treatment of children, slavery, infanticide, human sacrifice, torture, genital mutilation, rape, homicide, feuding, suicide, and environmental pollution. All these he says, "have sometimes [sic] been needlessly harmful." He defines harm or maladaptation as producing large proportions of dissatisfied individuals, or people who are physically or mentally ill, or anything severe enough to extinguish a community.

Edgerton's target is the school he calls "adaptivists," who hold that folk practices, even cannibalism, are guided by evolution, and who impute to early peoples unconscious problem solving ("immanent omniscience"). He demonstrates that optimal outcomes are not guaranteed. Poorly adapted societies caused environmental damage, rebellions, wars, arbitrary dictatorship, belief in witchcraft and taboos, foot binding, a eunuch class, female circumcision, false prophecies of the end of the world, and other blights ad infinitum. Confronted by this list, we might rather be led into the standard endeavor of economic historians, investigating how the astonishing benefits of living in the modern devel-

---

versity Press, 1996). Matthew Buttsworth's "Eden and the Fall: The Fallacies of Radical Ecological History" (Ph.D. dissertation, Murdoch University, 1998) is noteworthy for using the variety of anthropological medical practices to illustrate the randomness of cultural beliefs in the absence of scientific knowledge. These authors combat cultural-relativist romancing about the merits of early and tribal societies—romancing that, at least in some antidevelopment formulations, looks suspiciously like holding up distorting mirrors to reflect Western society in a bad light.

oped world were ever secured. The benign present, however fragile, seems as incredible as the deformities of the past from which it offered escape.

The point is not that the large-scale societies of the developed world have freed themselves from all failings. Maladaptive decisions are made everywhere, and crazy views are expressed in every population; it is a pastime of newspapers in other countries to report the claims of innumerable Americans that they have been abducted by aliens. It is easy to accept, however, that the chances of correcting these blemishes are greater than in closed societies where intellectual competition is restricted and dissent stifled. The contrast is especially marked with respect to medical practices. An encyclopedia of folkloristic "cures" can easily be collected, many of them capable of doing more harm than good, some of them unpleasant enough to turn the stomach, and none of them tested for efficacy. The belief was long entrenched in some quarters that for every illness and every noxious plant, God has placed on earth the remedy, like dock leaves next to stinging nettles to rub on the sting and lessen the pain. Dock leaves may indeed contain some mild antihistamine, but nettle beds do not invariably have docks ready to hand.

Folk remedies used locally available plants or animals, and in the absence of proper testing anxious patients complied with local norms. Maybe they remembered the successful cases when the pathological condition was in fact self-limiting. The side effects of herbal remedies could not be checked, records were seldom kept, and even in the developed world case histories were rarely published until quite recently nor were consistent rules developed. Maybe a proportion of herbal remedies did contain appropriate active ingredients: using digitalis for heart complaints resulted from William Withering observing a collector of simples in the eighteenth century, but this registers exactly the moment in time when pharmacology took over from herbal medicine. Only with the advent of modern medicine did old remedies fall into disuse, such as passing a child with a hernia through a hole in a tree. Yet not until 2004 did the British government decide to regulate herbal remedies.

Nothing like the random absurdities resorted to in remote regions is to be found in the modern pharmacopoeia, and to suggest otherwise is to parade something akin to the fallacy of moral equivalence. Whatever the failings of modern medicine, the weaknesses of which relate more to poor access than to ignorance or malpractice, science operates by a process of self-correction. The effort to understand and suppress disease is now international, and the teams of researchers in advanced countries are comprised of people from many lands. Obviously it takes time for cultures to shift from time-hallowed practices to scientifically tested ones. Inconsistencies can persist, like Isaac Newton elucidating the clockwork of the heavens yet spending years searching for the Number of the Beast, or the proliferation of New Age practices in once sober Western countries, where expectations have risen even faster than real incomes.[23]

[23] High disposable incomes have fueled the consumption of untested alternative medicines, dietary supplements, and New Age practices in Western countries. Among some young couples who have never seen certain diseases, there is a distrust of conventional medicine that is clearly against the public interest because they will not have their children vaccinated. They form the audience for semiscientific quacks, who can certainly find orthodox medical failures to trade on. These aberrations or pathologies of affluence may seem to disprove the notion that larger markets eliminate

Meanwhile less-developed regions are adopting advanced medical technology alongside older practices that have been given up or were never contemplated in orthodox Western medicine. While economic growth supports modern medicine, it also makes the older remedies more affordable—as well as providing ultrasound technology to make selective abortion effective in favor of the sons that peasant farmers once needed. The East Asian demand for parts of animals as aphrodisiacs may be growing, and it threatens several endangered species. There seems no evidence that these natural products work in the way intended, except possibly through autosuggestion.

A different topic where a functionalist explanation has also been offered is "scapulimancy." This is the practice among hunting groups, notably Eskimos, of burning the shoulder blade of a large animal in the fire, whereupon the shaman reads the cracks and directs the hunters to go off in the indicated direction. The shaman himself is sheltered from the consequences of failure by the shared belief in divination. The idea behind the explanation is that men are poor randomizers and will persist in hunting fruitlessly where they have made good kills in the past. Randomizing should offer greater long-run survival value than continually rehearsing the past. It is a nice idea. Unfortunately, as Edgerton points out, divination is seldom used by hunters.[24]

The law provides a final instance of where the inefficient methods of small markets have given way to better

---

inefficient practices; the response must be that we do possess a scientific establishment, and a majority of people does abide by its findings.

[24] Edgerton, *Sick Societies*, pp. 54–55.

ones.[25] Changes relate especially to identifying the perpe-
trators of crimes. Earlier methods asserted the raw power and
intellectual impotence of the judicial authorities. Lacking
codified rules of evidence and bodies of precedent; without
professional legal practitioners, without police forces; and
without techniques of forensic investigation, statements
were squeezed out of suspects (sometimes literally) by the
ordeal. When this approach was extended to identifying
witches, the victims were damned if they drowned and
damned if they floated.[26] Inefficient practices certainly had a
function here—that of finding culprits. The problem was that
they did not necessarily find the right ones. Driving such procedures into the outer darkness has been a long and uncertain journey. It has not been completed in the seventy-five
countries still practicing torture, at least if we assume that torture is designed to elicit confessions or information and not
merely to punish or for the pleasure of inflicting pain.

Some countries, including some former British colonies, have slid backward to politicized law. The legal systems
of very large societies like the Soviet Union and Nazi Germany were deliberately politicized, as the law still is in
China. To insist in the face of the persistence of torture and
judicial corruption that large, interconnected societies will
automatically eradicate evil practices would thus be wrong.
The open society with good information markets, in touch

[25] Richard A. Posner, *The Economics of Justice* (Cambridge, Mass.: Harvard University Press, 1981), pp. 119–227.
[26] There were growing numbers of rationalists in seventeenth-century
England eventually willing to curb the worst excesses. For an example of
the exposure of a fabricated case of witchcraft, see J. A. Sharpe, *Bewitching of Anne Gunter* (London: Routledge, 2000).

with similar societies, is the thread to follow when looking for the main direction of change. Legality is a consumption good that rising middle classes in all countries come to want. Even the collapsed balloon of a once-independent legal system, travesty though it may become, may be better than never to have had such a system at all. Where the forms of justice linger, their content can with luck be restored.

Is the world genuinely better off with larger cultural markets? According to Jared Diamond, the successful cultures of the modern world have been selected for economic and military success.[27] Their practices serve them for the moment but—here Diamond switches to denigrating American society—they bode ill for the future. According to him, adolescent turmoil, drug abuse, the poor treatment of old people, and gross inequality ought to rate as disasters. The Western world is an easy target for comfortable critics, and a Panglossian view of it would be out of order. But are we not being treated here to another fallacy of moral equivalence? Historically speaking, drug abuse has been as much a feature of the East as the West. Western societies were the first to reduce the grotesque income disparities typical of the ancient world and less-developed economies.[28] Western society is not the one to retain slavery. The scores of wars that have killed more people since 1945 than the Second World War, and which continue today as in the Congo, have not been Western wars. In its pluralism and multiple sources of power

[27] The first edition of Diamond's, *Third Chimpanzee* was published in 1991, and the book must have been written while the USSR was still in existence, making its anti-Westernism the more puzzling.

[28] For evidence on early wealth and income distributions, see Raymond W. Goldsmith, *Premodern Financial Systems: A Historical Comparative Study* (Cambridge: Cambridge University Press, 1987).

and influence, Western society possesses a more effective apparatus for correcting errors than its rivals do. It is not in the West that governments can, in Bertolt Brecht's phrase, dissolve the people and start again.

IV

Religion offers further evidence of the chameleonlike nature of belief and practice. Animism alone provides more than enough. There was backsliding in that direction within medieval Christianity, as there is today in the snake-handling churches of the United States. A Victorian divine claimed to find ophiolatreia or snake worship in every large country of the ancient world, interpreting it as a recollection of the events in Paradise.[29] The oak was also venerated, he said, adding sagely (p. 449) that this, "did not conduce to any national utility, as they never cut it down."

In the wilds of the theological literature every imaginable argument can be found, witness to the difficulty of bringing religious assertions to an agreed test. Beneath the tortuous theses written by Victorian theologians in their gothic colleges and rural rectories lay a universe of superstition. It lies there still. There are endless examples in travel books and an avalanche of literature on folklore. The persistence of superstition is shown by the tossing of coins into wishing wells, the strewing of rags on bushes, and (in another tradition) the stringing of beads on Turkish trucks to ward off the evil eye. And there was indeed a large element of snake veneration among the old chthonian forms of worship. The last elements of a snake cult survive today in the Black

[29] John Bathurst Deane, *The Worship of the Serpent Traced throughout the World* (London: J. G. & F. Rivington, 1833).

Forest, where house snakes are kept for good luck and to keep down vermin.

Largely omitted, if not actually concealed, in books about English churches is the existence of pagan insignia or at any rate images with no warrant in Christian liturgy. Thousands of medieval carved heads adorned with or comprised of foliage are to be found, though guidebooks rarely give them a mention.[30] Some of these "Green Men" are innocuous, others ugly and frightful "Wild Men." The Green Man at Sutton Benger, Wiltshire, is described as one of the great works of medieval Western European art. In a cluster of Devon churches there are carvings of three hares joined at the ears and supposedly implying fertility, as they do across Eurasia as far away as China.[31] The Devon examples are sometimes medieval and sometimes nineteenth-century copies. They often occur in conjunction with Green Men. Green Men also occur across the world in India and Burma. Such explanations as can be readily found of these repeated motifs, and why some things are portrayed but not others, refer vaguely to the persistent use of certain animals as symbols ever since people lived in caves.

Despite the puritanism which won a double victory in the Protestant churches of the seventeenth century and the Victorian age, erotic detail can also be found, besides grotesque carvings with no scriptural warrant. Whether the intentions were titillating or admonitory, what surprises is the

[30] Mike Harding, A Little Book of the Green Man (London: Aurum Press, 1998).
[31] Firsthand evidence of paganism coexisting with Christianity in Devon during the mid-twentieth century is given by Nancy Phelan in The Swift Foot of Time (Melbourne: Quartet Books, 1983).

presence and survival of so much overtly sexual imagery in the churches of a faith that for centuries at least has been fiercely puritanical in its expressed attitudes. Half-clothed angels on Georgian memorials could have been sculpted only by men with studios full of complaisant artists' models. In Victorian times, classical nymphs were driven out of the churches to adorn tombs in the cemeteries, but there they are sometimes flagrant. It all shows how ambivalent attitudes were even in the most puritanical of periods.

Some of the earlier carvings distort their subjects and seem calculatedly antierotic. Sheela-na-gigs are representations of women graphically displaying their genitalia, mention of which would be unthinkable at meetings of the Mothers' Union.[32] There are far more of such carvings than was once thought. The one close to the church door at Oaksey, Wiltshire, differs little from the type of pornographic image found scrawled in male lavatories. The church at Sapperton, Gloucestershire, has Jacobean pew-end statuettes of bare-breasted women of an Amerindian (Orinoco?) cast. There are topless women on seventeenth-century memorials at Burford, Oxfordshire, and on an eighteenth-century plaque in Bath Abbey. Once one's attention has been drawn to Green Men and other anomalies, it is hard not to notice them when visiting English churches, nor (to judge by websites) those in France and Spain. These survivals, so at odds with Anglicanism's antinatal stance, show how official literature can mislead about cultural attitudes.

According to an authority on the Elizabethans, the insignia are related to vestiges of cults of the generative pow-

[32] Jerome Burne, "Highly Selective Sex," *Financial Times Magazine*, 13 Sep 2003, a review of Catherine Blackledge, *The Story of V*.

ers, as in less prudish religions like Hinduism.[33] This seems not really to be so. The theory that an Old Religion of paganism lurked within Christianity has been rejected by modern scholarship, summed up in Hutton's immensely informed book on the pagan religions of Britain.[34] Continuity from paganism to Christianity was exceptional. Rather than adopting what had formerly been on offer, the church provided parallel services. Paganism in an organized sense became a ghost within Christianity, though Hutton admits that it bequeathed an enormous legacy of superstitions, literary and artistic images, and folk rituals to the culture of later times.

It remains utterly astonishing on the face of it that these things survived the Puritans and Victorians, who destroyed so much religious iconography and who were set against so much as mentioning sex or sexual pleasure. It is as if conventionally minded clerics and congregations almost literally ceased to see the images in their own churches. Of course, Christian society still uses the names of pagan gods for days of the week and has never bothered to replace them with the names of saints or apostles. Christianity may be notorious for its phases of cruel intolerance, yet its tolerance of ambiguity has been greater than one might expect. This may be because Christianity's early victory was so complete in England that no opposition was feared from organized paganism, which in its folk form was never theologically coherent to start with. Western thought in general is often said to be sharp-edged and not to countenance multiple religious

[33] A. L. Rowse, *The Case Books of Simon Forman* (London: Picador Pan Books, 1976), pp. 267–68.
[34] Hutton, *Pagan religions*, see n. 3, above.

allegiances like those of Japan. This may be true at some official level, but the evidence in the churches hints at multiple, Japanese-style ambiguities after all. Culture can be enormously plastic.

"With many superstitions," writes Goodwin, "there is no distinction between religions. Moslems and Christians often share in honouring sacred graves in which they put a saint of their choice."[35] Most remarkable—though there are other examples in the anthropological zoo—is the lapse of a Presbyterian community in the New Hebrides into worshiping a Duke of Edinburgh stone, sending a giant penis gourd to Buckingham Palace, hacking out an airfield for the Duke's aircraft to land, and reserving three bare-breasted teenagers as wives for him, to replace the somewhat older model he would presumably leave behind.[36]

Although cultural novelties can be accepted with surprising ease, people tend still to be marked by their upbringing: as the twig is bent, the tree grows. If their expectations are violated, the reaction may be pathological. In 2003 a Kurdish Muslim was convicted in England of murdering his sixteen-year-old daughter by stabbing her to death in an honor killing because she had a Christian boyfriend.[37] The police think there were at least twelve other such murders in 2003, estimates worldwide are of a minimum of five thousand, and no one can guess at the number of related hate crimes or the ostracisms and suicides of young people placed

[35] Godfrey Goodwin, *The Private World of Ottoman Women* (London: Saqi Books, 1997), p. 66.

[36] Alexander Frater, *Chasing the Monsoon* (London: Penguin, 1991), p. 213.

[37] BBC Radio 4, 29 and 30 Sep 2003. The woman announcer was audibly astonished as well as outraged at the murder.

under the stresses of cultural change. English society and its immigrant communities have been afraid to face up to such minority behaviors. Only in 2004 have the penalties been increased for female circumcision, at last described by the Home Secretary as an obscenity. The practice has been illegal since 1985, but there has never been a prosecution.

The clash of cultures is thus as evident in the religious sphere as anywhere else, and the violence with which the world religions continue to greet one another indicates conspicuously bad faith. Their story is one of discord leading at its extremes to outright massacres of opponents and fights over controlling sites sacred to more than one faith. Jerusalem springs to mind, and the temple at Ayodh. Theologians will retort that these clashes have no bearing on the truth of revelation, any more than have the disclosures of so much pedophilia by Roman Catholic priests or the contorted positions adopted in Anglicanism about women priests and homosexual bishops. Formally this is correct: religion soon becomes entangled in ethnic, national, and political disputes and can be blamed for them. A distinction needs to be made between its organized dimension, the churches, which are all too obviously prey to conflict, and its ethical and spiritual dimensions. The hierarchies of established churches have behaved just as Adam Smith predicted they would: elevating the role of learned men and elaborating theology, driving the less intellectual into less sophisticated, more participatory sects and cults.[38] Formal religion, Smith thought, would trap itself in this cycle.

The failure of any one faith to prevail in the world,

[38] Adam Smith, *The Wealth of Nations* (London: J. M. Dent, 1910), 2: 270–96.

even when comparative information is available, shows how rare it is to carry conviction about religion. When Christian settlers told American Indians that all humans were the children of one God, they remarked how odd it was that only white people had been given the news.[39] The closer proximity of incompatible systems in a world of population movements today has not yet led to an acceptance of Western values through the sort of ratiocination that the liberal media seem to expect. But notice more closely what had happened in the case of the unfortunate Kurdish girl. She had become "Westernized"—so her father complained, though both he and she were resident in England. A larger, more tolerant society had offered her options beyond those of her upbringing. She was a notably articulate young person and had seized her chance. Most, though not all, older people, captured by a single belief system when they were young, find it hard to weigh the alternatives dispassionately, change their ways, or permit change in others over whom they have power. Tragically, this young woman's father could not do so. Work on cultural adaptation indicates the frequent difference in generational adaptability but does not explain why the beliefs of some individuals are more malleable than others.

V

Christianity did not spread solely as a gospel preached by benign missionary monks who won the lottery from time to time when they converted a powerful ruler and cannily adapted the faith to pagan feasts and sacred sites. It also

[39] Forrest G. Wood, *The Arrogance of Faith: Christianity and Race in America from the Colonial Era to the Twentieth Century* (New York: Alfred A. Knopf, 1990), pp. 23–24.

played a part in obliterating predecessors and competitors, as Islam was to do more thoroughly. According to Richard Morris, Christian religious terror was unleashed around the ancient eastern and southern Mediterranean, as the faithful attacked temples, synagogues, and their worshipers, broke up shrines, chopped down sacred trees, and replaced the temples with churches.[40]

Yet the commoner story was one of accommodating pagan symbolism while providing similar but better comforts. Christianity provided a new identity, the chance of teamwork, and a clear-cut lifestyle in the insecure towns of the Roman Empire during late antiquity. In the pre-Christian countryside the farmers' gods were pagan and ancient. Pagan comes from *paganus*, a country dweller. The rural religion was propitiatory, as befits people dependent on the weather and the health and fecundity of animals.[41] Folk religion was on an annual cycle, ever renewed, and Christian festivals were synchronized with the same seasonal turning points. Heathen water cults at places like Bath and Wells were probably taken over by the church. Morris, the cautious scholar from whom these observations come, also traces the continuity of some church sites with pre-Christian sanctuaries. There is further evidence of this in continental Europe.

Paganism was not a structured religion. In Morris's words it was, a "cobweb of superstitions, tendencies, customs and relatively simple propitiary rituals" (p. 62). It was a loose amalgam of taboos, calendrical events, and brutal practices involving the ritual mutilation of animals. It was as much so-

[40] Richard Morris, *Churches in the Landscape* (London: J. M. Dent, 1989), chapter 2.
[41] Ibid.

cial as religious. There was a concern for genealogy, tracing the tribes to their divine ancestors. This "may be close to the sum of the whole issue," for paganism was more "a system of relationships than a system of theology." From the theological point of view, Christianity marked an advance over paganism, as all the world religions have done, by offering a more coherent philosophy. Yet despite the Christian codification of practice, its liturgies, and the panoply of churches and cathedrals, pagan beliefs and practices coexisted with it until the nineteenth century. Was this because people continued taking out insurance with the old gods rather than risk upsetting them? Was it because the population disliked being excluded from ritual, as they made plain during the Reformation, when the rood screens that had kept holy mysteries for the eyes of the priest alone were torn down?

VI

Sticky customs are not easily displaced unless new forces select against them. To that extent evolutionary processes are at work. As Richard Wilhelm states, stretching history only a little, "Chinese conservatism is not a symptom of rigidity but rather the result of adaptation to conditions which remained unchanged for thousands of years."[42] What disturbs the environment are new prospects, or, one might say, the falling price of information about alternatives. This takes place with migration, conquest, trade, and advances in the technology of communications. It expands the inventory on which random copyists can draw. The mathematical study of cultural transmission shows that changes come about

[42] Richard Wilhelm, *Chinese Economic Psychology* (New York: Garland, 1982), p. 45.

81

through random copying more than via Darwinian evolution, though nonrandomness prevails for a while when a fashion takes hold.[43]

Morris Altman has formalized the conditions that permit the survival of inefficient cultures.[44] Altman carries the argument further than Hallpike, and his work makes a suitable coda here. He makes cultural factors an additional variable in the production function, something that is seldom attempted in neoclassical theory. His particular contribution is to show how, even under competition, firms or societies with cultural values that do not conduce to economic growth may survive. Altman employs concepts now routine in industrial economics to the effect that firms (or societies) may be either X-efficient or X-inefficient. In the latter case they produce less than they might under relatively good conditions. Cultural norms that result in a less than full Weberian work ethic create X-inefficiency. Standard theory does not allow for this because it assumes that in any exchange economy all agents will be obliged by competition to become wealth maximizers. Altman points out, however, that where X-inefficiency stems from an actual preference for less competitive cultural norms, lower productivity will be offset by lower labor costs. This implies that labor, indeed society, will be voluntarily accepting lower material living standards than had it adopted a full-blown Weberian work ethic as its competitors did.

A decision to retain less competitive cultural norms

[43] *Economist*, 22 May 2004.

[44] Morris Altman, "Culture, Human Agency, and Economic Theory: Culture as a Determinant of Material Welfare," *Journal of Socio-Economics* 30 (2001): 379–91.

does not come without a cost; nothing does in economics. The opportunity cost is a lower material standard of living. Nevertheless, if it is willing to pay this price, a society with a less than fully competitive culture, and hence low productivity, can survive. Nevertheless, if information about the opportunity cost becomes widely available, the number of societies willing to retain their old cultures may be expected to fall. This is what the course of history reveals. More and more societies have modernized their culture. They have relinquished costly customs that, colorful or not, were baggage from the poverty of their past. Yet some mediocrity survives.

Luckily we do not live in a wholly mediocre world. Analogies may be drawn between cultural competition and competition in agriculture or industry. Agricultural and industrial histories are full of Schumpeterian gales of creative destruction, regional redistributions, and the emergence of rustbelts, all responding to shifts in comparative advantage. Were this not so, and had protectionists got their way, our leading industries would still include the manufacture of candles and crinolines, maybe of flint axes. Protectionist cries are ceaseless, of course, and we find ourselves still supporting lagging sectors, of which subsidized crop growing in the European Union and the United States is a glaring example. But free trade has not always lost, and material welfare has successfully increased over time.

A similar process has characterized cultural markets, sluggish though change in them can be. Despite perennial efforts to protect the churches, the arts, journalists, broadcasters, and cultural producers in general, novelties have repeatedly found their way in. Local producers are sometimes the ones who import them, if they think this will let them steal a march on their competitors. The division of labor may be limited by the extent of the market, as Adam Smith said, yet the extension of markets for information can work the opposite way. It can reduce the division of cultural labor by encouraging a synthesis of systems and eliminating mistaken beliefs. It can unify systems of ideas like modern science and medicine at the expense of the multiplicity of uneducated guesses and random treatments. The range of specialities within the new enlarged systems may expand, but with market integration the capricious diversity of mediocre practices will tend to shrink.

Chapter 4

The Means of Merging

Throughout prehistory and history the growing trend has been for societies, belief systems, and languages to come into contact, borrow from one another, and at times merge. The average size of cultures—groups who share beliefs and practices—has increased continually, though not continuously. When the degree of interaction rises, information becomes cheaper and available to more people. Because its price falls, more is consumed. Mark Casson remarks in an unpublished article that "in some cases the most important 'stylised facts' of history can be explained in terms of a simple hypothesis of falling information costs." Over time, information costs have been cut in many different ways and by successive new technologies, as the following brief survey will establish. The usual outcomes have been new syntheses in language, religion, and other domains and a reduction of local cultural diversity.

The late twentieth century brought somewhat nearer the possibility of a single world market for information that might permit universal cultural choice. A combination of information technology, air travel, container ships, and the liberalization of national markets restored the trend toward global integration that two world wars and the depression had interrupted. Although almost half the world's people still live in villages and have never used a telephone, the spread of mobile phones is rapidly reducing their isolation. But the prospect of one world is not yet practical politics. It remains less than elusive; it remains hypothetical, although on anything more than the shortest view the tendency toward coalescence is clear. Even the nastiness of modern conflicts testifies to increasing cultural overlap and the fervor with which threatened political classes resist competition and intrusion.

Among existing cultures, the American version is now far and away the most prominent. What is most distinctive about the United States is the syncretism of its culture. Every culture is replete with borrowings, but the American variety is openly a multiple hybrid. Its cultural products are put together by teams of people who have chosen to settle there from a host of other countries. An intensive exploitation of motifs from around the world results, along with the world's most energetic packaging and resale of cultural artefacts. American commercial society never stays still as it restlessly compiles a cornucopia of ingredients into new books, new art, and new blockbuster Hollywood movies. Most countries possess scholars, commentators, and publicists who are given to insisting that their society is unique and should not, cannot, be understood by reference to common traits. Only in the United States, the world's leading culture, does this become more than special pleading. George

Steiner once dismissed the United States as a "museum culture" lacking originality in most respects—he excepted jazz
and dance—but it is genuinely original in its aggressive meld-
ing of diversity.

Although it would now be physically possible for
everyone to share a single pool of information and ideas, the
mass of people in the poorer countries of the world as yet
come only indirectly into contact with Western lifestyles.
Hollywood and improved communications nevertheless
mean that they are made sufficiently aware of them to resent
either their very existence or the relative poverty of their
own lives, and to be confused and irritated by both these
things at the same time. The elites of the poorer nations seem
either to be striving to absorb American innovations, battling
to restrict their entry, or trying to prevent their own people
from hearing anything favorable about the American way of
life. They try to restrict the inroads of a global culture which
they see as an expression of American imperialism, Anglo-
Saxon capitalism, World Standard English, and Christian
or post-Christian values. They fear a cultural eutrophication
whereby the exuberance of Western culture might over-
whelm the offerings of their less fertile societies. Resistance is
at its height where there is an opposing culture that can be
mobilized in defense of particular readings of its own strictures. In the limiting case of Afghanistan, the Taliban draped
the bushes by the customs' posts with film ripped from video-
cassettes in order to keep out Western contamination.

I

About 50,000 years ago humanity, from its origins in the
warmer parts of Africa, had spread as far afield as New

Guinea and Australia. Another 20,000 years passed before people settled the colder parts of Europe. Siberia was reached only after a further 10,000 years and the Americas not for about 9,000 years after that. Polynesia was only settled between 3,600 and 1,000 years ago. These are notional chronologies that are sometimes hotly contested; archaeologists keep pushing them further and further back and now report finding very early, dwarflike people in Indonesia who scarcely fit the usual narrative. The details do not matter for our schematic purposes. During the great early expansions, our species behaved like other large mammals entering new territory. Populations separated and became culturally somewhat distinct from one another. The main interest lies in what happened when they met again.

An obvious mode of contact was trade, which had initially been self-organizing. One of its origins was the "silent trade," made famous by Herodotus. Nervous people crept out to examine goods laid out by another party, took what they wanted, and left their own offerings in return. More distant exchanges were hampered by the high costs of transport. Land carriage is said to have been typically fifteen times dearer than water-borne transport. Markets for goods only slowly extended their range, starting with the small, precious, lightweight baubles of early trade—"splendid and trifling," as Edward Gibbon called them—and exchanges of craftsmen and of high-born women given almost as hostages in politically-inspired marriages. There were setbacks enough, but long-distance traffic in everyday commodities began again whenever political calm prevailed. The most cited beneficiary was an Athenian at the time of Pericles. He could dine off food and sit among furnishings shipped from as far away as the Black Sea, Persia, and Carthage. Once shipping costs became low enough, trade extended from finished goods like these to unprocessed raw materials that were much heavier per unit value. Alongside the expansion of markets for physical items came strangers and news. Costs of learning about the habits of once-unknown societies fell as their goods were imported and their emissaries arrived.

The oceans as well as the land were crossed by preindustrial peoples. The Polynesians learned how to squeeze more navigational clues from wave patterns than one could imagine possible.[1] The Micronesians made an advance on this by devising extrasomatic caches of information that the Polynesians lacked, sources that did not die with the body and mind of the person who had created them but could be stored and transmitted across the generations. These sources took the form of charts of the sea's surface: three-dimensional models made from the ribs of coconut palms, the ribs bent to represent the curves and confluences of the main currents around islands that were denoted by shells.

Astonishing as this was, from the standpoint of information retrieval it was only a halfway house. Examining the charts in museums around the world, Harold Gatty found that those of the same area differed considerably. Nor were stick charts easily replicated. These early voyagers tended to lose contact with their homelands and altered their cultural habits according to the ecological potential of the new lands they found. They elaborated but did not collate the information available to them and in any case did not venture half so far as Captain Cook was to do. The European Discoveries really did inaugurate a new phase of global interconnectedness that established and sustained contact over

[1] Harold Gatty, *Nature Is Your Guide* (London: Collins, 1958), p. 159.

unprecedented distances. Only in the age of Cook, when findings were disseminated in the form of books, did reliable information about distant places become available in principle to all.

Exploration and trade have since confined absolute localism to holes and corners. It survives only in areas that lack overarching political authority. Michael Crichton describes the isolation he found in Baltistan in the early 1980s: the villages, sometimes no more than a couple of dozen wooden houses, were only five miles apart, yet they varied sharply.[2] Most of the year they were separated by deep snow as if they were hundreds of miles apart. They had different speech patterns and styles of housing. In Papua New Guinea, Crichton found people so separated by the mountains that customs differed from one place to the next and there were supposedly seven thousand languages or dialects. Although a pidgin had become a lingua franca, social cohesion across the New Guinea Highlands was slow to evolve. High earthen ramparts thread through the landscape like the Maginot Line, and there is an atmosphere of perpetual suspicion. This is the chrysalis from which it is conjectured the whole world emerged, sometimes thousands of years ago, sometimes only yesterday. How good a model New Guinea is for the early history of the world as a whole is not entirely clear, but the analogy is suggestive. Faint echoes of a similar localism can even be found in the remoter parts of Western Europe: in the 1960s Jan Morris found the same species of bird called by nine different names in nine neighboring Sardinian villages.[3] We may find parochialism quaint (travel literature

[2] Michael Crichton, *Travels* (London: Macmillan, 1988), pp. 203–4.
[3] Jan Morris, *Fifty Years of Europe* (London: Penguin, 1997), p. 200. Pos-

trades on it) or chilling (local demagogues trade on it too), but it undeniably impedes discourse between peoples.

The Pacific may have been a world of especially fragile contact but the borders of the Atlantic became firmly knitted together in early modern times, when the evidence ceases to be conjectural and becomes documentary. Letters detailing the products, flora, and fauna of the New World poured back to Britain from the American colonies. The transmission of information is symbolized by the way jointed wooden dolls dressed in the latest Paris fashion circulated not only around the European capitals but as far away as Boston, Massachusetts.[4] Astonishingly enough, some early American colonists revisited their homes in England, and at least one Somerset family kept this up for decades.[5] In the eighteenth century, making the trip back to England as a sort of Anglo-Saxon Grand Tour became routine for those wanting to spy out the secrets of advanced agriculture in the countryside and enjoy high society in the city. The Revolution was a surprisingly brief interruption, and further floods of correspondence came on its heels.[6] In the nineteenth cen-

---

sibly the white wagtail (*Motacilla alba*). Ornithological science depends on employing universally understood scientific names. Even the different bird names in national languages impede accuracy and communication. Regional and dialect names for birds survive in many countries, though their use is on the wane, making it easier to assess and compare records.

[4] Eric L. Jones, *The European Miracle*, 3d ed. (Cambridge: Cambridge University Press, 2003), pp. 113–14.

[5] Eric L. Jones, "The European Background," in S. L. Engerman and Robert E. Gallman, *The Cambridge Economic History of the United States* (Cambridge: Cambridge University Press, 1996), p. 104.

[6] Eric L. Jones, ed., *Agriculture and Economic Growth in England 1650–1815* (London: Methuen, 1967), p. 48.

tury, squatters from much further away, Australia, paid visits home too, to buy pedigree livestock and swan around the salons and fleshpots of London.[7]

II

The history of language illustrates the processes of unification. The boldest conception of the early fortunes of languages is by the evolutionary biologist, Jared Diamond.[8] Leading linguists counter that too little is known of the history of languages to align it with his, or indeed any, grand thesis, but Diamond imaginatively captures an essential mechanism by describing the occupation of the earth as follows: The geographical range of settlement was continually extended over thousands of years, yet small groups were always dropping out and settling down while the more adventurous leapfrogged over them to fresh frontiers.[9] Settlers and their descendants had limited contact with other communities, and each place developed its own language. In old settled regions, much of the diversity has since been erased by the expansion of centralized empires whose languages came to dominate. Languages consolidated into ever fewer groups, give or take some contrary instances during political breakdowns and the emergence of pidgins useful for commerce between separate populations. The most recently settled re-

---

[7] The formative knowledge transfers in Australia's case are detailed in Geoff Raby, *Making Rural Australia* (Melbourne: Oxford University Press, 1996).

[8] Jared Diamond, *The Rise and Fall of the Third Chimpanzee* (London: Vintage, 1992).

[9] See, for example, R.M.W. Dixon, *The Rise and Fall of Languages* (Cambridge: Cambridge University Press, 1997).

gions, New Guinea and the Americas, now hold about half of the surviving languages.

The conventional wisdom that the number of languages in the world is shrinking, though correct as to direction, is based on incompatible estimates. The consensus is that half the current total of 6,000 languages will disappear before A.D. 2100. This is doubtful, because there is no agreement about defining the stock of languages and estimates of extinction rates are exceedingly variable.[10] One authority, Robert Dixon, says there are 4,000 languages, not 6,000. Expectations of loss this century range between 300 and 5,400 languages—so extreme a range as to be meaningless. Part of the trouble is advocacy on behalf of preserving every language, no matter how few its native speakers. This involves absurdities such as equating the loss of languages with the extinction of biological species.[11]

Indo-European languages have become prominent, and among them much the most far-flung of the trading languages is English. As things stand, more people speak English than have ever spoken a single tongue, and those who speak it as a second language now outnumber native speakers. The common language of the European Union is said to be "bad English." Diamond's extrapolation of evolutionary theory implies that in the end English, too, may deliquesce into separate languages. The model for this is Latin, which lost political support at the fall of Rome and began to evolve into the group of Romance languages. The assumption is that

[10] Eric L. Jones, "The Case for a Shared World Language," in Mark Casson and Andrew Godley, eds., *Cultural Factors in Economic Growth* (Berlin: Springer-Verlag, 2000), pp. 226–27.

[11] David Crystal, "Things Left Unsaid: The Death of Languages," *Australian Financial Review*, 14 Jan 2000.

Latin was incapable of surviving without the prop of Roman power. English, on the other hand, may surely survive because of its use in world trade, though this is not to say its dominance is guaranteed.[12] Both centrifugal and centripetal forces are always at work in the realm of language. Prosperity, political ambition, political correctness, and reduced costs of transmission can work in favor of consolidation, but they may also rejuvenate local languages. The further advance of English may be blocked by other languages—Mandarin in East Asia, for example. Nevertheless, if the individual brush strokes are debatable, the larger picture is plain: English holds sway and brings more people into contact than ever before.

III

Religion is another topic that illustrates the long, uneven process of consolidation. Consider Europe: Christianity's triumph there was not inevitable, since Islam, Judaism, even Mithraism were all in the market. We have to turn to the initial calculus of choice in the cities of the Graeco-Roman world to become fully aware of the advantage of Christian values. A pre-Christian city was a chaos of poverty, overcrowding, ethnic conflict, epidemics, fires, riots, and downright brutality. Christianity had the potential to meet these problems through bonding the poor together and requiring high standards of behavior. It might not solve all problems, but it went some way toward assuaging them. There is no suggestion in this that the desperate troubles of city living

[12] Barbara Wallraff, "What Global Language?" *Atlantic Monthly*, Nov 2000, pp. 52–66.

caused the advent of Christianity, merely, as Rodney Stark says, that "its superior capacity for meeting these chronic problems soon became evident and played a major role in its ultimate triumph."[13] That triumph endowed the Western world with an organization capable of bringing about a considerable, though never absolute, standardization of religious practice. Even restricted standardization was a great feat, given the vast number of detached settlements and motley folk practices. As a secondary consequence, the church helped to renew the orderly diffusion of knowledge across Europe that might otherwise have ceased with the fall of Rome.

When Christianity spread, it diffused the main elements of Mediterranean culture present in the late Roman Empire: urban lifestyles, trade, Roman law and property rights, the written Latin language, Graeco-Roman literature, food, and dress, and so forth.[14] A complete uptake of all these items took centuries and often involved assimilating them to earlier beliefs and sacred sites; after an initially aggressive expansion, accommodation became the explicit policy of the church under Pope Gregory I (A.D. 590–604). This had the advantage of reducing the resistance that might have resulted from demanding too many outright mass conversions. The process was approximately paralleled where Buddhism and Islam spread, though Islam made a greater effort to eradicate traces of prior cultures.

[13] Rodney Stark, *The Rise of Christianity* (Princeton: Princeton University Press, 1996), p. 162.

[14] Richard Fletcher, *The Barbarian Conversion: From Paganism to Christianity* (New York: Holt, 1998).

IV

The writing of history in terms of information and communication systems was pioneered in 1950 by Harold Innis in *Empire and Communications* but not much taken up until the publication of Daniel Headrick's *When Information Came of Age* exactly fifty years later.[15] In the meantime the topic was commonly an appendage to histories of ships, railways, aircraft, telephones, and the like, or occasionally added to accounts of institutions such as post offices. The acceleration in information handling and transmission was not, however, directly measured by the increased speed and reach of this or that technological innovation.

Graphic anecdotes of the speed of communications at different periods may readily be found: news of the battle of Plassey in India in June 1757 took until February 1758 to reach England by a ship sailing round the Cape of Good Hope, while the report of Napoleon's death on St. Helena in 1821 took two months to reach London.[16] Whereas it took seven days for news of Washington's death to reach New York City, 68 percent of the American public heard of

[15] H. A. Innis, *Empire and Communications* (Oxford: Clarendon Press, 1950); Daniel R. Headrick, *When Information Comes of Age: Technologies of Knowledge in the Age of Reason and Revolution, 1700–1850* (New York: Oxford University Press, 2000). Another major classifier of information systems is Mark Casson; I quote in the text from his 1995 manuscript "The Historical Significance of Information Costs," which describes information costs as central to much of history. See also Dagmar Lorenz, "How the World Became Smaller," *History Today*, Nov 1996, pp. 45–50.

[16] Don Gifford, *The Farther Shore: A Natural History of Perception* (London: Faber & Faber, 1990), p. 114; Donald Read, *The Power of News: The History of Reuters 1849–1989* (Oxford: Oxford University Press, 1992), p. 7.

Kennedy's assassination within thirty minutes.[17] But these are anecdotes which, though they show the increasing pace of movement, do not directly track the falling cost of information. It is hard to find an overall picture of falling costs as opposed to compilations of speed records or vignettes of canals, steamships, and railways, and even individual locomotives, which are after all merely bundles of transportation services in successive physical forms.[18] The technology bias is akin to the "prize marrow fallacy" in agriculture, which awards prizes for the biggest or physically most perfect product instead of for economic efficiency or social outcomes.

Headrick analyzes information systems as a series of processes under the headings of organizing, transforming, displaying, storing, and communicating information. He identifies a revolution in information systems in the late seventeenth- and eighteenth-century West, involving such prodigious gatherers and classifiers of data as Linnaeus in botany and Johnson in lexicography. Their achievement long predated the mechanization of data processing in the postal and telegraphic systems of the nineteenth century.[19] The history

[17] Theodore Steinberg, *Nature Incorporated: Industrialization and the Waters of New England* (Cambridge: Cambridge University Press, 1991), p. 125 n. 89.

[18] Representative curves for the speed of successive modes of transport are available, e.g., as figure 8.1 in Barry B. Hughes, *World Futures* (Baltimore: Johns Hopkins University Press, 1987), p. 147. A diagram of electronic services, from telegraphy in 1847 to those of the year 2000, appears in Read, *Reuters*, p. 405.

[19] Additional material appears in Lisa Bud-Frierman, ed., *Information Acumen: The Understanding and Use of Knowledge in Business* (London: Routledge, 1994) and Shosanna Zuboff, *In the Age of the Smart Machine* (Oxford: Heinemann, 1988). See also Michael Porter and Victor Millar, "How Information Gives You Competitive Advantage," *Harvard Business*

of standardization throws further light on the unification of information markets.[20] Adopting a common calendar throughout most of the world regularized trade and intercommunication.[21] Clock time was coordinated by the exigencies of rail travel. The confusion of running trains across Canada, where every town set its clocks according to when the sun was directly overhead, led in 1879 to a proposal for twenty-four time zones, which were adopted by all North American railroads in 1883. In that year conferences in Rome and Washington adopted as international standards the Greenwich prime meridian and Greenwich mean time, including the international dateline, with its convenient minimum of bends and re-entrants.

Further and further jumps took place in the speed of transmitting information, means of processing it, and size of storage facilities (libraries for instance).[22] There were increases in the frequency and scale of public meetings even

---

Review, Jul–Aug 1985, pp. 149–60. Casual comparisons with the past occur widely, almost always designed to dramatize the technical superiority of successive inventions. For twenty-five years after 1945 encyclopedias were full of them. There was then a lull as technological triumphalism waned, only to resume in the 1980s and 1990s with the new triumphalism about electronic methods.

[20] An interesting argument that pivots the rise of the Western world on the unique coincidence of a standardized linguistic medium and a non-standardized message is Ulrich Blum and Leonard Dudley, "Standardised Latin and Medieval Economic Growth," *European Review of Economic History* 7 (2003): pp. 213–38.

[21] Jones, *The European Miracle*, p. 111.

[22] See Carlo Cipolla, *Literacy and Development in the West* (Harmondsworth, U.K.: Penguin, 1969), p. 110, for figures on the growing size of European and American libraries during the nineteenth century.

before radio and television reached audiences of a different order of magnitude. The immediacy of reporting stepped up—Gifford has argued for a turning point in the mid-nineteenth century, since the essay-like journalism of the 1840s gave way by 1870 to impressions of events reported minute by minute.[23] But Headrick is candid enough to observe that no one epoch marks a decisive break between the transience of oral cultures and modern electronic developments in the transmission, codification, and storage of data.

This is not to say that physical infrastructure was or is unimportant in tying markets together; that would be too extreme a view. The building of inland canals and railways and the construction of ship canals like Panama or Suez were heroic developments before the First World War. Investment in similar links has now returned to high levels. There are innumerable contemporary projects for high-speed railways, undersea tunnels, new roads, oil and gas pipelines, and the like, many of them international rather than confined to a single country. Much longer connections are in the offing around the world. Whether or not the more ambitious proposals, such as bridging the Bering Straits or tunneling between Morocco and Spain, prove to be viable remains to be seen. Celebration of comparable advances is chiefly to be found in books dating from the nineteenth century and the first half of the twentieth. Only engineering students seem enthused by them today. Search engines trump canals in other minds. Present-day writings about technology vaunt electronic communications, and the achievements of computer scientists above those of civil engineers.

[23] Gifford, *Farther Shore,* p. 51.

V

The precursor of the computer was the printing press. English-language histories of printing need, however, to be approached warily; they are slanted toward the experience of Europe, whereas the Europeans were in reality sluggards. China, Korea, and Japan employed movable type several centuries earlier. The reason late-coming Europe eventually forged ahead of them was less its somewhat derivative technological prowess than the emergence in the fifteenth century of a larger reading public. This was signaled ahead of printing by a rising demand for copies of handwritten manuscripts. In Italy this demand was precisely at its peak in the quarter-century before printing began.

Printing cut the costs of written material, but only widespread literacy could make this significant throughout society. It was much later before more complex demands on labor made it seem desirable to promote mass literacy and economic growth made it affordable.[24] Literacy is a term of inconsistent definition, and overconfident figures are bandied about in the highest quarters.[25] Even comparisons of modern levels of literacy often suffer from uncertainty as to whether they refer to reading or writing or both, and if so to what standard at what age. If we take what is available at face value, we may judge that about A.D. 1000 only 1 or 2 percent of Europeans were literate.[26] By 1850 the proportion may

[24] R. S. Schofield, "Dimensions of Illiteracy, 1750–1850," *Explorations in Economic History* 10 (1973): 454.

[25] For examples of improbable and inconsistent numbers published by UNESCO, see Eric L. Jones, "Cultural Nostalgia," *International Studies Review* I/3 (1999): 133–34.

[26] Cipolla, *Literacy and Development*, passim.

have risen to 50 percent, though probably half of those could read only poorly. By 1930 the figure is thought to have climbed to 90 percent, and by 1990 Western governments usually asserted that 98, 99, or in the most ambitious cases 100 percent of their populations were literate. One wonders, then, why they spend so much on adult literacy programs. Specialists in the field think that in reality only about 85 percent of the population in many developed countries are functionally literate—only 80 percent in Britain. Figures for the remainder of the world are much less certain, though without doubt literacy rates are lower in most non-Western countries.

Functional illiteracy means not being able to read even simple instructions or safety notices. Admittedly, information can be diffused by intermediaries, such as a tiny literate class. This was the Chinese historical experience, where ideas about new agricultural techniques reached the mandarins through the works known as Nongshu and were passed on by them to local farmers.[27] In this respect Chinese agriculture had the advantage over most premodern societies. But it did not retain the advantage over the West or Japan, where working farmers were often able to read, and knowledge and warnings could both spread quickly.

VI

In the nineteenth and early twentieth century came the telephone, an astonishing breakthrough by previous standards, although not by those of the present generation. As recently as 1966 only 138 simultaneous conversations could take

[27] Gang Deng, *Development versus Stagnation* (Westport, Conn.: Greenwood Press, 1993).

place between Europe and North America; Citibank hired squads of youths to sit all day in New York, dialing in the hope of getting through.[28] It was only the final decades of the twentieth century that saw a truly massive increase in "teledensity." The last jurisdiction without a telephone system was Tokelau, a New Zealand territory with a population of only sixteen hundred. It did not sign an installation contract till as late as 1996. By that date the enormous surge in the laying of landlines was being supplemented, and then supplanted, by satellite communication.

No doubt telephone, radio, and electronic communications have had more extensive impacts than other inventions subsequent to the devising of written scripts or the production of printed books.[29] By 1990 there were over two billion radio sets in the world and over one billion television sets. By that year 45 percent of these devices were in the non-Western world, as compared to only 20 percent in 1965. In India and China, where village isolation lasted almost to the present day, the spread of radios, televisions, and mobile phones means that huge populations are suddenly and for the first time being granted access to market prices, land ownership data, and national and global culture. Television may portray little more than sport and soap operas, but the temptations of the lifestyles it reveals will be giddying.

Despite exaggerated reports of the death of distance, or perhaps exaggerations of the speed at which this is occurring, modern technology is bringing about a staggering re-

[28] Robert Frank and Philip Cook, *The Winner-Take-All Society* (New York: Free Press, 1995), p. 48.
[29] Eric L. and Sylvia B. Jones, "The Book Industry," *Oxford Encyclopedia of Economic History* (New York: Oxford University Press, 2003).

duction in the price of communications.[30] There has never been such informational richness, especially for countries in the early stages of economic growth. The long-term effects are unknowable. Authoritarian governments are worried at their loss of control; about the reaction if an unbridled rise in expectations cannot be met; and about the shock of the new as peasant labor is forced from the cocoon of the ages into situations to which ancient lore is no guide. The Chinese workers who quit the factories in Guangdong when Britain relinquished control over Hong Kong in 1997 had no conception that such an event could take place peacefully. Their past had prepared them only for conflict between regimes, and they hired buses to take them back to their villages. Yet revolutionary changes in exposure to the world are in train, and student responses, at any rate, have already become much more knowing. Chinese students who were once suspicious worker-soldier-peasants are stylish travelers today.[31] A single generation has modernized them. The tran-

[30] Keeping calm in the atmosphere surrounding these changes was difficult. Although understandably enthusiastic, Frances Cairncross succeeded as well as anyone in providing a balanced appraisal in *The Death of Distance: How the Communications Revolution Will Change Our Lives* (Boston: Harvard Business School Press, 1997). Of the many skeptical comments on the creation of the "global village," Claude Moisy, "Myths of the Global Information Village," *Foreign Policy* 107 (Summer 1997): 78–87, is perhaps representative. He observes that the news sought by consumers was in reality becoming more local, a trend that apparently continued after 9/11 and maybe even after the Iraq War of 2003. See also Garrick Utley, "The Shrinking of Foreign News: From Broadcast to Narrowcast," *Foreign Affairs* 76/2 (Mar–Apr 1997): 2–10, which describes the pressure exerted on the media by the Chinese government and the additional self-censorship that results.

[31] This is not closely analogous to Western experience of travel since the

sition is having a striking impact on lifestyles and purchasing habits, as marketers are well aware, and this will trickle down to rural areas as they come to share in prosperity and rich information.

Culture and information accompany goods and services, migrations and conquests, as invisible baggage. They spread directly and indirectly via films, books, and broadcasts. Few societies can exclude all seepage from outside. Even China has begun to relax control, though its relaxations have an inconvenient habit of waxing and waning. The first correct daily temperature forecast was not broadcast until July 1999.[32] Previously, temperature predictions were never permitted to fall outside the range for efficient factory work. Unfortunately for the Beijing government, it was unable to maintain the fraud, because too many Chinese were now able to receive weather reports over the Internet.

When SARS struck, China tried to suppress the reports. Full data were not released for a disastrously long time; doctors were forbidden to talk to reporters; and even though

---

parents of current Chinese students had been confined to their own country by the Cultural Revolution—a restriction unlike any restriction Western civilians have suffered except between 1939 and 1945. Of course, travel may not so much broaden anybody's mind as lengthen their conversation: it has minimal effects on the attitudes of many Western holiday makers and had rather little on their grandparents and great-grandparents when they returned from overseas after wars. Travel may reinforce cultural stereotypes instead of eroding them. Longer stays may engender defensive chauvinism, even among university students. Instant conversions to wider sympathies and understanding are not to be expected. Most individuals, however, broaden their perspectives if subjected to fresh experiences over the longer term.

[32] *Australian*, 2 Aug 1999.

the first case occurred in November 2002, the visit of a WHO team was delayed until April 2003. That the lesson has still not been learned in Asia is revealed by the coverups and delays in reporting outbreaks of avian influenza in several countries during 2003–4. What may be of greater long-term significance is, however, that the Chinese surgeon who exposed the SARS scandal was able to do so via e-mail.[33] A view commonly expressed, though with less confidence today than at the height of the IT boom, is that new technologies will undermine authoritarian power by providing individuals everywhere with access to infinite knowledge. The Chinese examples, depressing though they are, support the idea that obdurate regimes may eventually be softened.[34] The authorities may be able to block the transmission of any term of which they disapprove, but even they do not have perfect foreknowledge, and a novel term may slip through the net of banned keywords.

VII

The world has never constituted a single market for ideas. The main civilizations and world religions long ago settled

[33] For the attempted cover-up, see any serious English-language magazine or newspaper for April or May 2003, for example, *Far Eastern Economic Review*, 10 Apr or *Economist*, 12 Apr. After a calculated interval the whistle-blowing surgeon was punished for quite different and not very credible offenses. For the inadequate precautions against SARS in China, see the account by a Westerner then present in that country, married to a Chinese and with a Chinese doctor for a mother-in-law, in *London Review of Books*, 5 Jun 2003.

[34] A bleaker impression is given by the fact that the mayor of Beijing who was removed for his part in the SARS affair was within a matter of months appointed head of the multibillion dollar project to divert water from China's south to the north.

down in effective isolation from one another. Their systems were never completely insulated but were generally proof against major incursions of foreign practices. Information costs were too high for the average person to learn much in detail about the other systems. There was too much inertia and there were too many vested interests to expect a wholesale adoption of novelty, short of conquest by the ardently religious or takeover by the ideologically driven. Even today many governments resist alien information flows and use technological countermeasures to protect what they claim are national interests, though these tend to be suspiciously well aligned with those of the ruling elites.

Is a world market for ideas truly struggling to be born? It is a long way off, as contemporary political convulsions attest, but the notion is not absurd given the potency of Western cultures and the scope of their commerce. On the other hand, non-Western civilizations may become more resistant as their room to maneuver is compressed. Is this not an element in the rise of Militant Islam? Timur Kuran has expressed the view that technology will in the end bring little change to the world.[35] His opinion may fly in the face of conventional wisdom but cannot be rejected out of hand. The argument is that we are already incapable of absorbing and processing everything we hear. Faced with overload, people may rely more, not less, on local social proofs than on dispassionate reasoning. They may retreat into conventional interpretations of the world around them and continue to defend the status quo. Traditional power groupings may be reinforced. The notion that more information must neces-

[35] Timur Kuran, "The Unthinkable and the Unthought," *Rationality and Society* 5 (1993): 501.

sarily lead to cultural coalescence, not to say to a convergence on Western forms, is thus a difficult one to prove. Historical precedent and even much contemporary experience cannot guarantee this will be the future. Yet overall they point in that direction.

Chapter 5

Institutions as Cryptogams

Cryptogams make up a class of flowerless plants named by the eighteenth-century Swedish botanist, Carl Linnaeus, in anticipation that their hidden means of reproduction would eventually be discovered. We can borrow the term to describe the cryptic potential of a number of early institutions in Europe and need not pursue the botany. In the 1730s Linnaeus became the first president of the Swedish Academy of Science, which had as part of its remit "Economics, Trade, Useful Arts, and Manufactures."[1] Had his concerns lain there, in social rather than natural science, he might have spotted the prospects of the institutions of his day. He might have predicted that nascent European institutions would one day outgrow their origins and reveal an expansible utility. Institutions elsewhere seldom seemed as promising; they

[1] Wilfrid Blunt, *The Compleat Naturalist: A Life of Linnaeus* (London: Collins, 1971), p. 134.

were commonly self-referring and not obviously tending toward the universal and impartial.[2]

Institutions and culture partly overlap. They do so twice: in fact and in scholarly usage. They sometimes incorporate one another, yet over much of their range the differences between them are crucial. Culture consists mainly of rules and practices learned fairly informally from parents or the surrounding society. Institutions tend to be conscious, even political, constructs including firms, trade unions, building societies, banks, codified legal systems, and other organized networks or sets of formal, embodied rules. Culture, though often able to bind, is relatively intangible; institutions have a more rule-bound existence.

The overlaps between culture and institutions are thus real and methodological. First, where chiefs or rulers or governments are able to assert their own wishes there is a distinctly political tinge to cultural practices, which do not then arise through long, slow, and misty choices by the population but are imposed upon them. To this extent aspects of cultural behavior are politically constructed rather than being quietly absorbed in the usual osmotic way. The second type of overlap occurs in the literature of institutional analysis, which often makes the term "institution" include underlying aspects of behavior such as degrees of honesty or trust. I prefer not to call attributes like these institutions at all but to leave them in the general category of cultural beliefs, values, or preferences.

Culture in its informal guise is hard to change, be-

[2] See, for example, Peter Munz, "The Two Worlds of Anne Salmond in Postmodern Fancy Dress," *New Zealand Journal of History* 28/1 (1994): 60–75.

cause it relates to personal matters and barely conscious forms of behavior, having been imbibed along with one's mother's milk and reinforced by upbringing. It evolves in almost unnoticed ways. Certainly it may shift rapidly on occasions (as in Harrisson's example of the penis bolt), but conditioning more often holds it steady in the face of all but the most striking stimuli or opportunities. On the other hand, institutions in the sense meant here are primarily political in origin, representing imposed or agreed routines or actual organizations. Institutions may fit with the culture (and will be under less stress when they do so), and may channel, support, or reinforce cultural practices and beliefs, but they have a degree of concreteness. However unthinkable it may be to alter them and however hard to do so in the face of resistance by the authorities, institutions are in principle always open to being renegotiated.

Without a stiffening by impartial legal and other institutions, cultural values of the types with which we have been concerned lack permanent foundations. There may exist a preference for growth, and growth may even take place, but it is vulnerable to silent reversal when men, not laws, have the final say over economic activities. In the last analysis, as Montesquieu and Voltaire knew, liberty and property are preserved by the law and not by values. By themselves, values are slippery. Their meaning may adjust covertly to circumstances. Institutions too can be changed, by agreement or fiat, but it is easier to tell when that has happened. The different effects of values and institutions are hard to demonstrate, agreed, because the relationships are broad, complex, fugitive, indirect, and not easy to observe. Much depends, too, on how long we allow for events to work themselves out; our conclusions may easily be premature.

Culture has been taken for granted or completely ignored, depending on the academic discipline; the history of institutions has lately reawakened from a couple of generations' slumber, but comparative institutional history has barely woken yet. In assessing the role of institutions we must make do with a preliminary sketch of the special character of the Western world, provided that we can find somewhere against which to benchmark the achievement.

Many histories of Western countries are given to detailing the ups and downs—the ups prevailing—of institutional development as it came to improve social welfare. A broader historical literature offers some "controls," mostly "Eastern," meaning Asian, above all Chinese. Ironically, some scholars who are unfriendly toward the Western world denigrate any effort at contrasting East and West. They impute unprofessional motives to the Western scholars who do so, claiming that the mere act of contrasting the histories of East and West "legitimated European domination over non-European areas."[3] This is incorrect and unhelpful: as Jan Luiten van Zanden remarks, "economic history is not a sports match" to be reduced to barracking for this team or that.[4] The critics go on to argue that only a more nuanced world-historical geography than the East-West contrast is acceptable.

There are two reasons for treating each of these great regions as a unit and not complicating matters at the outset.

[3] See, for example, Huri Islamoglu and Peter C. Perdue, "Introduction," *Journal of Early Modern History* 5/4 (2001): 271.

[4] Jan Luiten van Zanden, "The 'Revolt of the Early Modernists' and the 'First Modern Economy': An Assessment," *Economic History Review* 55/4 (2002): 632; cf. Eric L. Jones, *Growth Recurring*, 2d ed. (Ann Arbor: University of Michigan Press, 2000), p. 144.

First, the aim is to seek the central historical message. It is perfectly plain that diverse experiences are being swept together when the analysis is in aggregative East-West terms. But generalizations are not ipso facto caricatures: they can summarize what has so far been learned about the complexity of world economic history. They attempt no more than to capture the modal differences between great regions. It obfuscates matters to descend to local levels of description without returning to say what the main implications are. If we descend too precipitously into localisms, we will plunge into a welter of special cases, a sort of exceptionalism of everywhere, and risk concentrating on exceptions at the expense of the rule. The second objection to obscuring the overall differences between West and East is that it *was* the West that distinguished itself by industrializing first. The school that wishes to decry the West's achievement seems to be having it both ways, juxtaposing the performance of the West and part of China when this seems to be to Europe's detriment while declining to admit Europe's achievement by proclaiming that any East-West dichotomy must be false.

I

The very fact of Europe's primacy is under assault from a "California School" that hankers to explain away the rise of the West and replace it with the counterinstance of China. The most influential work of this school is Kenneth Pomeranz's, *The Great Divergence*.[5] Pomeranz's position is that

[5] Kenneth Pomeranz, *The Great Divergence* (Princeton: Princeton University Press, 2000). The membership claimed for the "California School" overlaps with a larger group of writers who are unimpressed by the West's performance vis-à-vis China's. Many of their views have, however, been

Western and Chinese economic performances were equivalent until after 1800. He argues this with reference to a phase of apparent quantitative success for one Chinese region in mid-Qing times and implies that its subsequent misfortune lay only in a lack of resource windfalls like those he thinks rained as manna from heaven onto Europe.[6] Pomeranz claims that the West had no "privilege," that its growth was the result of the double fluke of sitting on abundant coal reserves and seizing overseas resources. History's process is reduced to happenstance. Little or no credit is given to the positive role of Europe's institutions, not even to the workings of that prime institution, the state, and certainly not to the pattern of competitive states that made up the states system.

Nor does Pomeranz compare Europe's achievement with that of the whole non-Western world. Research by Robert Allen gives a little more perspective on the European-Chinese comparison, though even his Chinese data refer only to the delta of the Yangtze.[7] Allen claims that calculations of farm incomes and labor productivity in agriculture support revisionists like Pomeranz who urge that "Asia" was "doing very well." Yet were we to accept that the Yangtze

---

refuted by Doyne Dawson in "The Assault on Eurocentric History," *Journal of the Historical Society* 3–4 (2003): 403–27.

[6] A central role for natural resources cannot be completely excluded, especially when early industry was heavily dependent on iron (which is expensive to transport), but considerable doubt about the indispensability of resources is raised by the work of Jeffrey Sachs and Andrew Warner, "Natural Resource Abundance and Economic Growth" (Harvard Institute for International Development, Discussion Paper 517a, Oct 1995).

[7] Robert C. Allen, "Agricultural Productivity and Rural Incomes in England and the Yangtze Delta, c. 1620–c.1820" (2003), at www.econ.ku.dk/Zeuthen.

delta represents the whole of China, or all Asia, the comparison is belied by Allen's broader conclusions. Nor do the data overturn the standard view of Europe's superior performance, since what Allen actually shows is that in agricultural labor productivity England held a lead over even the Yangtze delta at the start of the nineteenth century. He also admits that the trajectory of change was quite different, with agricultural labor productivity rising steeply in England between 1600 and 1750 while remaining stagnant in China. Furthermore, the industrial structure of the Yangtze delta did not change, and Chinese real incomes fell dramatically. This is perhaps the key point: it was England, and eventually much of Europe, that was advancing, while China was falling behind. Allen candidly concludes (p. 16) that "incomes in England and the Yangtze Delta may have still been similar in the early nineteenth century, but the Chinese trajectory looks headed for a crash rather than an industrial take-off."

II

When did the great divergence between the West and the Rest take place? Joel Mokyr observes that while "the disparity in income [between Europe and elsewhere] may have been a relatively recent phenomenon, the disparity in a host of other economic variables was not."[8] He lists advances in sources of energy, transport, education, public health, a higher capital-to-labor ratio, advancing technology, and probably better economic management by European governments. Gunderson proclaims a similar achievement by the United States, pointing out that its level of income and

[8] Joel Mokyr, "Disparities, Gaps, and Abysses," *Economic Development and Cultural Change* 33 (1984): 175.

rate of change were already marked before industrialization: by 1800 the U.S. had a rate of growth almost as rapid as it was to become during early industrialization.[9] American growth was mainly an outcome of the widening of markets through transport improvements, meaning that, as in Britain, industrialization was the result of prior growth rather than growth's starting point.

A disparity in actual real income between the West and elsewhere need not have awaited Victorian times. Allen has reportedly shown that half the gap between northwest Europe and southern Europe (a 15 to 20 percent difference in real wages) was the result of sixteenth-, seventeenth-, and eighteenth century developments in the northwestern zone.[10] Angus Maddison has performed calculations indicating that the growth of per capita GDP in the West has been twice that of the remainder of the world ever since A.D. 1000.[11]

Even were we to accept Pomeranz's view that China had real incomes as high as Europe's into the nineteenth century, the question would remain: what happened thereafter to put Europe in the lead? Was it merely that Europe began to exploit coalmines and started to reap the ill-gotten gains of seizing American resources? The ability to do these things is what was pertinent. Resources do not guarantee their own

[9] Gerald A. Gunderson, *A New Economic History of America* (New York: McGraw-Hill, 1976), pp. 154–59.

[10] Cited in Jeffrey Williamson, "Living Standards in Asia before 1940," in A.J.H. Latham and Heita Kawakatsu, eds., *Asia Pacific Dynamism 1550–2000* (London: Routledge, 2000), pp. 31–32.

[11] Angus Maddison, in Ian Castles, ed., *Facts and Fancies of Human Development*, Academy of the Social Sciences in Australia, Occasional Papers 1 (Canberra: ASSA, 2000), p. 11.

development. It is not enough to be sitting on top of coal; one has to develop the technology and business practices to exploit it. It is not enough to haul back resources or engage in trade with distant regions; one has to ensure the resources are not squandered in the way that Spain and Portugal did in failing to utilize American treasure. One has to go on doing these things productively and cumulatively.

To achieve this in the sphere of technology, it was important to develop a broad-based society of tinkerers. There was an expansion of the class of (mostly) males who were interested in science and technology for their own sakes, and who, where they still exist, are either transfixed by the worship of obsolete machines like steam engines or, in the next generation, have transferred their passion to computers.[12] Institutions like the literary and philosophical societies made science and technology socially respectable as well as passably accessible to wide groups in industrializing Britain. Nor was the interest confined to industrial cities. There was a respectable scatter of like-minded individuals throughout the countryside and the glimmerings of a scientific approach to agricultural experimentation. This was no closed society but one with a great deal of intellectual interchange, where an interest in science and technology had become fashionable and was a foundation for economic growth.

All this predated as well as accompanied industrialization and, as surviving correspondence and movements of technicians from place to place show, the interest was by no

---

[12] Classics of the personality types were the fictitious William Rhodes in A. G. Macdonell, *England, Their England* (London: Macmillan, 1933), and the real Eric Lomax, author of *The Railway Man* (London: Vintage, 1996).

means confined to England. The special feature of both England and Europe in the seventeenth and eighteenth centuries was not merely rationality of a calculating kind but the ascending intensity of the rational search for novelty. Not all was gain. Much of the science subculture remained in the hands of tired or dilettantish or unlucky individuals. The field sciences were often diverted into the obsessive collection of specimens. Nevertheless, there was so very much activity, more than any culture has known before, that some seeds were almost certain not to fall on stony ground.[13]

This bottom-up evolution was what aided Europeans in making fruitful use of their opportunities. Coal and the Americas would otherwise have been inert. As Maddison observes, the *fundamental* change in Europe was "recognition of the capacity to transform the forces of nature through rational investigation."[14] It was institutions like postal services, clubs, and scientific societies that cemented the process together. Outside the West there seems to have been little by way of comparable, popular scientific institutions. Only in Japan does it appear that ordinary eighteenth-century farmers, for instance, read *and wrote* works of agricultural improvement. There appears nothing equivalent in the literature about China. The Chinese mandarins wrote about agricultural improvement in Nongshu, but they *were* mandarins and their recommendations trickled down rather than being grasped from below. Popular institutions of science that might have enabled Chinese society to broaden, regularize, and generalize its knowledge base and thus to tran-

---

[13] Eric L. Jones, "Subculture and Market," *Economic Development and Cultural Change* 32/4 (1984): p. 877.

[14] Maddison, in Castles, *Facts and Fancies*, pp. 11ff.

scend its acute troubles during the nineteenth century do not appear to have been created. It is neither possible to blame Western intervention for this lacuna nor to attribute the West's success to fluke or larceny.

III

We can afford to be generous: a *flow* argument that claims growth occurred in Europe before the nineteenth century is not indispensable to the case that institutions were vital to growth. All that is required is to speak in terms of *stock*, pointing to a prior accumulation of useful institutions, just as Mokyr pointed to an accumulation of infrastructure, available for whenever growth did take place.

The institutions founded in early modern Europe were intended to serve a variety of needs or protect particular interests and many were at first iniquitous as well as inequitable. They have understandably altered since then. Their special attribute was that they could be made progressively more positive. They could be, and eventually were, extended to incorporate wider circles of society, taking in workers and women. Extending coverage to new groups was always a struggle, yet society was not starting from scratch each time. Institutions were also exported to the colonies and—it is important to note—to a number of non-Western countries. Economic development arguably owed as much to regular administrative procedures and forms of governance as to imported technology.

Governance, policy, and the quality of institutions are all clues to economic adaptability, resilience to shocks, and the drive to growth.[15] Advanced technology by itself is no

[15] Tony Killick, ed., *The Flexible Economy* (London: Routledge, 1995).

guarantee of growth unless institutional conditions are right; it is merely more visible and appealing to the boyish imagination than office routines. As Albert Feuerwerker concluded in his study of the nineteenth-century industrialization of China, "one institutional breakthrough is worth a dozen textile mills or shipping companies established within the framework of traditional society and its system of values."[16] It was a commonplace of an earlier modernization literature that the average factory established in the Ottoman Empire remained in business for as little as eighteen months.

After observing that European institutions were not specifically designed to bring about industrialization, Bin Wong acknowledges that they did matter after all: they were useful for mobilizing investment, and European legal systems were specially able to handle complex contracting.[17] But outside Europe, he claims, they imposed standards that others were forced to meet. Other countries were obliged to amend their institutions in order to integrate with the West. Why that should arouse the resentment that so mars the historiography of this field is unclear. Furthermore, if the assertion that East Asian economies were *already* part of an interconnected world economy is correct, they should have been under no fresh compulsion to integrate with it.[18] In any case it is not the whole story, since institutional modernization in late Qing China sometimes had domestic purposes,

[16] Albert Feuerwerker, *China's Early Industrialization: Sheng Hsuan-Huai (1844–1916) and Mandarin Enterprise* (New York: Atheneum, 1970), p. 242.
[17] R. Bin Wong, in Patrick Manning et al., "American Historical Review Forum: Asia and Europe in the World Economy," *American Historical Review* 107/2 (2002): 419–80.
[18] David Ludden, in Manning, "Forum," p. 480.

such as the replacement of cruel and arbitrary justice. Likewise, Meiji Japan altered its institutions in order to transform its domestic economy as much as to integrate with the world economy, though of course it did that too. Japan's successful industrialization was the great early exception outside the West. May it not be that the absence of early industrialization in other Asian countries was partly because they did not modernize their institutions as vigorously as Japan? Unequal treaties or not, European intervention gave these countries access to technology transfer and international information of all kinds without which their subsequent modernization would have been impeded.

The California School denies any special credit to European institutions, as if institutions everywhere were plastic enough to adapt to whatever the economy demanded. Rapid adjustment like that may happen, but so may its opposite: institutions reacting defensively. Even Bin Wong's assertion that Western institutions were not necessarily superior implies that effective substitutes must have been present, or would arise, wherever growth occurred. In reality, China seems to have been undergoverned and to have witnessed in Qing times a withdrawal of state administration. To protect their property, individual villages were obliged to set up Societies for Watching the Crops. English villages had their constables, regularized into a formal constabulary at just the period when the Qing government was shrugging off responsibilities.

In this contentious realm, praise for Western institutions risks being rejected as Panglossian, presenting the West as flawless, which is far from my intention. My view of Western institutions is like Churchill's definition of democracy: the worst of systems, apart from all the others. Institutions are various, and one could debate for a long time which were the most significant where and at what periods. At the upper end of the institutional size-distribution were Europe's nation-states, the governments of which gradually began dispersing power among lower social classes, allocating it among different regions, and sharing it among constituent bodies. The United States went further and at the time of its birth formalized a decentralization of functions, geographically in the shape of states' rights and thematically in the separation of powers.

IV

For all the misuse of the laws, the rule of law itself was important to sustained Western development. In earlier centuries people were certainly transported, flogged, and keelhauled; men were broken in the way his officers tried to break William Cobbett. The late E. P. Thompson nevertheless felt obliged to plead in *Whigs and Hunters* that, although the laws were biased against the poor, no one should think of discarding them: independent law cuts both ways.[19] Thus, in the late eighteenth century, two private soldiers were able to take action at Winchester Assizes against the adjutant and a trumpeter of the Scots Greys for exceeding a courts martial order for 300 lashes and "accidentally" administering 325: each private received the then substantial sum of £20 plus costs.[20] A case relating to the same city occurred during the 1830 riots, when a man called Deacle brought an action for the unlawful arrest of his wife. He was protesting that she had

[19] E. P. Thompson, *Whigs and Hunters* (London: Penguin, 1977).
[20] M.T.H. Child, *Farms, Fairs and Felonies: Life on the Hampshire-Wiltshire Border 1769–1830* (Andover: privately printed, 1967), p. 23.

been literally carted off to Winchester in the course of the disturbances. Subsequently he petitioned Parliament about the matter.[21] While the Deacles were of higher standing and greater resources than the two private soldiers, both cases show that formal law could protect as well as punish. I came across these instances browsing in the records of a single county, and there is no reason to think others do not await discovery.

No excessively benign view is implied of the workings of the law as it stood in early nineteenth-century England. Obviously the general situation was monstrous. Men with power, money and connections could employ legal forms for their own ends as, to a degree, they still do. But it is unreasonable to complain of abuses if the distinction is not first made between societies where a system of formal, adversarial law existed and societies with little comparable. In a formal system there is always the possibility of defense as well as prosecution. Despite the savagery of punishments and the notorious injustice of enactments such as the game laws, the fact that independent law existed was a thread preserving through the dreariest of times a thin measure of protection that later could be, and was, broadened. For all their class bias, the lawyers' interest in earning fees would see to that.

In Europe independent legal systems evolved whereby even rulers were progressively restrained. "Who shall bind the ruler?" as Marc Bloch famously asked. *Quis custodiet ipsos custodes?* Europeans, and few other than Europeans, dared to

[21] A. M. Colson, *The Revolt of the Hampshire Agricultural Labourers and Its Causes, 1812–1831* (M.A. thesis, London University, n.d. [1936]), pp. 236ff. Admittedly, the man responsible for the arrest, a Baring of the banking and landowning family, cross-petitioned, and the case petered out in mutual recriminations.

ask. Autocrats elsewhere were disinclined to countenance such impertinences. Scholars have found complex systems of law in the non-Western world, and merchants managed their own legal disputes in remote places where the state would not, but the enforcement, universality, impartiality, and continuity of law were doubtful compared with the situation in Britain and increasingly in other European countries. McCulloch wrote in 1844, "the great defect of the Chinese, as of all similarly constituted governments, is the want of any effectual control over the inferior agents."[22] In China, Japan, and Turkey, the administration of the law by state authorities was "vindictive and sanguinary," and one can hardly claim that it is redolent of tenderness today. In the past it was disfigured by collective punishments extended to innocent family members and even to passers-by who had the misfortune to witness a crime.

The law in Europe was slowly made accessible to the larger populace. The law developed and codified by medieval clerics and fostered by a lay legal profession eventually took on a life of its own. Use of the ordeal gave way to appeals to evidence. Mainland European rulers made their royal courts adjudicate between competing interests. This was an advance, even if their original motive was less the protection of the peasants, *Bauernschutz,* than the undercutting of aristocratic rivals who might dispense justice in competition.

Support for independent legal systems came, ironically, from families who had obtained real estate by dubious

[22] J. R. McCulloch, *McCulloch's Universal Gazetteer* (New York: Harper & Bros., 1844–1845), 1: 629–30; 2: pp. 71, 970. See also Eric L. Jones, "A Long-Term Appraisal of Country Risk," in Ross Garnaut and Yiping Huang, *Growth without Miracles: Readings on the Chinese Economy in the Age of Reform* (Oxford: Oxford University Press, 2001), p. 79.

means. Aware that the rulers who had granted or sold them property were restrained only by convenience from taking it back, these families were eager to secure the gains for their posterity. They wanted stronger guarantees than the promises of princes, and the unintended consequence of their demands for legality was a measure of protection for others. At first the "others" were likely to be producers and entrepreneurs rather than wage laborers with no political connections, but the precedent was established. In England there were two cases in point: the first related to the land transfers consequent on the dissolution of the monasteries, when Henry VIII established property law in order to entice purchasers into paying his price; and the second was the security granted by the Crown to those who had bought land in the forced sales of Royalist estates under the Commonwealth. Charles II preferred to disappoint some of his own supporters rather than risk another upheaval.

By swelling the middle ranks of society, economic growth created more social classes that desired protection. This process began long before industrialization but was extended by it. In addition, part of the law's development was autonomous, the work of legal minds following the logic of debate wherever it led them.[23] An adaptive framework was capable of being extended to cover all social classes, while countries far outside Europe could later take it up. As the English barrister John Mortimer has noted, "in the countries which have received our law it often proves a most durable commodity, keeping a flicker of freedom alive when all else

---

[23] See the remarks of the jurist Otto Kahn-Freund, quoted in R. M. Hartwell, *The Industrial Revolution and Economic Growth* (London: Methuen, 1971), p. 256.

has broken down."[24] Mortimer instances South Africa, Nigeria, and Singapore. An unintended consequence of empire was thus its legacy of legal procedures. In short, English law proved to be a cryptogam. Nor should it pass unnoticed that most international laws, like most international institutions, are European or Western in origin.

We may allude briefly to one other important domain, the market for information, where the masses also eventually profited from changes that at first did not speak directly to them. The ability to discuss and criticize openly is vital if social problems are not to be swept under the carpet. Free access to information is needed for across-the-board creativity, though today China, Singapore, and other countries still do not accept that freedom is isomorphic. Whatever they may have achieved within their politicized systems during a few decades of heady and essentially imitative growth, in the long run the full blossoming of their creativity is likely to require unchained debate about any and every issue. Singapore, at any rate, has lately seemed more inclined to recognize this.

The book trade will do for historical illustration. Three forces militated against the wide consumption of information in printed form: lack of literacy, censorship, and high prices. Mass literacy owed much to the Protestant insistence on unfettered access to the Bible. In this sense, it may be urged that Christian culture played a role in the European achievement, at least as regards the demand for literature went. It was, however, the institutions of the law that safeguarded the supply of reading material. In the case of

[24] John Mortimer, *Clinging to the Wreckage* (Harmondsworth, U.K.: Penguin, 1982), p. 199.

England, the struggle against control of the press by state or church began even before the eloquent appeal of John Milton's *Areopagitica* of 1644. Censorship was forced on the retreat, witness the abolition of the Licensing Act in 1695. Even in the late eighteenth century, which was low tide in respect of popular literacy, some working people were reading the vernacular classics, and great publishing houses were soon founded by men of proletarian origin. A culture of working-class autodidacts and readers persisted for centuries. These are familiar episodes of the history of publishing, all of them derived from earlier achievements. Intellectual productivity rose well before productivity in manufacturing industry.

V

Writing European, or Western, history in terms of inequality and social exclusion, as is often done, is myopic. At the society-wide level, Europe institutionalized a creativity that *depended* for its energy on the social competition that is represented so negatively. More significant even than the character of individual institutions was the underlying pluralism, which is easiest to recognize when Europe is viewed in a comparative frame. In Europe, power was never wholly accumulated at the apex of society and never all across the continent at the same time, coming close to that result only in the ephemeral empires of Napoleon and Hitler. The actual outcome was the retention of numerous centers of economic and social decision making, and because of competition and emulation among them, the trademark propensity of European life was self-correction. Through the snowstorm of individual events can surely be glimpsed the general circumstance in which other people's errors could be avoided and their model solutions copied. Moreover, the chances of sidestepping or checking tyranny proved greater in a network of decentralized societies than under a unitary authority.

Whence did this polycentrism spring? One source lay in Europe's multiple political history, which resisted a takeover of the whole continent by overweening rulers. Another source lay in religious history: the Christian church in the West split like a troubled amoeba into Roman Catholic and Protestant halves, and then, on the Protestant side, into more and more sectarian subdivisions.[25] The suggestion that Christianity as a whole was a negative influence on economic growth misses two points. First, the multiplicity of sects opened different status pathways, contributing to a variety of competing opinion, personal questing, and intense curiosity. Second, the internalized fear of damnation inherent in Christianity may have restrained disruptive opportunism better than alternatives like the Confucian threat of public shaming.

There was once a tradition in economic history of dealing with these matters, a point instantly made by mentioning the names of Weber and Tawney. But, as Mokyr observes, these somewhat intangible issues have dropped from view.[26] Mokyr insists on the historical importance of reduced rent seeking and the adoption across Europe of a market ideology, essentially the political economy of the Scot-

[25] Further reasons for decentralization are discussed in Eric L. Jones, *The European Miracle*, 3d ed. (Cambridge: Cambridge University Press, 2003), chapter 6.

[26] Joel Mokyr, "The Enduring Riddle of the *European Miracle:* The Enlightenment and the Industrial Revolution" (Mimeo, Northwestern University, 2002).

tish Enlightenment. An expanded role for the market and a reduction in rent seeking were two sides of the same coin, since competition reduces the scope for corruption. Bribes to public officials, payments to secure favors, nepotism, and the like were all too evident in European history, and it was clearly efficient to restrict them by all possible means. Only European markets and states generated such reforms. Elsewhere the tendency was, as it were, to domesticate corruption and call it relationship business.

In reality a market ideology had emerged before anything that might be called the Enlightenment, Scottish or otherwise. Consider the guilds. Their protectionist powers had begun to be curbed by the courts of Elizabethan England.[27] A test case of 1599 involving the Dyers Company made it illegal for guilds to confiscate goods seized in the course of policing their trade privileges. In 1614 a guild lost a case against a man who had set up business in a trade to which he had not been apprenticed. By 1616 the power to compel nonmembers to join guilds was lost in two cases that became established precedents. Growth was already creating temptations to step outside the restrictions on enterprise and was at the same time raising up men who wished to seize the day. This did not guarantee that they would always succeed in overcoming the barriers, but by and large they managed to do so. That they did signals the early emergence of a market ideology defended by the law. The case of the guilds also shows that simply abandoning inefficient institutions was almost as helpful as creating new ones. Outside the West, the abolition of the guilds came much later.[28]

[27] Jones, *The European Miracle*, pp. 98–103.
[28] Eric L. Jones, *Growth Recurring: Economic Change in World History* (Ann

VI

A determined assault on the notion that Western states were "liberal-rational" and thereby especially favorable to economic development has been mounted by John Hobson.[29] Rational-legal states with centralized, impersonal bureaucracies and a separation of private from public interests should be at an advantage in terms of growth, but Hobson denies that early Europe possessed any such advantage. He points out that in eighteenth-century France and Prussia offices of state were sold to private individuals. Liberal-rational states would also be expected to have embraced free trade, but Hobson counters this with considerable evidence of European protectionism, in which warfare was financed from the proceeds of tariffs because, far from being governmentally strong, European states were too weak to rely on progressive income taxes. In addition, the liberal-rational state should be democratic, to which Hobson rejoins that democracy is a twentieth-century concept pushed back to the Middle Ages by Eurocentric historians. He has little difficulty in showing that there was no secret ballot in Europe before the twentieth century and that universal suffrage typically had to await the latter half of that century.[30]

Arbor: University of Michigan Press, 2000), pp. 102–3. Guilds in West and East were, however, different in their functions, and the contrast has to be drawn with care.

[29] John Hobson, *The Eastern Origins of Western Civilisation* (Cambridge: Cambridge University Press, 2004).

[30] In a more enlightened part of the West, the secret ballot was introduced in the nineteenth century and for a long time was known as the "Australian ballot." This was one of the five of the six demands made by the Chartists that were attained in Australia, which may be viewed as precociously working out tendencies that were British in origin.

Hobson weaves his case together with great skill. But even if we concede that he has shown it was late before many of the correlates of modern development were widely adopted, we are not obliged to abandon the idea that the attributes of the liberal-rational state were early inventions of the West, awaiting a more propitious era to be fully revived or generalized. There is little sign of the relevant institutions arising elsewhere.

Moreover, the relationship between institutional history and economic growth needs to be clarified. Modern experience shows what would at first appear to be congenial to Hobson's line of thought, that the inception of growth is possible outside the liberal democracies and without the institutions associated with their form of government. After all, Stalin's USSR forced through industrialization, though at a hideous human price, and East Asia came to outclass the world in its pace of development. These achievements represented the resource accumulation phase of development. The real test is yet to take place, for it is still to be demonstrated that growth in the quasi-authoritarian form can be sustained, or even carried on at all, without continually borrowing ideas. The collapse and still uncertain rebuilding of the former Soviet economy shows that persistent growth is not a foregone conclusion, nor is sustained recovery in East Asia or a successful future for China guaranteed without institutional and pluralist advances.[31]

The distinction between achieving growth and sus-

[31] Paul Krugman, "The Myth of Asia's Miracle," *Foreign Affairs* 73 (Nov–Dec1994): 62–78; Eric L. Jones, "China: A Cautionary Note from Development History," in Loren Brandt and Tom Rawski, eds., *China's Economic Transition* (forthcoming); Moises Nain, in *Financial Times*, 15 Sep 2003.

taining it has been made clear by Peter Lindert.[32] Western experience, so far the only test of long duration, suggests two phases, the first requiring limitations on the power of the ruler (Marc Bloch again) and the second mandating heavy investments in human capital, especially via primary education. Lindert demonstrates that until the early nineteenth century the establishing of secure property rights and enforcing of contracts was the link between institutions and growth. Even that achievement has seldom been satisfactorily replicated in the non-Western world. It has not yet appeared in China, for example, where despite improvements to satisfy foreign investors the law remains a creature of the Communist Party. It is no test to say that the exceptional scale of early industrialization in China ensures its future against political hazard; scale is not system. As to growth's second phase, Lindert shows that elite rule damages growth by underinvesting in egalitarian human capital relative to the levels of such investment in democracies.

The record shows that Western institutions helped to ward off internal violence and promote, generalize, and sustain economic growth. And if it be countered that in the past Britain and its offshoot, the United States, experienced bitter civil wars, three other societies closely derived from Britain—Canada, Australia, and New Zealand—achieved political modernization and economic growth without anything resembling these violent episodes. In the long run efficiency and equity are co-produced. This is not to say that material productivity may not be raised in the short run by amassing resources or bullying workers, only that societies

[32] Peter Lindert, "Voice and Growth: Was Churchill Right?" *Journal of Economic History* 63/2 (June 2003): 315–50.

that institutionalize inequitable behavior are unlikely to re-
lease as much talent, generate as much innovation, or re-
cover from shocks as readily as ones that are socially more
equal.

The institutions of the West were impersonal and decentralized; its institutional network held out the promise of
extension to fresh social groups and new societies; and last,
but not least, it evinced great powers of self-correction.
These qualities have not been replicated to anything like
the same extent outside the West. So far, so good—though
granted, the responsiveness of Western institutions may yet
be overwhelmed by either or both of two developments: the
decay of restraints on opportunism formerly provided by
moral and religious codes and the "illiberal democracy" that
replaces professional initiative by bureaucratic regulation in
the name of the mass electorate and its lobby groups.[33] Both
trends have been lamented in recent writings, and their conjunction is unprecedented as well as worrying. Resources are
being shifted into compliance and monitoring on a large
scale, with scarce talent allocated to conformist bureaucracies. As Robert Ellickson puts it, "lawmakers who are unap-
preciative of the social conditions that foster informal cooperation are likely to create a world in which there is both
more law and less order."[34] As Tacitus earlier put it, "cor-
ruptissima republica, plurimae leges."

[33] On illiberal democracy, see Fareed Zakaria, *The Future of Freedom: Illiberal Democracy at Home and Abroad* (New York: W. W. Norton, 2003).
[34] Robert C. Ellickson, *Order without Law* (Cambridge, Mass.: Harvard
University Press, 1991), p. 286.

PART II

CULTURAL COMMENTARY

Chapter 6

Cultures of Immigration

One way of testing how far cultures are fixed and the extent to which they are amalgams is to ask how immigrant societies develop. The question is, What travels? The "Great Experiment" of migration from Britain and Europe to Colonial America and the United States is especially illuminating. The flow of settlers was vast and lasted for centuries. At first glance, the process seems to have been a matter of transferring British society holus-bolus. Yet how much of the "invisible baggage" with which British colonists set out really did survive the trip? Did Britishness persist in some original or even ideal form, or were everyday ways replaced in the presence of new opportunities and challenges? That some people attempted to create a godly society in the wilderness suggests that alteration was intended. And how much in America was derived from practices the mainland Europeans brought with them? Similar questions can be asked about developments in other new societies, such as Australia, where there were some immigrants who wished to create a different type of society again, one of which the Chartists would have approved.

1

The issue is complicated by the fact that institutions as well as culture are transported. Certain types of institution traveled freely across the Atlantic, but others did not travel at all or reached only a few colonies, maybe fading soon after arrival. In the frontier circumstances of the New World, some British institutions seemed unnecessary or undesirable. While there were occasional exceptions and later revivals among them, craft guilds, sumptuary legislation, and common-field agriculture never established more than a tenuous presence in the American colonies. Standard explanations refer to a weaker sense of hierarchy than in Britain, the scarcity of labor relative to opportunities for work, and (what was almost but not exactly the same thing) the abundance of land.

The nationalistic bias of American history ensures that few of the older institutions mentioned rate much of a place in the textbooks. Also overlooked are the feudal tenures that were established in the Dutch patroonships of upstate New York and which lasted until the 1920s, complete with astonishing (or at any rate astonishingly neglected) shoot-outs over property rights of the type more familiar from movies about the Wild West.[1] American economic history concentrates on analyzing the past of features that have

---

[1] Henry Christman, *Tin Horns and Calico: An Episode in the Emergence of American Democracy* (New York: Collier Books, 1961).

persisted or which, like slavery, created massive traumas, and to that extent is presentist rather than historical. Even when the archaic elements are recognized, they are made to vanish as if they were mute curiosities that can tell us nothing about social evolution. Excluding particular Old World forms seldom seems to be conscious but arises from a self-fulfilling tendency to think Uncle Sam a more original fellow than he was.

Turning from institutions to broader issues of culture, David Hackett Fischer, in his significantly titled *Albion's Seed*, uses the term "folkway" for the normative structure of values, customs, and meanings. He lists two dozen of these "ways" that go to make up culture, including social, political, household, and sexual behavior, and sets out to trace the British regional origins of four American regional cultures or folkways.[2] The regions of the British Isles were diverse in terms of ecological setting and local society. They were always in a condition of slow social and technological development, altering through time as well as differing in space.[3] Hence, on what may be called the supply side, there were no permanent British cultures that could be picked up and set down intact: the home country's ways of life kept on evolving and altering the habits of successive generations until they became distinct from previous ones. People who spoke

[2] David Hackett Fischer, *Albion's Seed: Four British Folkways in America* (New York: Oxford University Press, 1989). I have used "origin" here and occasionally elsewhere, though the doyen of French economic history, Marc Bloch, pointed out that this term may confuse beginning and cause. When the distinction is needed, the context should make it clear which is meant.

[3] As documented in Ronald Hutton, *The Stations of the Sun: A History of Ritual in Britain* (Oxford: Oxford University Press, 1996).

different regional dialects were also nearly incomprehensible to one another. The stereotypically unchanging aspect of English villages is like the static backcloth of a theatre and should not be permitted to draw attention away from the activity on stage.

Given the differences in their origin, it is not surprising that American regional societies diverged from one another, at least initially. The spread of settlement across the Appalachians later weakened the connections between regions and began to threaten almost a Balkanization. Semi-isolated areas like "Franklinia" approached the verge of breaking away, though in the event road and canal improvements managed to keep them linked to the markets of the eastern seaboard. Subsequent population movements mingled the elements into a national style, more direct in manner, more positive and more entrepreneurial than among the British. Sheer opportunity amidst massive natural resources must have had much to do with the freer entrepreneurial drive. Yet, despite the more generous aspirations and expectations that soon distinguished typical Americans from Europeans, vast differences lasted or even became exaggerated by the American experience, witness the barely reconcilable attitudes of North and South. On what may be termed the demand side, the American colonies differed ecologically among themselves on a grander scale than do the regions of Britain or Europe.

In the terms used on the dust jacket of *Albion's Seed*, American regional cultures still control attitudes toward politics, education, governance, gender, and violence. The differences among American regions are greater than those between some European nations, though the fact that most Americans speak English helps to disguise the fact. Fischer argues for the persistence of regional cultures right from the time of settlement to the present day, despite the fact that over 80 percent of Americans now have no British ancestors at all. The process is layered: many non-British groups have preserved part of their own ethnic identity while nevertheless becoming undeniably American and furthermore assimilating to specific American regional cultures that were established early in colonial times.

Separating the inherited and evolving parts of the folkways is tricky. Fischer quotes Barrington Moore to the effect that for historians and social scientists the usual default option is continuity, which is considered to need no explanation, whereas change must be explained. Yet continuity is repeatedly challenged by events ranging from the birth of a child to political revolution. These events or shocks variously alter the way social roles are transmitted; affect the entire network of behavior; affect modes of control by elites; and influence those ultimate instruments of control, the uses of violence. We may suggest that the American regions have altered over time while nevertheless remaining different from one another in more or less permanent ways. Their adaptation thus coexists with an undercurrent of continuity. The most promising explanation, in Fischer's view, is institutional: each regional culture developed characteristic institutions and laws that stabilized it and aided intergenerational transmission. A complex interaction was always taking place between informal culture and constructed institutions. It would be premature to claim we fully understand this. Appropriate categories of information are hard to specify, and the interactive effects are hard to measure.

Finally, Fischer distinguishes among three underlying conceptions of American regional cultures, presumably again implying that the main channels were regionally specific institutions. First came the "germ theory," as Midwestern historians called it, in which European culture was transmitted to America, lock, stock, and barrel. This was a fixity thesis and was reputedly favored by scholars of Anglo-Saxon descent, whose social origins it celebrated. It was succeeded by Frederick Jackson Turner's "Frontier Thesis," which looked to new circumstances on the western frontier to account for the free institutions of the United States; this was supposedly more attractive to scholars living in the continental interior, nearer to the frontier. Later, the Turner thesis was replaced by a pluralistic migration model said to appeal to eastern scholars who were neither of British nor frontier stock. Perhaps "racial" validations of cultural theory like these indicate the changing ethnic origins of graduate students at successive periods; whether they have any real substance is another matter. Fischer himself opts for a partial germ theory, emphasizing the significance for the United States of its British origins. He considers religious denominations, social ranks, dialects, building styles, means of carrying out the everyday business of life, and conceptions of political power, order, and freedom. All of these are described in his book as differing systematically among the four main waves of immigrants, who imported them from distinct regions of Britain. In essence this is a modified fixity thesis.

II

Founder effects are evident in the social organization of the various American regions. The attributes of the first comers suffused the regional societies they founded, without necessarily conferring any special fitness through superiority over habits drawn from other parts of Britain. The founder effects blocked the emergence of forms with which later comers had been familiar in their home regions of Britain, obliging them to imitate what the first settlers had established. There is a sense in which this may have promoted survivals of the mediocre or produced what in economics is called multiple equilibria; there was no all-American competitive marketplace that could ensure the dominance of a single set of cultural practices. Immigration and later westward movement laid down chains of settled rural societies. Greater competition among them had to await an increased density of settlement, the improvement of communications, and the advent of political union. Certain forms of behavior would then become typically American whereas other forms would remain associated with particular regions. Overall there was a bewildering mixture of persistence and mingling.

Moreover, continental European influences were present from far back in the seventeenth century, offering other, less mainstream role models. African slaves, too, had more of an impact than was once acknowledged, especially as regards cuisine and music. Native Americans also exerted some influence, and although the role of the indigenes was long played down in the official ideologies of all European overseas settlements, late twentieth-century historians have redressed the balance to the point of overcompensating. All told, a parallel may be suggested between the history of colonial countries and the history of religion. In both cases, informal practices risk being written out of the record. Religious history is often presented as the formal history of churches, with folk practices and unofficial observances given short shrift. In much the same way, histories of former colonial areas emphasize elements conducive to the building of the new nations. They have a habit of describing the central tendencies of social development and pruning away the contributions of minorities as if they were eccentricities.

III

To imagine that the United States contains a wholly new society would be outlandish. The opposite position was most vigorously stated by Jonathan Hughes, the leading student of institutional transfers.[4] Hughes documented the carryover of English law. He quoted observations by American judges to the effect that the law of the United States was purely and simply the common law of England. Chief Justice Morrison Waite proclaimed that "when the people of the United Colonies separated from Great Britain, they changed the form, but not the substance, of their government." Chief Justice Marshall added, "It is too clear to require the support of argument that all contracts and rights, respecting property, remained unchanged by the Revolution." Like the Restoration of Charles II in England or the Glorious Revolution that brought William of Orange to the throne, the American Revolution was predominantly conservative. For a very long time it was a breeze playing around the country's legal foundations, not a gale sweeping them away.

The nativist view, which sees American society and culture newly minted by the westward movement, is best conveyed by Frederick Jackson Turner's Frontier Thesis.[5] This proclaims that the urgencies of life away from the effete

[4] Jonathan Hughes, "A World Elsewhere: The Importance of Starting English" (mimeo, Northwestern University, 1985).
[5] Frederick Jackson Turner, *The Frontier in American History* (New York: Henry Holt & Co., 1920).

East Coast and its English echoes rubbed at the European patina until only a shining new American society was left. We have seen that some imported institutions did not last long. The Frontier Thesis celebrates novelty but downplays the invisible baggage that people of British or European origin could not help but carry with them, parts of which they might drop but the bulk of which would persist. Nor was the frontier an archipelago of islands abandoned in a sea of nothingness. Its inhabitants remained and stayed connected with the East, and via the East with Europe, because supplies of store-bought goods came from there and the export market for agricultural products lay in that direction. They condemned the sophistication of the eastern states while remaining secretly admiring of it. Their inverted snobberies may be sensed in *Tom Sawyer* and *Huckleberry Finn*. The frontier demanded new efforts and created new ways or new amalgams of old practices, just as it created drawling new accents. But it was never wholly cut off and never quite able to rid itself of the hangover of older ways that were endlessly reinforced by the chains of contact.

Walter Prescott Webb turned the Turner thesis on its head.[6] No one could have been more impressed than he by the scale of frontier settlement, but Webb saw this as producing, not a totally non-European society, but a bond between Europe and the American frontier, because it supplied food and raw materials that the European market desired. The implication is again that the forces making for novelty were dampened by the persistence of market exchange.

Against Turner's thesis may also be set the Hartz the-

[6] Walter Prescott Webb, *The Great Frontier* (Boston, Mass.: Houghton Mifflin, 1952).

sis.[7] This has the merit of embracing the experiences of several of Britain's colonial areas around the world within a single scheme, but it is nevertheless an extreme fixity theory. Louis Hartz sets out to explain why the colonies differ socially and politically from one another despite their common origin and same general coloration. A crude summary is that each constituted a "fragment" of Europe, from which it was effectively sealed off at its own particular formative period. Each region could work out only the guiding ideas imported until that period. Subsequent homeland philosophies were a closed book. Much depends, of course, on agreeing on the date of the formative period: in the case of the United States, the England that was recreated was supposedly that of John Locke. Still more depends on believing that colonial systems of governance and ways of life thereafter stifled, in some essential but slightly baffling fashion, their own capacity for absorbing later English thought. Even the most convinced Hartzian could scarcely claim that information flows were blocked after each region's formative moment.

Another writer mightily impressed by the enduring legacy granted during what he calls the "English moment" in history is Claudio Veliz.[8] He sees English culture as outlasting what he describes (presumably in overreaction to the temporary industrial troubles of the 1970s) as England's decline. Veliz labels as Anglomorphs those many people all over the world who, whatever their personal origins, affect the English manner, consume goods associated with England, and play its sports. It is hard to see how Scotch whisky and

[7] Louis Hartz, ed., *The Founding of New Societies* (New York: Harcourt, Brace & World, 1964).
[8] Claudio Veliz, "A World Made in England," *Quadrant*, Mar 1983, pp. 8–19.

golf, to which he refers, can be attributed to the English! But the point is probably that for a prolonged spell the English, or rather the British, put themselves in a commanding position for marketing their culture. The role of cultural marketeer rather than ultimate progenitor is one that the United States is nowadays accused of playing. This misses the point that all cultures are syncretic, though some may be more open or energetic than others at mixing and developing borrowed and indigenous ingredients.

A powerful reason for similarities between the United States and Britain is strangely absent from most accounts. It is that the two countries remained subject to common influences. On both sides of the Atlantic, urbanization and industrialization drastically altered previously rural communities. During industrialization, it has been suggested, labor law was amended in both countries in favor of employers.[9] Although preindustrial employers had also needed little prompting to press for legal changes in their own favor, the basic point is well taken. Given that the two countries were initially alike, since one had been settled from the other, and given their shared language and common-law tradition, it is not surprising that they responded in approximately similar ways to comparable shifts in economic structure.

IV

Culture is an intricate assortment of the enduring and the novel; adaptations to new challenges and opportunities can

[9] Peter Karsten, "'Bottomed on Justice': A Reappraisal of Critical Legal Studies Scholarship Concerning Breaches of Labor Contracts by Quitting or Firing in Britain and the U.S., 1630–1889," American Journal of Legal History 34 (1990): 213–61.

be quick as well as slow. Diet is usually taken as an indicator of deep cultural preferences: "man is what man eats." Consider on the other hand the almost immediate uptake of maize by Puritan farmers. Since their English small grains grew poorly at first, they were quick to plant and eat maize, Native American fashion. Whatever their cultural preferences, the Puritans preferred survival to starvation. Occasional novelties were also adopted from mainland Europeans: the Dutch, Germans, French, and Spanish. In the Mississippi valley there was an imprint of French law, and in California Spanish-style property rights are still discernible in boundaries and marker trees.

There seems no theory to account for the pattern of borrowings from these other settlers. In view of the inconclusive record of such things, we may never be able to generalize precisely, so to speak, about the persistence and mingling of traits. Some suggestions do emerge from thinking in evolutionary terms, the assumption being that traits were retained only as long as they were superior to the alternatives: a selectionist form of evolution. From time to time men did sit down and decide whether to change their institutions or methods of farming, but formal choices like that were rare, or rarely recorded. But if institutions in the realm of politics, the law, and agrarian organization were occasionally weighed in the balance, fundamental values were not consciously chosen from a checklist, however much preachers in their sermons might wish it otherwise. Habits were habitual. In short, conscious choices were seldom made in an atmosphere of "anything goes." Manners and social values remained the province of unconscious upbringing and stealthy imitation.

At first glance, it seems reasonable to suppose that even blind imitation would select what was expected to be most useful in the new circumstances. Yet the overall selection environment was seldom harsh. Competitive pressures allowed surprising latitude. The weak selection environment may be why British regional traits persisted for so long, not merely a generalized Britishness—mainland European observers were in fact disappointed at how very British American lifestyles remained. A few specialized methods of coping with the landscape might be copied from the Native Americans, but no obvious advantage was to be had from their tribal customs, which were disdained. The rural lifestyle of most British regions coped with American conditions with surprisingly little alteration. This statement has of course little meaning without a sense of what would have been possible. Far more adaptation could and doubtless would have taken place had it been as advantageous as the switch to maize.

There are admittedly objections to evolutionary explanations in social science. A great many appeals to evolution turn out to be only metaphors, and the difficulty of agreeing on the unit of selection is a serious problem. Jack Knight avoids selectionism or functionalism for another reason: he says the results are not guaranteed to be allocatively efficient.[10] He envisages both institutions and conventions (read customs or cultures) as outcomes of power struggles. Their continuing development is, in his opinion, a mere by-product of struggles over distributional gains. All conflict and politics are about distribution, and self-interested motivations are not necessarily socially efficient. The best man neither makes infallible choices nor does he inevitably win; the most powerful man wins.

[10] Jack Knight, *Institutions and Social Conflict* (Cambridge: Cambridge University Press, 1992), especially p. 89 n. 3.

This rather stringent objection thus replaces a process of selection by the self-interested choices of the most powerful actors. The argument does not precisely invalidate the notion of "selection against," because there is nothing in evolutionary theory to require that outcomes be efficient in all respects. The actors are permitted to make mistakes. An evolutionary mechanism may operate without any expectation that it will give socially optimal results. Nevertheless, Knight is making the interesting point that the selection environment seldom seems to have been severe enough to eliminate demonstrably inefficient practices, unless, tautologically, anything that has been eliminated is termed inefficient.

V

As regards American culture, the result was a long hangover of British traits and an even longer tail of British terms for American customs. The process of replacing imported habits and terms was slow and not entirely unidirectional, which is consistent with a surprisingly weak selection environment. But in the end it was fairly sure.

Today, despite large migrations from less familiar sources, the argument has arisen that only a handful of American states is being transformed.[11] So much for the melting pot. During the 1990s two-thirds of the Hispanic and Asian populations were to be found in California, New York, Texas, and Florida, while other Americans were moving to states in the "New Sun Belt." This flight was not

[11] Christopher Caldwell in *Financial Times*, 20 Sep 2003, summarizing the work of William Frey of the Population Studies Center, University of Michigan.

equivalent to the "white flight" from the cities to the suburbs during the 1950s, since blacks and long-established immigrants were also moving. All the New Sun-Belt people, "are seeking protection against global modernity as surely as Camembert makers in France or foxhunters in England. The difference is the use of exit rather than voice, since whereas Europeans protest, Americans simply move away. That, after all, is how we got here in the first place," says Christopher Caldwell.[12]

This interpretation of the history of American immigration may be appealing but it is misleading. The melting pot has already done the job of creating fertile new cultures. Of course, the process was never smooth. There was plenty of agitation about immigrants in earlier American history—about the Roman Catholic Irish in the 1850s, about southern and eastern Europeans, who also tended to be Catholics, later in the nineteenth century, about Asians in the twentieth century—but the objections largely passed into history. The generational cycle turned, and converted crass incomers into passable Yankees, if not quite into WASPs. It is conventional to say that each wave enriched American culture in the process. Conventional and true.

At the start of the twenty-first century the scare in the United States is that the big contemporary immigration by Spanish-speaking Hispanics will split the nation in two.[13] Hispanics are said to be keeping themselves apart, avoiding the use of English, and declining to absorb on the spot the "core" Protestant and individualist values that underpin the

[12] Ibid.
[13] Samuel Huntington, "The Hispanic Challenge," *Foreign Policy* Mar–Apr 2004 (Internet version).

149

American way of life. There will be adjustment costs for both sides, it is correct to say, but it is only fair to take equivalent account of the gains. Xenophobia is bred by short time horizons, but precedent suggests that young Hispanics will eventually merge their Latino identity in the larger American one, just as previous streams of immigrants have done. They will be able to embrace both cultures. It is encouraging to find The *Economist* reporting that they are already doing so.[14] Only 10 percent of them still rely mainly on the Spanish language.

VI

The best-known theory of cultural persistence tends to deny the effectiveness of the melting pot in America and elsewhere. Thomas Sowell argues that imported cultural differences can persist for generations.[15] His *Economics and Politics of Race* made this case as early as 1983, at a time when public debate and the academic world automatically took the cultural-relativist line. Sowell's method was to compare the performance of individual ethnic groups in a range of immigrant countries where all incomers supposedly faced similar conditions. His conclusion was as definite as it was politically incorrect: "racial and ethnic groups differ enormously

[14] *Economist*, 6 Mar 2004. The supposed counterinstance of prolonged separateness represented by American blacks is based on highly selective examples and overlooks the experience of members of this group when they are outside the country. For all the race problems of the United States, American blacks in African countries usually recognize that their identity is American after all, and that is how they are perceived by indigenous Africans.

[15] Thomas Sowell, *The Economics and Politics of Race: An International Perspective* (New York: William Morrow, 1983).

in their economic performances, whether in their respective homelands—where climatic and geographical differences complicate comparisons—or in other countries under the same climatic, geographic, legal and political conditions."[16]

Sowell cites as an example the Germans in Australia, the United States, and Brazil. In Australia they made contributions to family farming, science, and technology; they were not simply shaped by the host culture. (But now it is a rare place where one can detect any strong German influence.) In the southern states of Brazil during the early twentieth century, almost half of industry was owned by people of German descent, compared with the mere one-fifth owned by descendants of the original Portuguese settlers. (Yet surely the Germans arrived with more capital and commanded better technology than the earlier Portuguese settlers.) As to people of Irish descent, Sowell states that they were seldom businessmen in early twentieth-century America, supposedly reflecting the pattern in Ireland itself; they were, he says, overrepresented in politics, including crooked politics, supplying 50 of 110 presidents of the AFL unions.[17] This he links to purported Irish characteristics of human warmth, wit, and oratory.

Politics has a lower entry price than business and impecunious immigrants might have been expected to gravitate toward it and use the political system to offer one another support. Group cohesion may confer little external status in the new country, but it does promise insurance against ill fortune and help to compensate for lack of local advantages. Some degree of cultural persistence is only to be

[16] Ibid., p. 135.
[17] Ibid., p. 71.

expected. Nevertheless, even where there is, statistically speaking, a population difference underlying such stereotyping, it commonly washes out over time—which is why a historical approach to culture is so appropriate. Even if we grant some descriptive truth to Sowell's observation about the Irish in the United States, its lack of generality would be exposed by the situation in Australia. The Irish there show no sign of having brought oratory with them from the Ould Sod; they have accommodated to the comparative inarticulateness of other Australians.

This point is worth elaborating. The first generation of people born in Australia, the currency lads and lasses, were better built and longer in the limb than their convict parents. They were great all-rounders. According to one admiring visitor, "they could do everything but talk."[18] The point, then, is not that cultures do not exist in some sense (as can be seen by the rapid formation of a similar accent and social manner from one end of Australia to the other) but that they are mutable. Certain features may persist, like the relative lack of fluency mentioned, but most will blur into the common run. Immigrants, whoever they are, are far from certain to retain every alleged peculiarity of their behavior at home. Sowell's emphasis on persistence, real though that can be, risks the common failing of cultural studies: picking and choosing among criteria.

Few came forward to agree with Sowell. The most prominent scholar to take a similar line at the same period was the development economist Peter Bauer, who insisted on the catalyzing role played by Jews and nonconformists in European history, Chinese immigrants in Southeast Asia,

---

[18] Kylie Tennant, *Australia: Her Story* (London: Pan Books, 1964), p. 42.

and Indian and Levantine traders in East and West Africa.[19] Any economic historian could add other communities who clung together, offered each other deals and daughters in marriage, and achieved collective successes that lasted for at least a few generations. Religious affiliation is commonly the tightest bond, as is seen with the Amish, Jews, Huguenots, Quakers, Old Believers in Russia, and Sikhs, who marked themselves off as cultural groups in their own countries, not merely when they were immigrants adrift in new and potentially unfriendly lands. The Amish are almost a caricature case of a lump the melting pot has not dissolved, though even the Amish are not the same in every respect as they were even a generation ago. The logic that emphasizes the advantages of clinging together has also to accommodate the awkward fact that, while such groupings may last for generations, they do not last forever, and at no time does every individual stay within the group. If the advantage of togetherness is so real, why should it ever be given up?

Sowell and Bauer were forerunners of those who, around the turn of the millennium, sought to revive cultural explanation in economics. An effort needs to be made to modify their position by placing it in historical context. Admittedly, common observation goes a long way toward supporting their notion of immigrant communities that keep their identities while remaining apart from their host societies and from one another. Throughout the centuries regimes often ensured that foreign traders were housed in their own quarters of cities, for which "ghetto" would not always be a fair term. Some of these communities of metics

[19] Peter Bauer, *From Subsistence to Exchange* (Princeton: Princeton University Press, 2000).

held tightly to their old ways, though the institutional element underlying their togetherness should be recognized:
the privileges they were granted tended to keep them together. People from the same European localities often
pitched together when they settled overseas. Thus, in Nor-
wich, where the Strangers included Walloons, Jews and
Netherlanders, the last sermon in Dutch was not preached
until 1900. German-language services were held just north
of Chicago until the 1920s. At Thomastown, now a suburb
of Melbourne, gravestones were wholly inscribed in German
as recently as 1970, and there are still descendants of mid-
nineteenth-century immigrants from Germany who hold the
annual festival called Kris Kringel. Notice, however, that the
distinctiveness of these communities has faded, until their
memory is little more now than an aspect of the nostalgia or
tourist industry.

VII

Most Western countries contain substantial numbers of recent immigrants, some countries more than others and Australia most of all. Anyone who has lived in the cities of a recipient society knows of ethnic districts and communities,
though we should beware: some of these are in the process of
merging into the larger society as their younger, more energetic, and more successful inhabitants move out. Often they
persist more by repute than reality. In Australia an impression of Balkanization—never more than faint—is sustained
by the fact that old ethnicities are replenished by ones from
new sources. There is a cycle in these things. When their
numbers are small, immigrants tend to marry "out," return to
marrying "in" when the community grows, and disperse

again in another generation when young people feel themselves secure members of the larger society. They then pair off with individuals from any group, selecting for personal attractiveness rather than origin. Behavior is thus partly a function of the size of the marriage market and the position of individuals in the generational stream of settlement.

This is the situation in Australia. Immigration there has been a roaring success. The nasty, brutish, short, and overreported life of an anti-immigrant party that formed in rural Queensland rang few bells in the southern cities, where most Australians actually live. The best test of homogenization for which statistics are available relates to the marriage patterns of second-generation immigrants.[20] The data show that fewer than 10 percent of brides of western European origin marry within their own ethnic grouping, and the figures for second-generation migrants from some parts of Southeast Asia, Africa, and the Pacific islands are also low. Certain other ethnic groups do continue to marry within their own communities and will undoubtedly continue to do so into the third and later generations, but not necessarily forever.

Taken overall, only one-quarter of the second generation marries into its own ethnic community. The remainder generate the Australian ethnic mix, a large development that is disguised somewhat by the practice of taking the father's name as the family name; this creates the illusion that people adhere to the communities indicated by their patronyms. The illusion is dispelled if the mother's maiden name becomes known since increasingly this denotes a different

[20] Charles A. Price, "Ethnic Intermixture in Australia," *People and Place* 1/1 (1993): 6–8.

origin. Already by 1988 there was an ethnic mix of at least 37 percent of the population, and this proportion is growing. None of the postwar immigrant groups that have been added to the earlier Anglo-Celtic population of Australia has been numerically dominant; the largest, the Italian, made up only 6 percent of postwar net migration. As Charles Price says, this provides Australia's "best protection against becoming a battle-ground of 'warring tribes.'"[21]

During the past thirty years my experience of thousands of Australian—and at intervals hundreds of British and American—undergraduates, scores of whom have discussed their personal circumstances with me, indicates that they are not much affected by the origin of either parent. It is usually of secondary importance to individuals, many of whom show an astonishing unconcern, even ignorance, about where their parents came from and why they left. Instead the young New Australians display the obsessive concern of the entire nation with sports fixtures; that is to say, with the local culture. The predominant sense of identity that the children of immigrants adopt is simply Australian. Older people from long-settled families will more willingly lay claim to the cachet of overseas descent, and nowadays even convict ancestry confers status among them. This mild form of inverted snobbery is merely a variant of the interest in genealogy found in all the English-speaking countries. It leads to no significant reverse migration and does not undermine the self-image of Australians. A large number of Australians is domiciled in Britain, perhaps as many as a quarter of a million, but their main reason for returning is seldom because their ancestors came from there.

[21] Ibid., p. 8.

I am more struck by the speed of adoption of new identities by immigrants (in the United States and elsewhere, as well as in Australia) than by their continued separateness: by globalization rather than ghettoization. Admittedly, children from immigrant families can become embroiled in conflicts with cloying mothers and authoritarian fathers when neither parent is much at ease in the new society. Fortunately, the misery that this creates—the attempts to restrict the children's choice of marriage partners—seldom lasts more than a generation. In the long run, cultural identity is a Potemkin village. The main exception to assimilation, at least as signaled by the extent of intermarriage, seems to be the Islamic community, but for the great majority of young people of other faiths, new identities are swiftly formed and local loyalties internalized.

Sowell, on the other hand, is impressed by the differential efficiency of cultures, which he defines as distinct bundles of ways of undertaking tasks and solving problems. Another way of putting this would be to say that culture may influence transaction costs. Sowell sees each overseas culture as influencing, and almost (though not quite) determining, how its members perform in new settings: wherever they go, they perform according to the signature of their home culture. This is a strong path-dependent position. It is not wholly incorrect; we should expect a carryover of imported ways for any number of reasons. Sowell's strongest cases are where advantages (the endurance and frugality of the Overseas Chinese) or disadvantages (the lack of skills for entering the urban economy on the part of rural black Americans) seem to account for prolonged separatism. Perhaps there are population differences of these kinds; a belief in them is part of the common lore. Yet the thesis remains leaky. It cannot tell us how long assimilation may take nor what else in the whole range of social pressures may be reinforcing the sup-posed propensity. We should expect to see a carryover of original advantage or disadvantage, but we should just as def-initely anticipate that this will dwindle over time. There are innumerable cases where it has washed out, while in others what actually persists may be more superficial than it seems.

Over time groups tend to lose their pure identities, though continuing to attract prejudice to their old names. A strong thesis of cultural persistence does not allow for the generational progression whereby many in most groups inte-grate almost unnoticed into the host societies. Sowell him-self notes that over three-fifths of German brides in Australia married non-German grooms between 1908 and 1940.[22] The proportion will be vastly greater since then. Even peo-ple who remain in their communities may pick up new val-ues as a result of learning-by-doing and cognitive dissonance. The theory of cultural persistence tends to confuse ethnicity and culture. In the very long run, ethnicity is culturally ir-relevant because culture can be acquired. People of all back-grounds share cultures and contribute to them. I once heard Glenn Loury, a black American economist, give a talk in which he made great play of the fact that he, too, is an heir of Western civilization. And so he is.

The early stages of migration invariably arouse preju-dice. Germans in the Roman Empire were accused of a "nau-seating stink." They were permitted to be servants or soldiers but not to intermarry with Romans. Maybe they did stink; it would not be surprising given their circumstances. Many first-stage migrants all around the world are young men with

---

[22] Sowell, *Economics and Politics of Race*, p. 58.

the energy and lack of finesse this may imply. Poor migrants have little education or money. They work in unpleasant jobs that locals do not want, such as those on building sites. They do not look like acceptable suitors for the daughters of dignitaries. The complaints about them scarcely alter over the ages: they are unwashed, crude, do not speak the language or speak it with barbarous accents, they are criminal, diseased, and chase the local women. In the era of the welfare state, they are accused of becoming burdens on the taxpayer. What else is to be expected than complaints of these kinds, however exaggerated they may be?

These protests were heard in the Roman Empire and recur everywhere today, in Europe, in Malaysia, in the southern Chinese cities. The ethnicities and nationalities of those whose reputations are besmirched go the rounds, but there is little change in the litany of accusations. Undoubtedly there are social costs associated with each new wave of migration, including migration from countryside to town within the same country. Successive groups, if they manage to secure a foothold, recycle the complaints against the next-comers. The employers of cheap labor do their best to pass the costs on to the community.

Much of this resistance to immigration is vulgar protectionism, as can be seen when it comes to the Jews and other commercial groups: then the objections are turned on their heads, and the complaints are of excessive competitiveness, not of what Sowell calls "the classic patterns of social pathology" found among those without urban skills.[23] Once migrants are successful they may still cling together for a time, but increasingly they adopt the manners of the larger

[23] Ibid., p. 132.

society, each wave adding a coloration of its own. Their characteristics change, and their opportunities of contributing to society increase. Too little is known about the details to say precisely what will be added and what will be left behind, but the dynamism of the process is evident. Culture exists as a succession of transitory phases that attract a great deal of comment and anguish at the time. Since history takes place during these interludes, they cannot be completely dismissed. But on the time scale that nations must take into account, cultural persistence is not so persistent after all.

Chapter 7

East Asia's Experience

Much the greatest economic experiment of the past two generations has been the rise of East Asia. First came the British industrial revolution, second, the industrialization of Europe, third, the industrialization of the United States, and now, fourth, the "East Asian Miracle." The transformation of East Asia can be seen as technological catch-up but is remarkable in its own right because of the grand scale, extreme rapidity, unexpectedness, and range of countries involved.[1]

In the aftermath of the Second World War, other parts of the world had been thought far more likely to achieve growth. East Asia was seen as held back by the dead, or at any rate conservative, hand of Confucianism, which over the millennia had not been systematically associated with economic growth. This dismissal on cultural grounds

[1] Eric L. Jones, "The East Asian Miracle," *Business History* 45/3 (2003): 119–24.

was not merely Western prejudice; it was accepted as late as the 1960s by some of the region's own intellectuals. The massive shift that took place amounts to an experiment in cultural as well as economic change. It touches explanations of growth in terms of Asian Values; the transformation of society and culture through industrialization, urbanization, and steeply rising incomes; and the future possibility that growth may alter authoritarian regimes until they become pluralist, maybe eventually democratic.

The material results of the East Asian Miracle are plain. Whereas thirty years earlier the region held 20 percent of global foreign exchange reserves, by 2003 it held 70 percent, and this despite the Asian Crisis of 1997. The Asia-Pacific economies as a group are the fastest-growing in the world, generating one-quarter of global gross product (GGP) and a similar share of merchandise exports. Much of coastal East Asia has been industrialized and urbanized, and millions have been lifted out of poverty. In one East Asian country after another, urban populations have been scaling the "ladder of consumption" whereby consumers attain successive income thresholds and buy more elaborate goods in sudden waves. Tourism is speedily growing: six million Chinese traveled abroad in 2002.

China, which had taken the lead from Japan and the smaller Tiger economies, was by then attracting much the largest share of international investment. Its manufacturers were buying raw materials on a scale that was tempered only by limitations of bulk carrier and port capacity at home and abroad. In three heady weeks of September and October 2003, freight rates soared by 50 percent. Cargoes of iron ore dispatched to China from Brazil cost more to ship than they did to buy. At that date all the talk was of how Japan, South Korea, and Taiwan, besides distant countries like Mexico, were being obliged to restructure their economies to match the competition and seize the opportunities presented by the Chinese market. Economies in East Asia were scrabbling to move factories to China and turn themselves into hubs supplying that country with services and advanced inputs. Argentina and Brazil were galvanized as resource exporters. Australia's resources sector boomed. China could almost be seen as the center of the world, the "Middle Kingdom" it once claimed to be.

Bourgeois societies are in the making there and elsewhere in East Asia, but the social costs of breakneck change have been high. For instance, there were 100,000 deaths in traffic accidents in China in 2002.[2] The urban/rural divide has produced the fastest-growing income inequality in the world. The ratio of average incomes in country and town, which had been in the order of 1:1.8 in 1985, may have widened to 1:6 by 2003. The resultant pressure to get ahead is said to be creating more anxiety disorders than did the Cultural Revolution. In China there are only 2,000 qualified psychiatrists, compared with 105 per million of the population in the United States. Suicide is the leading cause of death among 18–34 year-olds: over 250,000 per annum. In Japan one in forty households contains a young loner, a total of one million individuals who seldom venture out of the house. In Asia as a whole, WHO states that five of the ten major causes of disability are mental illnesses, which are a greater burden on the economy than cancer, and predicts

[2] *Time*, 24 Nov 2003.

that depression will become the leading disability. As if these were not problems enough, an AIDS epidemic is under way, though its true scale is difficult to gauge because in China the data are still "national secrets."[3]

1

Was the economic success of East Asia produced by its culture? Many articulate Asians think so, and a smallish but dogmatic lobby of Westerners agrees with them. Asian values, or rather customs, are held to explain the region's rise, amid proclamations that they offer superior alternatives to rule-bound Western methods of doing business. Western commentators who were willing to believe that their own economies were falling behind had first lavished praise on Mao's China, then on Japan's Ministry of International Trade and Industry (MITI), and finally on the manner in which Overseas Chinese businesses operate. During the early 1990s the Asian Values interpretation was promoted by Lee Kuan Yew and Singaporean bureaucrats (the "Singapore School"), followed by members of the elite in other Southeast Asian countries.[4]

Writers who suppose that early rates of growth in developing economies will never falter are often inclined to attribute them to culture, despite the fact that the societies concerned have mostly languished for centuries under despotisms seldom given to safeguarding human rights or the status of women. "I have to confess that I found this theory [Asian Values] appealing at first, since I am of Indian ori-

[3] *Economist*, 22 Nov 2003.
[4] See, for example, Lee Kuan Yew, "The East Asian Way," *New Perspectives Quarterly* 9 (1992): 4–13.

gin . . ." remarks Fareed Zakaria. "But then I wondered, if being Indian is a key to economic success, what explained the dismal performance of the Indian economy over the four decades since its independence in 1947 or, for that matter, for hundreds of years before that? One might ask the same question of China, another country with an economy that performed miserably for hundreds of years until two decades ago."[5]

The central Asian Values argument is that Asians, primarily the Chinese, have beliefs and behaviors that distinguish them from Europeans and Americans. They work for the benefit of the community; they work hard; they are thrifty; they respect education. Notice that the veneration of the elderly, an aspect of Confucianism proper, is not included; the appeal to conservatism was dropped because tradition seemed to interfere with economic success. In Singapore, Western commercial law was adopted, and judges were paid vast salaries to reduce the incentive to take bribes. This created a hybrid that can scarcely be termed "Asian" culture. The Asian Values push was in reality an implicit defense of soft authoritarianism, accompanied by gloating references to the anticipated decline of the West.[6] The advantage to employers and governments of hard-working, high-saving workforces is obvious.

This euphoria never carried with it all informed Asian opinion; it was resisted by Kim Dae Jung in Korea, Martin Lee in Hong Kong, and Lee Teng-hui in Taiwan. The

[5] Fareed Zakaria, "Asian Values," *Foreign Policy*, Nov–Dec 2002, p. 1 (Internet version).

[6] Eric L. Jones, "Asia's Fate: A Response to the Singapore School," *National Interest* 35 (Spring 1994): 18–28; Eric L. Jones, *The Record of Global Economic Development* (Cheltenham, U.K.: Edward Elgar, 2002), p. 142.

last-named said Chinese history was being misread; there are only values, not specially Asian ones.[7] While collectivism may have been tolerable during the early phase of rapid growth in East Asia, it was only one choice among several philosophies indigenous to the region. Asian Values arguments misrepresent or submerge the democratic elements in China's past, especially traits associated with Buddhism and the self-governance of villages.[8]

Nevertheless, a number of Western advocates were swept off their feet, including members of the New China Lobby, who based private consultancies on the contacts they had made during the course of working in China for their own governments. The motives of others were obscure, though some hankered for the docile workforces and uncritical support which they believed East Asian governments gave to business. Others were persuaded that, by contrast, individual rights were destroying social cohesion in Western countries.[9]

Although there was a brief, gleeful recurrence after the Enron and other business scandals, less has been heard of all this since the Asian Crisis. Commentators began to

[7] Jones, *The Record*, p. 142. For the views of Kim Dae Jung, see "Is Culture Destiny? The Myth of Asia's Anti-Democratic Values," *Foreign Affairs* 73/6 (2004): 189–94.

[8] See, for example, Steven Muhlberger and Phil Paine, "Democracy's Place in World History," *Journal of World History* 4 (1993): 23–45.

[9] See, for example, Reg. Little and Warren Reed, *The Confucian Renaissance* (Annandale, Australia: Federation Press, 1989). See also David Howell, "Don't Blame Asian Values," *Prospect*, Oct 1998, pp. 14–15. Howell claimed that the Asian Crisis would be even worse for the West and last much longer than predicted. It was surprising to find a British Conservative Party figure championing a system that relies less on the law and more on intervention than Britain's own economic system.

point out that so far from authoritarianism being better able to get things done, at least no democracy has ever suffered a major famine, an observation that can be traced back to Amartya Sen. The same cannot be said of China, which experienced a colossal famine under Mao Tse-tung in 1958–61. The November 2002 issue of *Foreign Policy* actually dumped Asian Values among its candidates for the "dustbin of history." More recently, Peter Lindert undertook an econometric study that disposed of Lee Kuan Yew's assertion that autocracy works best.[10] Surveying East Asia between 1960 and 1998 revealed a positive, not negative, correlation between democracy and economic growth. Lindert concluded that, "[Lee Kuan Yew's] hypothesis is based on a self-congratulatory contrast of successful Singapore and (pre-democratic) Taiwan with anybody growing more slowly under a different regime."

Leading Japanese scholars have resiled on former interpretations of their own Miracle. The Ministry of Finance now follows academic opinion in stating that MITI's protectionist policies actually retarded growth in textiles, aircraft manufacturing, and chemicals, while the industries that did grow succeeded precisely because they eluded government intervention. This interpretation is very hard to "sell" to older businesspeople, who continue to admire what they think of as the Japanese industrial system, despite being obliged to admit its prolonged spell in the doldrums.

The notion dies hard that Japanese exceptionalism (*Nihonjinron*) accounts for the country's success. A book by Ann Waswo puts exceptionalism in its place, together with

[10] Peter Lindert, "Voice and Growth: Was Churchill Right?" *Journal of Economic History* 63/2 (2003), especially pp. 339, 345.

the assumption of superiority it embodies.[11] She prefers explanations based on observable trends and events rather than purportedly unique and enduring cultural traditions. Interestingly, she notes that the Japanese establishment has repeatedly invented and reinvented supposed traditions whereas actual norms, values, and behavior have continued to alter autonomously. "Japan today," Waswo states, "possesses a distinctive culture, but that culture has been and remains no more static than in other countries."[12] Ian Buruma adds that far from their system being entirely indigenous, the Japanese embraced German theories on racial purity, European-style excuses for colonialism, and the realization derived from Christianity that a single overarching deity (in Japan's case, the newly restored emperor) could motivate soldiers better than a looser contingent of Shinto gods.[13]

II

More apparent nowadays than the fading idealization of Japan is admiration of Overseas Chinese businesses. If their contributions to the economies of Asia were added together, the Overseas Chinese would make up a great economy of their own. Today some of their larger firms are starting to be managed by a younger generation returned from American business schools, who are introducing more regular and self-

[11] Ann Waswo, *Modern Japanese Society 1868–1944* (Oxford: Oxford University Press, 1996). In 1896 a Japanese bureaucrat argued that Japan could avoid the "sad and pitiful" history of industrialization in Britain (p. 26). To judge from material on the Japanese environment in Alex Kerr, *Dogs and Demons: The Fall of Modern Japan* (London: Penguin Books, 2001), and my own observations, he was doomed to be disappointed.

[12] Waswo, *Modern Japanese Society*, p. 4.

[13] Ian Buruma, "Japanese Spirit, Western Things," *Economist*, 12 Jul 2003.

critical managerial practices, but the typical business remains a family concern founded and dominated by a patriarch. Fluid, adaptable firms are spread over a range of industries, wherever the temptations of a takeover or start-up appealed to the boss.

Like family firms everywhere—the commonest type of business in the world—Overseas Chinese companies are secretive. No eye need be kept on shareholders or the capital markets. Account books need not be over-nice, apart from those prepared with the tax collector in mind. The founder's advantage is that he can immediately commit his own capital. This independent market power is useful where the courts cannot be depended on to enforce contracts fairly, meaning that transactions and agency costs are high. Low costs are incurred for motivating and monitoring a family workforce, and it is relatively easy for the proprietor to allocate rewards. Those involved will one day inherit the company, though uncertainties as to what the assets really are mean, ironically, that some of them will end up fighting over their shares.[14] Family businesses are not all sweetness and light, and international economic integration is exposing them to demands for a more transparent legality.

Rather than impersonal rules, the principle governing contacts with suppliers, customers, clients, and government officials are sets of relationships called *guanxi*. These can be traced historically to the need to identify those who could be trusted. The five levels of Confucian relationships, whereby individuals doing business become progressively closer in personal terms, provided a means of shaking out the crooks.

---

[14] See, for example, Rajeswary Ampalavanar Brown, *Capital and Entrepreneurship in South-East Asia* (New York: St. Martin's Press, 1994).

Guanxi represent a logical solution to the problem of trust, though they remain second best to independent law, for which demand is now stirring in China. The reciprocal gift giving that accompanies personal relationships is corrupt to Western eyes.

The atomized nature of Chinese society—the "sheet of sand"—is still very evident. Peter Hessler reports that on-lookers gape at road accidents and offer no help, nor will they involve themselves if someone has their pocket picked.[15] Families and small groups look after one another, but Good Samaritan traits are conspicuously absent. A reference to the Good Samaritan is, however, potentially misleading. West-ern behavior may still be guided to some extent by the over-hang of Christian ethics but may also owe much to the con-fidence imparted by the West's long history of personal comfort and security.

A defense of Chinese business practices, coupled with criticisms of Western ones that have become almost routine, has been put forward in a paper called "Challenges of China's Economic System for Economic Theory," by Gregory Chow, a Princeton economist and adviser to the Chinese govern-ment.[16] Chow asks whether all contracts *should* be enforced, implying that guanxi permit continual "realistic" adjust-ments via personal relationships as opposed to the costly court battles common in the United States. (He rather con-fusingly takes the United States to be synonymous with the West.) In practice the distinction between business behav-

[15] Peter Hessler, *River Town: Two Years on the Yangtze* (London: John Mur-ray, 2001), pp. 111–12.
[16] Gregory C. Chow, "Challenges of China's Economic System for Eco-nomic Theory," in Ross Garnaut and Yiping Huang, eds., *Growth without Miracles* (Oxford: Oxford University Press, 2001), pp. 492–98.

ior in East and West is less marked than this may make it appear. Chow himself quotes Oliver Hart to the effect that American contracts are only starting points for further negotiations, and it may be added that Ulrich Witt observed some time ago that many Western deals are in fact made on a handshake.[17] The difference is that when informal agreements go wrong in the West, there is the fallback of impartial, black-letter law.

Chow asserts that informal personal relationships may—note *may*—better solve contractual problems. He does not demonstrate that this is so. Nor does he attach instrumental or ethical value to the concept of equality before the law. As a result he does not recognize that guanxi surrender disputes to the respective power positions of the parties concerned—that guanxi are politics rather than law. Chow does not acknowledge that the number of complex exchanges with long gestation periods may be restricted by these cumbersome arrangements. There are high marginal costs to establishing personal relationships before business can be done.[18]

Late Qing times saw business retreat from using the courts and the customary law that had become quite widespread.[19] Republican times were scarcely more propitious. Shareholder power was sidelined, and the biggest corporations tended to become personal fiefs. Then, between 1937 and 1945, entrepreneurs were confronted by Japanese mili-

---

[17] Ulrich Witt, "Evolution and Stability of Cooperation without Enforceable Contracts," *Kyklos* 39 (1986): pp. 245–66.

[18] To overcome the problems, the People's Republic of China (PRC) is at last adopting sections of impersonal international law.

[19] Parks M. Coble, *Chinese Capitalists in Japan's New Order* (Berkeley: University of California Press, 2003).

tary and puppet governments and in response intensified the practices they had already devised to evade interference by an untrustworthy state. If they kept no accounts, or kept them secret, or fabricated them, this was understandable when what was at stake was the survival of their companies, the security of their families, and the preservation of their own lives. They were at risk of being killed by the Japanese for not collaborating or being murdered by Nationalist agents for looking as if they might do so. Secrecy and relationship business were adaptations to these dreadful circumstances. The business culture of Nationalist China was reimported by the PRC (People's Republic of China) in the late 1970s, after Deng Xiao-ping's opening of the country, courtesy of the Overseas Chinese who had carried it away from the Communist regime in 1949.

In Southeast Asian countries where the Chinese formed tiny minorities, envied, hated, and sometimes massacred, they continued to behave in a defensive manner. In Indonesia under Suharto, the Chinese were said to own 70 percent of commercial assets although they constituted only 3 percent of the population. One way of protecting their assets was to pay off politicians; another, not resorted to until well into the 1990s, was for some Indonesian-Chinese companies to contemplate listing on the New York Stock Exchange in the hope of entangling American investors in their affairs, and through them the U.S. government. Only a powerful threat could have persuaded the Chinese to open their books to outside investors.[20]

[20] The opacity of company accounts in mainland China means, accord-

After Suharto fell, Chinese shops were attacked and thousands of Chinese were slaughtered: my students in Australia showed me the desperate e-mails from family, friends, and neighbors they were receiving every day while this horror was taking place. The Western students looked on disbelievingly, but in truth it was nothing new. It had happened in Malaysia in the 1960s. As a friend told me, "They killed my dog, and I left because I thought they were going to kill me next." No wonder the Chinese habit is to spread risk by establishing family members in each of several countries.

Individual personalities vary, as they do in any group, but harsh experience or the harsh experience of one's parents can induce suspiciousness and other disagreeable attitudes. Western teachers sometimes encounter in Chinese students an unwillingness to take part in class discussion, an inability to accept that marks have been carefully assigned and in fairness cannot be altered, the opinion that Western democracy and all it entails is a dream or a confidence trick. Students of Chinese descent from several countries, including the PRC, have fortunately begun to respond more positively now. This can be attributed to environments that are more secure as well as more prosperous than in the past, and to a better grasp of English than many of those previously studying overseas had.

There is nothing genetic or racial about the attitudes, and even calling them cultural gives them too definite an appearance. The attitudes are cultural only in the sense that

---

ing to the *Far Eastern Economic Review* (8 Jan 2004), that creditworthiness remains almost impossible to assess, notwithstanding the eagerness of Western rating agencies to rank firms there.

they have been learned over quite short periods and are susceptible of rapid alteration in sunnier times. Moreover, the behavior apparent in the classroom is not specific to the Chinese but is shared by students from many lands. It is an effect of growing up in hierarchical societies and being schooled in an authoritarian, rote-learning manner.[21] Confrontation with excessive power rather than intangible cultural heritage is the crucial variable. And because defensive behavior is learned, it can be unlearned, give or take the difficulty of deconditioning people whose responses became engrained when they were young.

An investigation of decisions affecting health and safety is apposite. It suggests that Chinese and Americans have similar perceptions of what is fair, but the Chinese avoid making decisions on that basis, inclining to tell their superiors what is expedient.[22] This would seem to confirm common stereotypes of the two nations, but whether or not these capture reality at any given moment, they are clearly not fixed. They are age-related rather than national: strikingly, young Chinese management students make choices much more like those of Americans than do middle-aged Chinese professionals. Another cross-cultural study found that the "Chinese were less tolerant than residents of six other countries, but the differences among Chinese and oth-

[21] Maria Spizzica, "Cultural Differences within 'Western' and 'Eastern' Education" (paper presented to the First National Conference on Tertiary Literacy, Victoria University of Technology, Melbourne, 15–16 Mar 1996).

[22] Wen-Qiang Bian and L. Robin Keller, "Chinese and Americans Agree on What Is Fair, but Disagree on What Is Best in Societal Decisions Affecting Health and Safety Risks," *Risk Analysis* 19/3 (1999): 439–52.

ers were less substantial among people of similar educational levels."[23]

Investment by the Overseas Chinese led China's own economic recovery. They found fertile ground. Why the Communist Chinese, notably the peasantry, proved so responsive to economic incentives after a quarter of a century under a command economy has rarely been investigated. A paper by Tom Rawski is an important exception.[24] Earlier phases of reform during the Communist era, he notes, had produced nothing like the same breakthrough from extreme poverty to new levels of output, productivity, and income. While skeptical of broad appeals to underlying Confucian culture and eager to "avoid the romantic and mysterious imagery that often surrounds the discussion of Asian economic matters," Rawski finds the traditional Chinese economic culture of late imperial times and after to have been unusually rich in market experience, market institutions, complex organizations, popular religion, and family and personal life. Despite the absence of a system of dispute resolution comparable to Western commercial law, there were customary substitutes without which the rural economy could not have operated. Individuals were trained to respond in the marketplace as an unintended consequence of the arrangements he describes; a comparable training was absent from many other less-developed countries.

Rawski is not surprised by the carryover in China

[23] Andrew J. Nathan, "Is Chinese Culture Distinctive? A Review Article," *Journal of Asian Studies* 52/4 (1993): 930.
[24] Thomas G. Rawski, "Social Capabilities and Chinese Economic Growth" (mimeo, University of Pittsburgh, Apr 2002, 16 pp.).

from earlier times to the recent past. A desire to differentiate oneself despite tight group norms persisted in the most restrictive days of the Cultural Revolution; it is as though people desire to be one of the gang, only more so.[25] We should also recognize that there must have been a vast amount of preference falsification during the Maoist period, with real attitudes deeply camouflaged.[26] I recall that my son attended a concert in China performed on traditional instruments by men who had buried them during the Cultural Revolution; they had not forgotten where they were any more than Scottish Highlanders forgot their claymores hidden in the thatch. Family loyalty, though severely tested under the mad reign of the Red Guard, survived the Maoist assault. "Vulgar Confucianism" survived the anti-Confucius campaign. Had Maoism lasted twice as long, deconditioning might have been much harder, as is suggested by the slowness with which *Homo sovieticus* in former East Germany converts to *Homo economicus*.

Considered in these terms, culture is internalized by many people at each historical stage—under a command economy, by all who wish to survive—and can be described as a layered compound of their reactions. But it is not hard and fast, to be admired or disparaged in the case under review as indefeasibly Chinese. The "Chinese characteristics" of which so much is made are contingent, as cultural features tend to be; we can identify the conditions to which they were originally adaptations and the new circumstances to which

---

[25] See, for example, Jung Chang, *Wild Swans* (London: Flamingo, 1993), p. 492.

[26] For the theory of preference falsification, see Timur Kuran, *Private Truths, Public Lies* (Cambridge, Mass.: Harvard University Press, 1995).

the Chinese are adjusting. The men my son heard at the concert were all elderly; few young people are coming forward to play traditional music—they find new attractions. The Chinese no more live outside history than anyone else, nor are they creatures from outer space set apart from the workings of social science. They possess their own codes of ethics, modes of behavior, and sets of values. These features are real, but they are not facts of nature; they were conferred by particular histories.[27]

Ironically, it is some of the Chinese students, whether from the PRC, Southeast Asia, or even those of Chinese descent now resident in the United States, who are among the hardest to disabuse of the notion that they possess a permanent "Chineseness."[28] They are too young to have experienced the transformation from cohorts traveling overseas from the PRC at the end of the 1970s as "worker-soldier-peasants" in Mao jackets to (twenty years later) well-heeled urban consumers, with many of the attitudes (although a more avid approach to shopping) of their fellows from other countries. Their position is at least as much political as cultural, since they have embraced nationalism in lieu of Maoist-Leninist ideology, of which they know next to nothing. Sometimes their attitudes seem responses to the disorienting experience of being outside China for the first time, trying to cope with what must seem mystifying classroom

[27] It is interesting to note that Nathan ("Is Chinese Culture Distinctive?" p. 926), in struggling to locate an answer to his own question refers at one stage to continuity but soon recognizes that something as apparently timeless as, say, ancestor worship varied under different dynasties.

[28] Coble, *Chinese Capitalists*, pp. 205–6, for the recent uncritically enthusiastic embrace by Chinese Americans of official Chinese nationalistic positions on China's history.

procedures conducted in a foreign language. But only in limited respects may their identity be said to be defined by a unique and timeless culture.

IV

Asians may seem to be imbued with unchangeably different values from Westerners when they are compared at the same period. Yet a cross-sectional view is unhistorical by definition and likely to mislead. Nor is it correct to assume a constant relationship between values and economic performance. Countries that share an underlying Confucian-Taoist philosophy have grown at different times and rates. Values like those of Singapore's neo-Confucianism are associated with a specific phase of growth. When incomes were low and welfare almost nonexistent, the opportunities created by growth-promoting policies may actually have selected for traits favorable to growth (or, better put, selected *against* the indolent and spendthrift). The causation may run from growth to values as much as, or rather than, the other way round.

The values of which the Singapore School makes so much, like hard work, thrift, and educational self-improvement, were characteristic of Britain during its nineteenth-century industrialization. At the very least, these things were then approved, as becomes clear once we mention Samuel Smiles or the fact that before the National Act of 1870 the working class already paid out its pennies to have children educated. The Protestant Ethic comes to mind. There is nothing specifically or permanently Asian about hard work, thrift, or learning, but there may be something special about the relation of these qualities to early economic growth.

The more precise charge by Asian Values proponents

is that the West no longer exhibits these traits while East Asia displays them in abundance. This neglects the dynamic context. Britain and other Western countries once gloried in similar values, but commentators quickly came to fear they might be undermined by the very success of growth.[29] Already in the eighteenth century, John Wesley fretted that when Methodists prospered they would slacken their efforts and relinquish self-denying values in favor of lives of ease. In the early twentieth century, Joseph Schumpeter persuaded himself that capitalism's success would undercut the moral foundations on which it was built. Prosperous societies would not need to work as hard as their forebears who had created prosperity in the first place.

Whether or not one thinks the opinions of Wesley and Schumpeter deserve the status of prophecies, borne out by the unseemly mixture of affluence, indolence, and criminality now apparent in some Western countries, is not quite to the point. At least Wesley and Schumpeter did not think that values were independent of the economic stage. They agreed with the Singapore School that certain values were instrumental in fostering growth but looked ahead to the prospect that these would fade once they had brought about growth. Theirs is a correct reading of the main direction of influence: not from culture to eternal prosperity but from rising incomes to cultural change. Robert Samuelson, on the contrary, grasps the wrong end of the stick in stating that "Asia's success offers at least the hope that capitalism is sufficiently malleable to be made compatible with different cultures."[30]

[29] Jones, "Asia's Fate."

[30] Robert J. Samuelson, "Seeking Capitalism's Spirit," *Australian Financial*

The strong assumption behind the Asian Values story is that, unlike Christianity, neo-Confucianism will prove immune to the blandishments of wealth. Once Charles Darwin had, in a manner of speaking, dethroned the Almighty, the certainties and fears that had driven the West's accumulation phase began to evaporate.[31] Western countries purportedly began to slide into social dysfunction, opportunism, and free riding, abetted by the easy living of the welfare state. Leaving aside the question whether this negative view of life in the West is fully justified, it is unclear why beliefs in East Asia should respond otherwise to material prosperity. In reality signs of dysfunction have already become evident there.

Ironically, it was Singaporean politicians—Wesleyan and Schumpeterian look-alikes?—who were among the first to notice this. Their enthusiasm for the topic of Asian Values peaked about 1994, but soon afterward they were raising the alarm about "affluenza," meaning the loss of the work ethic among young people brought up in comfort. Singapore may actually have the least need to worry. I see no special indolence among my Singaporean students—quite the contrary, despite the fact that most of them attended schools where instruction was heavily by rote. Their English is usually the best among people from the region, while in 2004 Singapore topped the world examination league for mathematics and science. Classroom drilling is clearly effective at transmitting existing knowledge. On the other hand, the independent mind-sets needed for entrepreneurship and work

Review, 19 Jan 2001 (reprinted from *Foreign Affairs*). Samuelson was writing a favorable review of Harrison and Huntington's *Culture Matters*.
[31] This is the variant of the Asian Values thesis propounded by Deepak Lal in *Unintended Consequences* (Cambridge, Mass.: MIT Press, 1998).

on research frontiers may require less disciplined approaches, which are indeed now being introduced into schools in Singapore.

Whether rising levels of wealth have also been accompanied by expectations that pluralist politics, human rights, and other liberal (a.k.a. Western) notions will enter the region is unclear. Earlier, Lee Kuan Yew had said that he was "not sure that in 50 years China will have yet accepted American-style human rights," but he seemed to believe that economic growth would bring a degree of political change, adding that "once they are well above the poverty level there will be less of the kind of barbarism where a man's head is chopped off or he is shot in the back without a proper trial."[32] Another close observer, the journalist Richard Hughes, asserted that Western-style democracy would never establish itself in East Asia since constitutions cannot be dispensed like Marshall Aid or gifts from the squire's lady.[33] But his observation was made some years ago, when incomes were lower. More prosperous cohorts have since arisen, freed from the scarifying experiences their grandparents endured and less afraid to announce their personal preferences.

The debate continues, with some writers still asserting that Western norms are unsuitable for Asia but others being committed to exposing the "fallacies, confusions, and mistakes involved in the defense of Asian exceptionalism."[34] Li Xiaorong, whose aim this is, refers to the idea that

[32] Lee Kuan Yew, "East Asian Way," p. 11.

[33] Reported in Norman MacSwan, *The Man Who Read the East Wind: A Biography of Richard Hughes* (Kenthurst, Australia: Kangaroo Press, 1982), pp. 177–78.

[34] Li Xiaorong, "'Asian Values' and the Universality of Human Rights," *Business and Society Review*, nos. 102/103 (1998): 86.

norms originating in the West are inappropriate for Asia as "the genetic fallacy."[35] I agree that it is a fallacy: it is a special case of the theory of cultural fixity. Proponents draw on highly contingent examples of the alleged preference of Asians for authoritarianism. Excessive attention to differences between societies tends to produce a dogged belief in cultural exceptionalism. Consider the final sentence of a paper by Andrew Nathan in which he asks whether Chinese culture is distinctive: "Although *anyone who studies it must be convinced that it is*, we have far to go to state clearly how it is distinctive and to prove it empirically."[36] Experience suggests that changes in economics and demography will bring about continued adaptations of cultural forms. The debate about Asia's future too often takes place without reference to social dynamics. Chinese culture may remain distinctive in the sense of continuing to differ from other cultures, though the gap will be smaller in the future than it is now, and *the cultures from which it differs will include its former self*. From its past will be drawn a general shape and a host of details, but the past will not be repeated.

V

It would have been extraordinary had the economic upheaval in East Asia not altered its cultures. Peasant societies were industrialized wholesale, occupations were reordered, average incomes soared, and cities metamorphosed into mega-cities of over 10 million inhabitants each. In 1998 there were nine mega-cities in Asia, with a total of 126 million inhabitants, a number that continues to rise and is ex-

[35] Ibid., p. 83.
[36] Nathan, "Is Chinese Culture Distinctive?" p. 936; italics added.

pected to reach 382 million by 2025. The capital cities of several countries account for a truly giant share of national output. Even the shantytown fringes in which rural incomers live during their first years of urban life are economically productive, not inert slums.

The growth process was generally reminiscent of the British industrial revolution, though there were significant differences. What had been a prolonged transition in the West was compressed into a few decades in East Asia. Demography responded much faster to rising income. Life expectancies rose. Fertility rates fell: Japanese birth rates are now the lowest in the world, and the cities of southern coastal China are following suit. Together these forces have produced population aging comparable with that in Western countries—in the case of Japan, exceeding it. Young urban couples have not always resisted the temptations of spoiling an only child or bundling their own parents into retirement homes, like Western yuppies. According to Radio Netherlands (19 November 2003), China has built twenty thousand homes for the elderly in two years, because they "prefer" to live by themselves. Singapore has passed a law requiring children to take financial responsibility for their aged parents. The need for such measures would have been unthinkable in earlier Confucian societies.

The most conspicuous sign of social change has been the increase of consumerism, for which the prospects in Asia are very marked indeed. The falling birth rate will take time to have its greatest impact, and meanwhile the number of young adults will continue to climb. Whereas in Europe and even the United States the equivalent cohort will shrink in size, the number of Asians between thirty and fifty-nine years old is expected to rise from 1.2 billion in 2000 to 1.7 billion by 2020. This offers an enormous market. In some respects, national markets are already starting to merge into a pan-Asian market—intra-Asian trade and bilateral treaties to encourage it became noticeable in 2003. Cultural products, though in some ways the easiest to resist, are beginning to cross borders. For example, after a long period during which Japanese pop music was banned in South Korea in symbolic rejection of Japan's former colonialism, its import is now allowed. In return "Korean Wave" music has caught on across East Asia.

I always question my students about their hobbies. The answers tell me a lot about Western students but many Asians are, or were, inclined to leave the space blank or answer only "shopping." A few years ago a student of Chinese origin, the daughter of a Thai diplomat and educated in two Western countries, told me privately that Chinese students did not understand a concern with hobbies. According to her, they preferred to pass any spare time eating meals with their families or shopping. In Southeast Asia, malls have overtaken parks, mosques, and temples as venues for social gatherings. In several countries the newly rich find their identity in nontraditional dress and food and judge one another by what they buy, just as many do in the West. In China there are already 10 to 13 million customers for luxury goods; Chinese women are said to buy fashionable brands in an effort (surely paradoxical) to assert their independence.[37] Armani plans to open twenty or thirty new stores in China. Chinese tourists spend their time overseas shopping, and in response luxury stores in Paris are hiring Mandarin speakers. The Chinese are in this respect being called "the new Japa-

[37] *Economist*, 19 Jun 2004.

nese." The craze among Chinese and Japanese city dwellers for celebrating Christmas, the origin of which few of them can define, is part of the same frenetic consumerism.

Notwithstanding this, the behavioral cycle continues to revolve. Many people may be expected to revert under prosperity to the ancient pastimes of their civilization, for instance, calligraphy and painting. Western classical music has a vogue, and the usual spare-time interests of well-heeled, educated townsfolk will no doubt expand. In this respect the cultural dynamics of Taiwan are indicative.[38] The Japanese occupation of Taiwan was a civil administration and did not inspire the hatred that the military government provoked in Korea. As a result the typical Taiwanese home looks Japanese in its display of visual arts, crafts, and ceramics. For fifty years the Nationalist government fostered a conservative view of Taiwan, stressing links with pre-Communist Chinese life and blocking other traditions. In reality Taiwan is an immigrant society that has been absorbing foreign influences for centuries. Now that mainland China is increasingly competitive in industry, the Taiwanese government has switched to promoting culture as an alternative. The minister of culture is herself a former concert pianist trained in the Paris Conservatoire.

The manifestation of extreme shopping by the Chinese is an understandable phase in the life of peoples who have been deprived of so much until almost this generation. Certainly consumerism will not halt; after all, there are plenty of materialists in the West and scope for further acquisitiveness everywhere in the world. Nevertheless, the *relative* significance of consumerism is likely to decrease, de-

[38] *Financial Times*, 15 Feb 2003.

spite the comment of Li-Ning Wilson Xu, marketing manager of the largest sportswear firm in China, on a report that only 15 percent of mainland Chinese aged between fifteen and thirty-five play sport as a hobby compared with 50 percent in the United States. Mr. Xu said, "Most Chinese people believe that success is about academic achievement and making money."[39] Against this is the finding of surveys that younger Chinese have become very interested in sport and other hobbies and are starting to make time for them. Whereas 36 percent of urban people over fifty-five years of age express no interest at all in hobbies, 81 percent of those under thirty-five now state that hobbies are very important to them.[40]

For the present, the number of lives devoted to consumerism, though impressive in absolute terms, remains only a fraction of the whole Asian population. What is to be noted, however, is the direction and pace of the change and the demonstration effect it is having. This is a general tendency, a reflex of rising wealth; the impact can be seen even in India, where income growth has lagged behind East Asia. There, "Rolex has replaced religion," and a "second unification" is happening, in which the affluent young now define themselves by a shared consumer culture and not solely by caste, creed, and language. They are starting to marry within *that* subculture, which is spread by television, now reaching half of Indian homes.[41]

In the countries of Asia education is drawing the af-

[39] *Economist*, 2 Aug 2003.
[40] *Far Eastern Economic Review*, 12 Dec 2002. I admit that this does not seem to extend as yet to those who take business studies.
[41] *Economist*, 3 Jan 2004.

fluent young together, unifying the rising generation in opposition to its parents' values. The shift toward universal values consonant with city living is plain, though apparently
not to all observers. For instance, David Edwards states that
"Africans or Asians cannot be expected to believe in or behave like Europeans or Americans, *or those who are educated
in a modern style like those who are not.*"[42] Note the implied
contradiction: non-Westerners are different but less so if
they are educated.

In East Asia change was symbolized by McDonald's,
which helped to revolutionize personal habits.[43] According
to James Watson's classic study, in Hong Kong the chain
catered to the wealthy in the late 1970s, but within twenty
years it served the working class, for whom the restaurants
were less fast-food outlets than reliably clean leisure centers,
as they have become in Beijing, Seoul, and Taipei. Fast food
is not new in China, having been available in Kaifeng, capital during the Song dynasty (tenth to thirteenth centuries
A.D.). The novelties are the leisure-center aspect and the
draw-card of American style. Yet far from imposing uniformity, McDonald's attends to minor differences in the expectations of different Asian peoples, and studies of the
McDonald's phenomenon rightly make much of its simultaneously multilocal nature. Elements of "global" uniformity
are provided, on the supply side, by generalizing American
managerial practice and, on the demand side, by importing
an unfamiliar conception of manners. The way people are induced to eat in McDonald's converges on Western table

---

[42] *Guardian Weekly*, 13 Nov 2003; italics added.

[43] James L. Watson, ed., *McDonald's in East Asia* (Stanford: Stanford University Press, 1997).

manners. East Asians are socialized to queue, keep the lavatories clean, and give up hawking and spitting in public. Westerners off the farm once had to learn these things too.

The standard view is that societies in the West are leading the world culturally, like the metaphorical flying geese whereby Japan led other East Asian countries into economic development.[44] An alternative view is that cultures are path dependent, shaped by their own heritages. The term "multiple modernities" is used. Since only demagogues think globalization is entirely obliterating local cultures, this view smacks of choosing the half-full rather than the half-empty pot. Variation about the mean is real but secondary to the central tendency of modernization. East Asian cultures are evolving very fast indeed. Consider the matter of queuing. The habit is perhaps being exported to Asia from the West, but in the West it is neither a universal nor permanent feature: a German visitor lamented its absence from England in the 1850s, I noticed its absence from Germany in the 1950s, and it is declining again in twenty-first-century England. Asian Values exponents might say that McDonald's is exporting civilities like queuing to East Asia precisely when they are fraying in the West. This is too despairing. Cultures are always in flux, but in general East Asian public behavior has been lifted in the direction of higher Western expectations.

What is happening is not wholly unlike the early improvement of Western manners via the trickling down of upper-class practices, as the work of Norbert Elias made familiar. Each and every source of new behavior in East Asia is not Western. There are always cross-currents in the trans-

---

[44] See the discussion in Grace Davie, *Europe: The Exceptional Case* (London: Darton, Longman & Todd, 2002), pp. 155–57.

mission of taste and behavior, and all of them are damaging to notions of cultural fixity in general and beliefs in permanent East Asian habits in particular. The Taiwanese have some Japanese tastes, just as Hong Kongers have British ones, few realizing their origins. The French supermarket chain Carrefour did not do well in Japan at first, because Japanese customers wanted French delicacies at high prices, not cheap Japanese fare. The Italian fashion house Armani painted the door of its first shop in Beijing red, an auspicious color to the Chinese. But shoppers wanted fashion, not tradition. "The customers hated it," wrote the proprietor himself, "they wanted Giorgio Armani of Milan. I won't make the same mistake again."[45]

Behavior has also altered in more damaging ways. Demography and sexual habits are cases in point. In 1955 two-thirds of Japanese couples met through arranged marriages, but by 2003 fewer than 10 percent did; many Japanese were scarcely meeting the opposite sex at all. The fertility rate has fallen far enough to threaten the viability of the population, down to 1.29 births per female. This is the extreme case of a trend common in developed countries. Thus, in Japan, provincial governments worry that not enough young people meet and marry. Despite attitudes to sex that are lax in terms of the West's puritanical conventions, "dating is fairly new to the culture." Since the late 1990s hiking trips and cruises for singles have been officially sponsored, so far to little effect. Exhortations by so-called celebrities have proved equally ineffectual, laughably given that celebrity nowadays is merely an index of sex appeal.

Young Japanese women are marrying on average as

[45] The Economist, *The World in 2004* (London, 2003), p. 119.

late as twenty-nine, previously unheard-of in Asian cultures, where most women were married at puberty. Since the wealth explosion of the late 1980s, women have become frantic consumers, belonging as they do to the first generation with no experience of wartime deprivation.[46] Many of them had U.S.$2,000 per month to spend on themselves by the 1990s. Perhaps their extreme shopping is a *Leerlaufreaktion*, a vacuum reaction; the young men are said to be exhausted from work, an observation borne out by their catatonic state on commuter trains. The peak of exhibitionism on the part of the OLs (office ladies) was the "bodi-con" (body conscious) craze of 1993. After work thousands of them changed out of their company uniforms into G-strings and a few furs and feathers, to dance en masse under strobe lights at discos. At one gathering young men gawped listlessly at as many as fifty thousand women.

Women in Japan and East Asia generally "are emancipated if they remain childless but imprisoned by traditional male attitudes if they do not." Fewer and fewer are having children: "This is the war of women against male chauvinism. Women are winning. If the men who dominate these countries do not surrender, they will soon not have much of a society left," suggests Martin Wolf.[47] One might add, especially now that Japanese women have at last been given legal access to the pill. Much discrimination against women persists in Japan, and delaying marriage and not having children seem gestures of resistance. On the other hand, they may be features of a transitional period and eventually swing

[46] *Australian*, 22 Apr 1995.
[47] *Financial Times*, 7 Jan 2004.

back toward previous norms, although the great change in context argues against a full reversal.

A sexual revolution has been sweeping China, accompanied by the state's retreat from decisions over private life, such as choice of marriage partner and the right to divorce.[48] Birth rates have fallen sharply here too. More sex, fewer offspring: advertisement hoardings playing on sexual themes confront the millions of young people pouring into the cities from the countryside. The government has softened film censorship that banned sex scenes. Sex shops have opened in Beijing and Shanghai. Premarital sex has become frequent, as have divorce and cohabitation among the elderly, who may be financially dependent on children who object to them remarrying. Fifty percent of remarriages in Shanghai end in divorce. The pendulum began to swing in this direction in the early 1980s, soon after economic reform, and has now reached the opposite extreme from forty years ago, when love and sex were denounced as bourgeois decadence. All this has been accompanied by an upsurge of sexually transmitted diseases, including HIV/AIDS. There are many other signs of dysfunction in formerly conservative societies throughout East Asia.[49]

It is impossible to reside amidst fast-burgeoning prosperity without making some accommodation. Previous beliefs can scarcely be held in the presence of so much tumult; the extent of mental illness already mentioned is doubtless related to the confusion of old and new norms—cognitive dissonance as new values struggle for acceptance involves

[48] *Australian Financial Review*, 18 Nov 2003.
[49] Jones, *The Record*, pp. 137–40.

personal disturbance by definition. Obviously modern East Asian culture owes more to the region's past, in the sense of the grandparents' culture, than it does to that, say, of New Yorkers. Yet modern culture does not encourage beliefs familiar to the grandparents' generation. If they are still alive, they may have had to adjust too. Part of the apparent survival of old attitudes is just that: apparent.

Whole new identities are formed in circumstances like these, as is shown by a study of the experience of country girls from Sichuan coming to work in an electronics factory in Shenzhen.[50] Factory managers and local townspeople laugh at their rural accents, unfashionable jeans, lack of make-up, pastime of knitting, and habit of sharing everything. Popular culture and factory work favor sexually independent young working women, which (faced with both carrot and stick) is what the once-rustic Sichuanese soon become.

Asian immigrants in Western countries face even greater social pressures but at the same time confront immense resistance to change. Conservative elements in their own communities would like them to cling to their old identities. In the United States, at least, the larger battle has been won by the host society; most married Asian Americans under the age of thirty-four are said to have non-Asian spouses. However, at the level of community politics, discomfort is still caused by those whom Eric Liu calls "Profes-

[50] Ngai Pun, "Becoming Dagongmei [working girls]: The Politics of Identity and Difference in Reform China," *China Journal* 42 (1999): 1–18. The actual distaste of urban Chinese for Sichuanese immigrants is made clear in Hessler, *River Town*, p. 250.

sional Asian Americans."[51] There is in truth no reason except small-mindedness why individuals should not adopt multiple identities along with more than one passport. Liu wrote *The Accidental Asian* to announce his refusal to "accept the party line of identity politics." "The end product of American life," he declares, "is neither monoculturalism nor multiculturalism; it is omniculturalism." His own children will be Chinese-Scottish-Irish-Jewish, and, as a reviewer of his book says, "the task of distinguishing between 'Asian' and 'American' may be academic sooner than we think."

[51] *Australian Financial Review*, 5 Jun 1998 (reprinted from *New York Times Book Review*).

Chapter 8

Economic Changes, Cultural Responses

In 1946 George Orwell sat in English pubs projecting the austerity that then gripped Britain into the totalitarian horror of *1984*. Most of his compatriots found his predictions all too plausible. Certainly, few imagined the prosperity of the late twentieth century, much less the freer lifestyles that accompanied it. Postwar wintriness took time to thaw, yet thaw it did. Americans call people who came to maturity in the 1950s "the generation that never showed up," but even among their anxieties and pieties a more hedonistic existence was starting to seem possible, in much the way that rigid late Victorian and Edwardian society can now be seen to have contained the seeds of the astounding shift in behavior during the First World War.

Since Orwell's day, individual choice has expanded immeasurably throughout the modern West. It can be interpreted as people doing what they wish to do in the presence of further and further relaxations of constraints such as limited income, community sanctions, and restricted markets for information that once made it hard to get in touch with individuals of a like mind. Internet search engines have enabled individuals with particular tastes, indeed the most peculiar tastes, to find one another. The greater commercialization of social and private life has extended choice in unheard-of directions. In consequence attitudes have changed—no doubt by a learning process and by cognitive dissonance. Cultural values adapt to opportunity. Behaviors once unthinkable become new norms. The culture of no two generations has ever been identical, if only because history serves up different "traumatic imprinting events" to each cohort. Compared with their forebears, baby boomers and younger cohorts have experienced a minimum of social traumas and an unimaginable abundance, with all the choice, freedom, and personal excess that this permits.

Services of all types can now be located with ease. As the branding consultant, Brian Boylan, says, "You can have a funny art museum in a funny town in a funny part of Europe—the Guggenheim in Bilbao—and people know about it."[1] Of longer standing has been the retailing revolution that has multiplied the range of goods on offer in supermarkets a hundredfold since the end of the Second World War.[2] Dinner party opinion and street protest may deride supermarket shopping, but it is this that has enabled everyone to live like princes of old. The real price of food has fallen substantially, even where the EU holds taxpayers to ransom to

---

[1] *FT Creative Business*, 13 Jan 2004.

[2] See Eric L. Jones, *The Record of Economic Development* (Cheltenham, U.K.: Edward Elgar, 2002), pp. 175–97.

support farm incomes. As Boylan observes, the 1960s are back—but this time, "things that used to be reserved for the rich or trendy London types are now for everybody." Tesco, the market leader among English supermarkets, has "done for ordinary folk what M&S [Marks & Spencer] did for the middle classes. They say, 'Joe Bloggs—you are rapacious in your desire and we serve you' . . . The elitism in certain types of shopping has gone."

Historically, indulgent behavior in the West and elsewhere was checked by lack of opportunity. Only the rich escaped constraints. Their friends might tut-tut but could be ignored. Other people, unwilling to risk the little they did possess and restricted to living in one place, were not so free. Today, on the other hand, the mass of the population in Western countries feel they too have the opportunity to indulge themselves without invoking much, if any, public disapproval. Rising incomes, technological developments, and the sheer availability of information mean they believe they can engage with impunity in activities that their parents or grandparents saw as off-limits or could scarcely imagine.

It is believable that if one's sources are the press and television, one can have no idea of the scale and nature of the Internet pornography now being consumed in Western countries.[3] Apparently, the most watched film in Britain in 2004 was not *The Lord of the Rings* or the latest *Harry Potter* but a stolen home movie in which a former children's show presenter has sex on screen—a movie downloaded by six million people. This is a prime area where recent changes in Western countries have moved them away from the public

---

[3] *Australian Financial Review*, 11 Mar 2005 (reprinted from the *New Statesman*).

attitudes of less-developed countries just when, in other respects, economic integration has been bringing the world closer together. What might paradoxically be called the mass individualism of Western societies, reflected in its cultural products and transmitted overseas, has become a greater potential source of international conflict.

Where Western developments show up most sharply is with respect to gender, the status of women, and personal sexual behavior. Ask women of thirty (the age of my MBA students) why their set has so few children or none, or has deferred the decision to start families. Their response is that they "can't afford it," which is ludicrous given that they and their partners together—or sometimes individually—will earn as much each year in real terms as their great-grandparents earned in a lifetime, and these great-grandparents raised families of seven, eight, nine, or ten children. Quickly recovering from the implausibility of their first answer, the women account for their behavior in terms of their expectations of autonomy, development of their potential, career prospects, exotic holidays, and material consumption. Would their great-grandmothers not have liked these choices? Should the question be, not why modern women have so few children, but why their great-grandmothers had so many? Great-grandmother lacked the option not to. She had to choose a husband early, from a shallow pool of possible partners, in order to secure a living and find a home; the lack of effective birth control meant that a large family usually followed.

Admittedly, there may have been calculated motives in peasant societies for having large numbers of children. Big families were the means of providing enough sons to work the farm holding as well as to offer the insurance of keeping the parents in their old age. Agricultural progress and state pensions have dissolved these motives in the developed economies, just as careers and independent incomes for women have disposed of the other insurance need: catching a husband to get a living. What the great-grandmothers' generation was obliged to do translated into the oppressive fact that it was what their society expected of them. Although some of the present cohort of young women will be unhappy when they find, too late, that their childbearing years have slipped away, it would be condescending to criticize their decision. It is what society in the developed world encourages and approves.

Marriage is nowadays often delayed and to some extent rejected. Childbearing more so. This is not a war against recreational sex. It is not *Lysistrata*. A shift in sexual behavior predated the pill and was starting to emerge during the officially repressive 1950s. It had a prehistory in lax wartime behavior. The pill, however, expunged the fear of conception. Was previously more circumspect, not to say more terrified, behavior and the punitive public attitude that heightened it part of true culture? No, it was contingent on a lack of opportunity inherent in restricted possibilities for copulating safely. Testimony by Elspeth Huxley makes this plain.[4] Huxley was an undergraduate at the University of Reading during the mid-1920s. She wrote in the 1960s, "I suppose it is the motor-car that has liberalized the morals of students; and the fact that students have become rich enough to own cars, or at least to know someone who does. . . . People talk a lot about the decline of morals, collapse of religion and so

---

[4] Elspeth Huxley, *Love among the Daughters* (London: Quality Book Club, 1968), p. 64.

on among the young. It was not religion or morality that kept most of us relatively chaste, but lack of facilities."

Another indication of the greater choice now within reach is the change in the relative ages of marriage partners. The average age gap may remain two years, but the dispersion around this has widened considerably.[5] Twice as many British men today choose an older bride than in the 1960s. A gap of five years or more between marriage partners now occurs in over 50 percent of cases, as against 36 percent in the 1960s. Marriages take place five years later on average, partly because of divorce and remarriage. Marrying an older man is no longer a young woman's only route to security and status. She is able to fulfil her personal goals and marry whom she will. Her sisters are not so autonomous in the less-developed world, where half the population, certainly half the female population, still lives in villages. In a village one is stuck with whatever restricted or idiosyncratic practices the elders or the community select, whereas in the cities it is possible to graze a behavioral smorgasbord.

Fashion is even more plastic than courtship behavior. The introduction of the miniskirt, for instance, was greeted with utter horror by matrons in the 1960s, but ten or fifteen years later, when the fashion changed again, it was women of matronly age who were left wearing miniscule skirts while their daughters took to long ones. The standard economist's view is accordingly more right than wrong: culture is labile and can be explained by external factors, which is not to say that during its ghostly transit through history it does not exert some powerful influences on lives and expenditures.

Civility has decreased. Civility, meaning good man-

[5] *Financial Times*, 12 Dec 2003.

ners, can be interpreted as a form of conflict avoidance, like the even more formalized deference and bowing in Japan—which has little to do with concern for the recipient. And in the West since the Second World War, more than civility and deference have declined: threatening behavior, graffiti, vandalism, criminal damage, and roistering at night are evident, certainly in Britain. By the end of the twentieth century, they were making life miserable for many, and an MP, Frank Field, responded to the pleas of his constituents by writing *Neighbours from Hell*.[6] Worse than this, a seven-centuries' long decline in violent deaths in England had begun to be reversed as early as 1950.[7]

Is one to lament the reduction of civility and deference? In some respects, the answer is surely yes. Disorder and violence on the streets and in the schoolroom are to no one's benefit. In general, however, the answer is surely no, since the society that formerly demanded deference cramped the lives of so many. Their newfound opportunities now permit unprecedented numbers of people to behave in creative ways that were denied to their forebears, such as supporting their children's education or engaging in cultural activities—witness the vast growth of hobbies like archaeology, bird watching, painting, and the visiting of museums and country houses. This is genuine liberation for people who two generations ago had little leisure or discretionary income. Even British society is kinder than it was, more tender toward women, minority races, sexual minorities, and so forth, though still not to other social classes.

[6] Frank Field, *Neighbours from Hell* (London: Politico, 2003).
[7] T. R. Gurr, "Historical Trends in Violent Crime: A Critical Review of Evidence," *Crime and Justice* 3 (1981): 295–355.

Yet individualism, opportunity, and choice cut two ways. As Jean-Paul Sartre said, today we are condemned to be free. In the United Kingdom 250,000 people are reported to use psychotherapy, nothing like the number of Americans who do so but witness to depths of unhappiness that family and church support cannot assuage. Psychotherapy and such-like techniques center on the individual, not on the group as church services do. David Martin Jones cites several writers about Southeast Asia who found that rapid growth during the 1960s "generated identity confusion at both a personal and a national level."[8] It hardly seems fanciful to see role confusion overcoming many Westerners during the modern hypertrophy of affluence. Since one-quarter of its population takes mood-altering prescription drugs, the unhappiness must be particularly great in France.[9] The disintegration of the French family has had a high cost, being partly responsible for the fifteen thousand deaths during the heat wave of August 2003—the highest civilian disaster toll since the 1918 "flu" epidemic. Disproportionately hit were the elderly and solitary—those whom their families had deserted for the beach.

The hyperindividualistic tendency is not intrinsically unstoppable. A big economic depression might reverse it, and so might ideological revolution or religious revival. For the present, however, the trend is toward individualism and the heady mix of opportunity and danger that it represents. Whether or not these things are harder to live with than the problems of the past, which I doubt, they increasingly dis-

[8] David Martin Jones, *Political Development in Pacific Asia* (Cambridge: Polity Press, 1997), p. 141.
[9] *Guardian Weekly*, 13 Nov 2003.

tinguish Western countries from their own past and set them decisively apart from the less-developed world.

I

Let us consider for a moment contemporary changes on the religious front, where the underlying issue is less the current extent of divergent behavior within the West than whether the differences will persist. The primary distinction is between America and Europe. The United States is much more prominent than Europe in church-going and formal religious adherence. Church membership grew for two hundred years after the eighteenth century, throughout long periods of rising wealth, and is only now slowly declining. Europeans often speak as though American religious practices are bizarre oddities to find in the largest of the rich countries. From a European perspective it is easy to poke a kind of aghast fun at the creationism and televangelism of the United States, while political commentators make endless digs at the religious right. Europeans tend to doubt American good faith, arguing that a weaker welfare state must predispose people to join churches for reasons other than religious belief. Using churches as support groups seems to many Europeans outdated. From their perspective, poorer health services and social security payments mean Americans are not liberated enough to eschew religion. This is unduly cynical, because the United States, where the constitution disallows an established church, is a haven for religious experimentation, as indeed Europeans are prone to complain. The United States offers enough liturgical variety to satisfy the most outlandish religious consumer. If America's churches were nothing more than insurance agencies, we would expect consumers to crowd into the handful of stable ones with large resources. It might also follow that, were the United States to adopt more generous welfare policies, the extent of church-going would drop.

The case has been made by Grace Davie that it is Europe which is the religious oddity, not just in Atlantic but in world terms.[10] Church attendance is soaring in poorer parts of the world, but falling in the mainstream European churches. The widely held European opinion is that the remainder of the world, including the United States, must eventually get in step with Europe. This is merely secularization theory, which holds that religion is superstition and will fade away, not so much as a result of scientific doubt as because fear has been reduced (or in the case of death, deferred) by rising life expectancies, kinder medical procedures, and the escape from oppressive communities that more pay and greater job and geographic mobility permit to the individual. Davie concludes, on the contrary, that "secularisation is essentially a European phenomenon and is extrinsic rather than intrinsic to the modernising process per se." (It might rather be thought that it is religious adherence that is intrinsic to modernization, since churches offer spiritual comfort and social support, and are—temporarily?—attractive to people in the throes of unnerving change.) Davie demonstrates that modern Europeans barely possess the vocabulary to discuss the topic and find it hard to conceive that their post-Christian society is not the face of the world's future. However, Europeans may have ceased to *attend* but they have not ceased to *believe*, and she observes that this leaves

[10] Grace Davie, *Europe: The Exceptional Case* (London: Darton, Longman & Todd, 2002).

open the possibility that Europe may converge on other regions rather than vice versa. The possibility does not, however, seem strong, since the attractions of church membership in poorer regions of the world may fade once new generations are secure in modernized societies. This depends, of course, on taking an extremely contingent and long-term view of religious adherence.

Meanwhile, in the Western world as a whole, religious belief has failed to prevent a shift toward free-thinking, postmodern, and self-actualizing values. As an example, large numbers of Roman Catholics remained within the church while ignoring the strictures of Pope John Paul II against artificial means of contraception. There has been a general move toward greater expressions of individualism, as attested by the World Values Survey.[11] What seems to have diminished is the internalizing of values that planted a self-monitoring conscience in everyone reared as a Christian unless they explicitly rejected it. In the past, for all the preference falsification and backsliding, the belief that God "sees every sparrow fall" was a more efficient internal deterrent to opportunism than any police force or laws could be. The censoriousness of society worked externally to the same effect. All this has tended to evaporate except within specific religious communities.

II

A major development in Western countries during recent decades has been the accelerated decline of manufacturing and the expansion of employment in the service industries.

---

[11] See, for example, Paul R. Abramson and Ronald Inglehart, *Value Change in Global Perspective* (Ann Arbor: University of Michigan Press, 1995).

Services require and create white-collar workforces with technical or tertiary education. The values of Western society increasingly reflect those of this sophisticated sector; the media and cultural industries diffuse them. Differences among the Western nations in these respects are not necessarily profound; some may simply indicate the relative levels of income attained so far. International communications and trade seem likely to narrow the differences in future. All countries are responding to two sets of forces: firstly, similar demographic, economic, environmental, and geopolitical influences that affect each one slightly differently, and secondly, global competition. The unique path that each country supposedly takes—and to some extent really does take—derives from patterns sketched out in a less integrated world economy. Continued globalization will erase some of them and introduce still more standardization in material and social provision. It will reduce costs and inconvenience by increasing certainty. There is no need to anticipate dull uniformity—the world is far too complex for that—but over the decades a further degree of convergence is to be expected, making the concept of a single developed or Western bloc even firmer than it is already.

The West's exports include images and newsprint redolent of nontraditional lifestyles and above all of freedoms for women. An excellent example of the consequences relates to Brazil. Writing from the Harvard Center of Population and Development Studies, George Martine attributes the drop in the rate of Brazilian population growth to the influence of American-style television soap operas introduced in the 1970s.[12] The transmitting of "soaps" was more pow-

[12] *New Scientist*, 20 Mar 1996.

erful than a family planning program was likely to have been. In Brazil, television diffused middle- and upper-class city values throughout the country and "made people conscious of other patterns of behaviour and other values, which were put into a very attractive package."

The effect in Brazil has been a shift in the direction of soap-opera lifestyles, in which women have glamor, independence, and purchasing power. "Credit programs" whereby poor people could buy small items such as shoes on the installment plan also led, according to Martine, "to an enormous change in consumption patterns and consumption was incompatible with unlimited procreation." An annual population growth rate of 2.99 percent between 1951 and 1960 was cut to 1.93 between 1981 and 1990. This is not to say that Brazilian women were silly enough to expect to be wafted fully into *Dallas*, nor that soaps were the sole contemporary influence, but women saw the advantages of birth control for their health and quality of life. They began to target lower completed family sizes, just as Europeans had done a century earlier.[13] Conservative men were not ecstatic about the shift in respective gender roles.

Portuguese-speaking Brazil is not however a mass exporter of television; it is the United States which excels at that, and it was the United States that first influenced the Brazilians. The American entertainment and educational establishments set the goals for the remainder of the world.

---

[13] Susan Cotts Watkins, *From Provinces into Nations: Demographic Integration in Western Europe, 1870–1960* (Princeton: Princeton University Press, 1991). Watkins is able to exclude the role of standard economic variables and comes to the conclusion that female networks communicated to one another a more desirable nuptial outcome.

The only serious exceptionalism is American exceptional-ism. Other countries respond by imitating this—at the same time struggling to replace with their own products the slicker ones coming out of Hollywood and Harvard—or by resisting its influence, as some authoritarian countries do and as French officialdom strives to do. The entertainment offered by Hollywood seems increasingly characterized by simple plots and stark characterizations, which is part of the reason for its success, but it is also full of the vacuous, violent, and pornographic. This makes it a parody of American life. Many studies have shown how much less religiously observant American media personnel are than their own countrymen. In depicting gross and amoral versions of life, they know not what they do. The gap between what is available from the world's biggest entertainment and communications indus-tries and what is thought appropriate in the ideological camps of the less-developed countries has thus widened. The less salubrious products of the Third World itself, like mar-tial arts and kung fu films, have not attracted the same op-probrium; they do not have behind them the force of Holly-wood's distribution machine.

The American media are interested in profits and, un-like state monopolies of the media in more authoritarian countries, have no direct political motives. They can scarcely have understood the implications for more traditional soci-eties of the gender imagery carried routinely in their films and television shows. Hollywood would or could not have censored itself. It was competing in a raucous domestic mar-ket. In the term used by forecasters, it "mirror-imaged" and appears to have supposed that foreign consumers either did or would conform to American taste. Commercial interests and the young in the remainder of the world may certainly have been willing to accept Western productions, but the political and religious authorities do not agree.

Politically unacceptable broadcasts and downright pornography can no doubt be banned by the offended countries, just as China, Vietnam, North Korea, Saudi Arabia, Iran, and Syria block many Internet sites. But that misses the point, for even merely routine images of Western life may be disturbing. We have noted the raw power of television soaps in a Brazilian context. Standards of living in the West excite envy; the dress, deportment, and status of women provide enticing role models for females elsewhere, besides inflaming male lust. To patriarchs, religious leaders, and social conservatives, Hollywood films and Western television are Trojan horses harboring alien values.

The most ordered philosophy which the West's louche images offend is Islam. Strictly speaking, there is no single Islam to affront, since local circumstances so much influence practice and, in Marcus Noland's words, "attenuate the impact of Middle Eastern traditions."[14] Nevertheless, there is a degree of commonality. No one seems to have anticipated the extreme backlash in Islamic countries.[15] There, sexual politics figure large, and the young men are

[14] Marcus Noland, "Religion, Culture, and Economic Performance," http://www.iie.com/publications/wp/2003/03-8.pdf.

[15] An exception is René-Jean Ravault, "Is There a Bin Laden in the Audience? Considering the Events of September 11 as a Possible Boomerang Effect of the Globalization of US Mass Communication," *Prometheus* 20/3 (2002): 295–300. The *Economist* (26 Feb 2005) notes, however, that "it is not just inadvertent imagery that can induce a certain restlessness," since Arabic television itself, beamed by satellite from the more liberal Arab states, is having a demonstration effect through portraying elections and a higher status for women.

commonly frustrated.[16] It may be easiest for them to reject the West and its works altogether in favor of the certainties of radical Islam, while easing their sexual frustrations by watching satellite broadcasts from the West.[17] The version of modernity thus peddled seems to fundamentalists to be stealing Muslim identity and trying to replace it with one that is bland, secular, or worse, Christian.

Were the conflict between the West and Militant Islam simply a materialist clash about economic growth, the West might not be the first target. It has gone largely unnoticed that we might expect Muslim rage to be directed at East Asians rather than Westerners. Starting from not dissimilar levels of development soon after the Second World War, East Asia's growth has convincingly outclassed MENA (the Middle East and North Africa) and other predominantly Islamic regions, such as Indonesia and Nigeria. The West was ahead from the outset. Although Jason Burke does remark in his monograph on Al-Qaeda that "the recent economic success of East Asia, for example, is felt as *wrong*. It is not fair, right or just. It is humiliating," only a tiny fraction of the resentment has actually been turned eastward.[18] East Asia probably escapes the bulk of the censure because it exports goods, not cultural services.

III

Much of the world has not yet shared the all-transforming economic growth achieved formerly by the West and re-

[16] Jason Burke, *Al-Qaeda: Casting a Shadow of Terror* (London: I. B. Tauris, 2003), p. 246.
[17] *Guardian Weekly*, 23 Oct 1994.
[18] Burke, *Al-Qaeda*, p. 245.

cently by East Asia. The rub comes with the greatest lag-gards, which (leaving aside the chaos in much of sub-Saha-ran Africa) are the largely Islamic lands of the Middle East and North Africa (MENA). These have made little eco-nomic headway and are at the bottom of any league of qual-ity of governance. Between 1985 and 2000 real income per head in MENA rose on average only 0.5 percent per annum, far below the 6 or 8 percent achieved in East Asia. Capital flight is extreme, with residents holding offshore anywhere between $100 and 500 billion.[19] The regimes are typically corrupt and unaccountable. Military spending at 6 percent of GDP is the highest in the world. Although many of the countries have abundant natural resources, this has con-ferred little blessing on their inhabitants, who are victims of the "resource curse" that has led to endless squabbling over rents from the oil fields. Meanwhile, population growth has created a reserve army of unemployed young men. Their anger threatens to be a real destabilizing force.

MENA's economic problems are typical of the less-developed world. It is, however, improbable that they are to be attributed to religion or culture, any more than the un-derlying inspiration of Al-Qaeda is religious rather than po-litical.[20] Neofundamentalism and jihadism ultimately derive from sociological changes in the Muslim diaspora rather than the permanent values of Islam. Marcus Noland of the

[19] This estimate is cited by Eva Bellin in "The Political-Economic Co-nundrum: The Affinity of Economic and Political Reform in the Middle East and North Africa," *Carnegie Papers* 53 (Nov 2004): 3.

[20] For a rejection of what he calls "culture talk" about terrorism and an in-sistence on its contemporary political origins, see Mahmood Mamdani, "Whither Political Islam? Understanding the Modern Jihad," *Foreign Af-fairs*, Jan–Feb 2005, pp. 148–55.

Institute for International Economics in Washington certainly absolves the Islamic religion from responsibility.[21] He finds no evidence that countries with the largest Islamic populations grew more slowly or had lower productivity growth than other developing countries. Their two defects, neither of which is confined to Islamic countries, are low levels of education (though literacy even for females is at last rising in several Arab lands) and overlarge government sectors. Noland's results "aroused suspicion, bordering disbelief, among [his economist] colleagues when he first produced them." Nevertheless, his conclusion is that "if one is concerned about economic performance in predominantly Islamic regions or countries, conventional economic analysis may yield greater insights than the sociology of religion," a result that seems more likely to be right than wrong, although he may downplay the roles of politics and rent seeking the way that economists tend to do.

The *Financial Times* commented that "some sociologists have argued that the tendency of Islamic education to rely on reiteration of a finite set of information, together with the disapproval of lending money at interest, has restricted innovation and growth in Muslim countries." These are separate, partly cultural possibilities, both of which have long been acknowledged by economists as well as sociologists. One leading writer on Islamic underdevelopment, Timur Kuran, who is an economist, urges that the problem is not demonstrating the existence of particular Islamic beliefs, which is readily done, but explaining why marginalized individuals in Islamic countries have not seized the opportunities for economic action that the mainstream has passed

[21] As discussed in *Financial Times*, 8 Dec 2003.

by.[22] Kuran concludes that the nature of public discourse under Islam keeps individuals from questioning or even noticing social inefficiencies, a limitation reinforced by the vicious circle in which intellectual incuriosity demands only a few books and in turn reduces the need for printing.

This cultural position can account neither for the fact that Islamic science flowered during what was in European terms the Middle Ages nor for the selective eagerness with which modern Islamic societies seize on innovations in military hardware and information technology. It may be better to steer between Noland's approach, in which culture is largely beside the point ("cultural nullity"), and Kuran's more cultural line ("cultural fixity"). Cultures may be envisaged as sets of filters through which economic action has to pass; the filters are potentially capable of slowing the action down but are in the end altered by feedback from the economy. This interpretation is "cultural reciprocity," in which culture and the economy continually react on one another.

Yet while politics and economics are likely to trump ideology in the end, doctrinally there is next to no room for maneuver. The unity of Islam is founded on the message of the Koran and the hadiths, which are all the later sayings deemed acceptable. Further elaboration virtually ceased once the "Gate of Interpretation" was closed in the tenth century (Christian calendar). Culture may change; it is more difficult, though ultimately not impossible, for theological interpretations to do so. Extremists can always hark back to hard-line versions.

[22] See especially Timur Kuran, "Islam and Underdevelopment: An Old Puzzle Revisited," *Journal of Institutional and Theoretical Economics* 153 (1997): 41–71. For a more extreme fixity approach, see David Pryce-Jones, *The Closed Circle: An Interpretation of the Arabs* (London: Paladin, 1990).

Given the ambitions of radical Islam to establish a new Caliphate, a superstate in which Sharia law reigns, the sort of fudging in which the secular rulers of Islamic countries currently engage is under challenge. Nor do the theologues want any truck with secular universalism of the type enunciated by a secretary-general of Amnesty International: "we hold that the same standards must apply in every part of the world, irrespective of the degree of economic development. The alibi of cultural specificity doesn't work any more. There are universal values, like human rights, which all great religions have."[23] So much for cultural relativism.

The greatest cultural war in recent history was the Cold War.[24] Because this turned hot only in distant places, struggles over culture were of overriding importance. The West prevailed because it granted cultural producers more chance to strut their stuff; the Soviet side conceived art as narrowly political and insisted on dictating the terms on which it could be disseminated. The struggle with Islamic extremism is more one-sided. Islamic ideas are readily accessible in the West, and minority populations build mosques in every country. Deep pockets have been willing to fund such activities, the Saudi royal family's being among the deepest. But Islamic interests lack global communications networks, and even the Al Jezeera television station is based on Western models. Arabic may be the lingua franca across North Africa, the Middle East, and into Asia but does not have the scope of English for reaching minds all round the world.

[23] Interview with Pierre Sane, *Guardian Weekly*, 2 May 1993.
[24] David Caute, *The Dancer Defects: The Struggle for Cultural Supremacy during the Cold War* (New York: Oxford University Press, 2003). For a firsthand account, see George Clare, *Berlin Days, 1946–47* (London: Pan, 1990).

IV

Does this prognosticate perpetual conflict? Here, the fundamental questions are how readily cultures may change and how long the units of analysis are. A suggestive mechanism was advanced some decades ago to account for attitudinal change, specifically the increasing activism of American voters over air pollution.[25] The real level of pollution was actually falling, yet for a generation fortunate enough to have high incomes and job security the matter became casus belli. The parents of that generation had been concerned with bread-and-butter issues, but the new one could afford to concern itself with the quality of life. Significantly, problems of urban land use and pollution were likewise to be the first to radicalize the newly prosperous citizens of Taiwan, South Korea, and Japan, as well as the disgruntled rioters of the heavily polluted Zhejiang province of China.

The connecting theme is the Product Cycle. As economies move round the cycle to successive core industries with more complex technologies and higher and higher added value, they require and elicit more skilled and better-paid technological and managerial workforces. The children of these professionals grow up secure, in material comfort, and with better formal education than their parents. The Western experience was that some fraction of the bourgeois children of bourgeois parents and farm-worker grandparents began to ask more of life than additional possessions. They began to speak of nonmaterial gains like those to which the middle classes always aspire: environmental cleanup, more participatory and pluralist politics, a freer press, and an im-

[25] Matthew A. Crenson, *The Un-Politics of Air Pollution* (Baltimore: Johns Hopkins University Press, 1971).

partial legal system. Why should people elsewhere in the world lack these aspirations? A very strong theory would surely be needed to demonstrate that non-Westerners will in the long run refrain from expressing such common human aspirations. In East Asia they have already started to express them. And there is no reason why the process should be limited forever to the West and East Asia, leaving the less-developed world to trudge forever down a quite different historical track.

No one pretends that every nonmaterial desideratum can be secured immediately in every society. There are always political squabbles over such things. Authoritarian regimes try to manage change, oftentimes meaning to frustrate it. Take China. At this early stage of its development, we might anticipate that the emergent middle classes would be easily bought off with consumer goods. No doubt many are. The moneyed elite is comfortable with the current mode of governance and accepts that it is told the news honestly—say, with respect to SARS, despite the fact that foreign media were the ones to expose its presence.[26] There is still no freedom of speech or religion and no law independent of the polity. For all that, even the Chinese authorities are experimenting with pluralism, tightly controlled but real, because they sense that, with more feedback from the public, policy errors can be better corrected.[27] Of course, this can be presented as managerialism or an oriental version of Bismarckian socialism. Minxin Pei argues that the Communist Party continues to believe it can have its cake and eat it too, but if the flagship pluralist experiment in Shenzhen is not a gen-

[26] *Far Eastern Economic Review*, 20 Nov 2003.
[27] *Financial Times*, 13 Jan 2003; *Economist*, 5 Apr 2003.

uine step toward freedom, the danger for the authorities is that it may have opened Pandora's box.[28] Meanwhile, in Taiwan and South Korea, authoritarian regimes have given way to forms of parliamentary democracy that may be flawed but that compare not unfavorably with Western countries at similar stages of development.

The possibility that economic growth will lead to political liberalization in East Asia has been stoutly denied, notably by David Martin Jones.[29] His objections are that the middle classes are passive, conformist, and willingly dependent on illiberal regimes. They are content to be managed. Capitalism has supposedly reinforced the consensual, communitarian values of traditional Confucianism, Taoism, Buddhism, and Islam. It is not clear from this why Christianity, communal enough in the Middle Ages, eluded the straitjacket, nor why we should believe that no other system of values can ever transform itself. While it may be unfair to expect Jones to provide a comparative history of the world's religions, the fact that Christian Europe was able to generate individualism and pluralism during economic growth suggests that this is a live option for other parts of the world. Furthermore, the accommodation between Christian ethics and capitalism occurred over a long period. Comparable Asian experience has been far shorter, even if we include Japan; it seems too brief to justify a blanket assertion that non-Christian value systems are incapable of adjusting to

[28] Minxin Pei, "China's Ruling Party Cannot Have It All," *Financial Times*, 14 Jan 2004.

[29] David M. Jones and David Brown, "Singapore and the Myth of the Liberalizing Middle Class," *Pacific Review* 7/1 (1994): 79–87; David M. Jones, *Political Development*.

capitalist values. Nevertheless, the rapid pace of change impresses more than sluggishness.

Jones draws the claim from Ernest Gellner that "whereas Protestant individualism and its contingent democratic politics may have initially favoured the modernized industrial order, once that order 'has come into being, and its advantages are clear to all, it can be better run in a Confucian collectivist spirit.'"[30] On the contrary, the superiority of pluralism over collectivism has been firmly demonstrated by Peter Lindert.[31] The point about pluralism and a fortiori parliamentary democracy is that these are not winner-takes-all systems but ones of constrained conflict, in which governments that lose elections automatically go into opposition and make way for the winners. Jones and Gellner were, of course, both writing before the Asian Crisis came within a whisker of stripping the Mandate of Heaven from the rulers of Southeast Asia.

V

Can Asian Values adapt to capitalism? Will Asian societies take up pluralist politics? They have already begun to do so. After all, they have coped with other major transformations: Japan, the Tiger economies, and China have adapted large parts of their behavior and beliefs to accommodate economic growth; China turned to face the capitalist way in Deng Xiao-ping's time; and all these countries have been adapting to rampant consumerism. It is easy to suffer from as-

[30] David M. Jones, *Political Development*, p. 160, quoting a 1994 comment by Gellner.
[31] Peter Lindert, "Voice and Growth: Was Churchill Right?" *Journal of Economic History* 63/2 (2003): 315–50.

sumption drag. Appearances change slower than realities. The candid Singaporeans now admit the need for individualism in order to establish a creative economy and compete with Hong Kong as a service hub. They are investing in the arts and have invited young Australians to come and share their ideas. Lee Kuan Yew has appealed to his countrymen to take longer over lunch and create a buzz. Although all such authoritarian regimes want to have their cake and eat it too, Singapore's response to economic currents is remarkably fluid. Notions of cultural fixity allow neither for reactions like this nor the possibility of "Quebec effects," in which rapid, unheralded social change takes place in the most unexpected places.

The problem toward which this discussion leads is knottier. If Confucian East Asia is already adapting its values to a cascade of economic changes, can Islamic countries ever follow suit? Despite the obvious difficulties, general considerations say yes. Admittedly, economic growth and social change in MENA would need to be faster than they are at present. The Arab states have failed to convert their oil wealth into economic development and structural change. In 2000 average schooling in Arab countries was approximately four-and-a-half years, in contrast to almost ten years in the Asian Tigers.[32] Internet penetration is very low, under 10 percent in fifteen of eighteen countries. Severe restrictions on female activities persist, and in Arab countries only 33 percent of women have jobs, compared with 75 percent in East Asia.[33]

Yet these problems are amenable to policy solutions,

[32] *Financial Times*, 21 Oct 2003.
[33] *Economist*, 19 Jun 2004.

and already there is more heartening—though contentious—change than there seems at first sight. Female literacy has risen considerably in several countries. Seventy percent of university students in Qatar and Kuwait are female, and 55 percent even in Saudi Arabia. Since 1970 female life expectancy has risen, and in the past twenty years the average number of children per woman has fallen to little above world norms. In a generation the proportion of Arab women marrying at twenty has dropped from 75 percent to 38 percent, and many delay marriage until their thirties. Most telling may be the aside that rich Tunisian men are now seeking brides in the villages because they think city girls too independent.

Successful economic growth should not be thought of as the outcome solely of a pair of triumphant ethnocentrisms, Protestant Christianity and Confucianism. Other regions are too glibly dismissed, explicitly or implicitly, because they seem to lack either Protestant or Confucian values. Where these ideologies are professed, growth has succeeded, but this does not prove that the saga of economic history is over and done with. Who in 1750 expected the industrial revolution? As late as 1776 *The Wealth of Nations* talked scarcely at all about industrialization. Who after the Second World War expected the East Asian Miracle? There were precious few credible prognostications of these developments, but there are plenty of post hoc rationalizations that put the emphasis on their presumed cultural foundations. If other parts of the world succeed in achieving growth, we may be quite sure that writers will discover unsuspected merits in their cultures too. Indeed, *post hoc ergo propter hoc* interpretation has already started. Growth rates in India languished for decades after Independence but have picked up in recent years; Amartya Sen wryly notes that India's ancient tradition of accounting has already been dusted off and presented as the cause.[34]

David Martin Jones has laid out the fixity line, this time with respect to Islam, in the course of another attack on treating liberalization as an outgrowth of development.[35] He argues that Southeast Asia is moving into a closed world of Islamic sectarianism, taking care to carry with it modern technologies to spread its message. On this reckoning, Islam's "social character" becomes a great exception, fatally different from the Christian West and Confucian East Asia and scurrying back into a cul-de-sac of history.

Jones's account of the way university-educated Islamic males have retreated from the doubts that their scientific studies may have been expected to cast on fundamentalism is faithful to the record as it stands. Many of these men have turned their backs on a world run according to universal rules in favor of one pinned together by alliances of the faith. Islamic extremists believe the West's tolerance is a sign of its weakness, but this contempt is the type that the enemies of pluralism always display. It is likely to be wrong this time too. I quote in support the following remarks by Hugh Byas, who was correspondent for *The Times* in prewar Japan: "They think democracies are constitutionally 'soft.' That a nation can be pleasure-loving, extravagant, for ever running after novelties, pacific, loathing war; that an unbridled press, radio and cinema may ceaselessly reflect and magnify all

[34] Amartya Sen, "Asian Values and Economic Growth," in UNESCO, *World Culture Report 1998: Culture, Creativity and Markets* (Paris: UNESCO Publications, 1998), p. 41.

[35] David M. Jones, "Out of Bali: Cybercaliphate Rising," *National Interest,* Spring 2003, pp. 75–85.

these things; and yet that such a nation may be revengeful and 'tough' is something the narrow Japanese military mind does not comprehend."[36]

The fundamentalists do not speak for all in Islam any more than the military spoke for all Japanese (or retained their loyalty after the defeat of 1945). Fundamentalists can be seen as warring against moderate Islamic regimes as much or more than against the West. The economic problems of Islamic countries can be read in reverse, as an enormous opportunity for catch-up growth. Islam exhibits plenty of traits favorable to commerce and was, after all, founded by a merchant. The present cultural wars are exacerbated by the West's increasing individualism and sexual laxity, but what has happened in the West is no reason for supposing that Islamic values cannot adapt to rapid economic growth. That Islamic values may prove malleable is a bold proposition, and common opinion argues against it. After an Arab businesswoman delivered the address at an international forum on economics in Jeddah in 2004, she was denounced by the highest religious authority in Saudi Arabia.[37] The woman had dared to speak before men with her face uncovered, and her picture appeared in newspapers the next day. The grand mufti said all this was prohibited: "Allowing women to mix with men is the root of every evil and catastrophe. It is highly punishable. Mixing of men and women is a reason for greater decadence and adultery."

But his outburst can be read the other way round, as coming from someone whose authority is already threatened.

[36] Hugh Byas, *The Japanese Enemy* (London: Hodder & Stoughton, 1942), p. 81.
[37] *Financial Times*, 22 Jan 2004.

A struggle is under way to reform Saudi society and confront its religious extremism. In 2002 the religious establishment in Saudi Arabia was stripped of its control over girls' education. Further change is not impossible.[38] The gradual advance in the status of women that is observable constitutes a "swell of the ocean" change. Notwithstanding the fact that even women vice-chancellors of Iranian universities must ask their husbands' permission before going overseas, it is inconceivable that the stratum of educated women emerging in several Islamic countries will not alter their societies. Islamic culture has flowered before, and it is unhistorical to think it can never flower again.

[38] The possibilities are indicated by the move to denounce in every Turkish mosque so-called "honor" killings of women as contrary to the Prophet's teaching on clemency. There are currently dozens of such killings every year for offenses like going to the cinema with a man other than one's husband. *Economist*, 21 Feb 2004.

Chapter 9

Cultural Protection

"All classes of society are trades unionists at heart, and differ chiefly in the boldness, ability and secrecy with which they push their respective interests," wrote Stanley Jevons as long ago as the 1880s.[1] We still live in a world of multiple distortions, where groups of producers engage in rent seeking and attempts to block trade and competition. As Mancur Olson observed about such coalitions, special interests brook no limitation on what they seek to take out of society's common pot.[2] Apart from the dead hands of the farmers, those who come top for relentlessly trying to socialize risk while privatizing profit, fending off foreign competition, and

[1] Quoted in Henry Phelps Brown, *The Origins of Trade Union Power* (Oxford: Clarendon Press, 1983), p. 12.
[2] Mancur Olson, *The Rise and Decline of Nations* (New Haven: Yale University Press, 1982). For a summary of the implications of coalitions, see p. 74.

levying claims on taxpayers' money are now the producers of art and entertainment. Their methods swing between generalized panhandling and assertions of specific grievances. Outside the United States they seldom go long before making Hollywood a target, and often their pitch is couched as emotional nationalism.

Spokespersons for the entertainment business presumably believe that the public will either be swayed by their appeals or find them too expensive to resist. Cultural producers, with all the public relations help they can command, have the advantage. They realize how much they stand to gain or lose. Dispersed consumers have little recourse beyond writing to the newspapers and hoping against hope that politicians will defend free trade and competition in the face of lobbying by special interests. The benefits of capturing the business of making films, especially, can be enormous. "Wellywood," the satirical name for the New Zealand companies that made the three *Lord of the Rings* epics, was for a time the biggest private employer in the country.[3] Part of the competitive advantage was that the Kiwi dollar was then cheap relative to other currencies, and it was worth nurturing a skill base in the hope of hanging on to filmmaking against the exchange rate becoming less favorable.

Australian interests have long been piqued at New Zealand competition, and their demands neatly indicate the hyperbole of cultural protectionism. Pique turned to outrage when a trade agreement forbade excluding New Zealand television programs from the Australian market.[4] A spokes-

[3] *Economist*, 6 Dec 2003.
[4] Eric L. Jones, *The Record of Global Economic Development* (Cheltenham, U.K.: Edward Elgar, 2000), pp. 171–72.

person for one Australian opposition party claimed that New Zealand competition threatened not only the cultural identity of Australians but their human rights. The Australian government lamented that the trade agreement prevented it from excluding the competition but swore that local content quotas would insulate Australia's "world class" (yet somehow tragically vulnerable) television networks from fresh foreign assaults over the next decade. Filmmakers in Australia have not been greatly comforted by this promise. One of them demanded, to rapturous applause, that American movies be kept out because they will not tell Australian stories.[5] He insisted that the government "take culture off the negotiating table entirely." An actress speaking for a film institute added that what was wanted was for the film industry to be exempted from the proposed U.S.-Australia free trade agreement, for the sake of Australian culture.[6] She did not, of course, define Australian culture—this sort of argument usually refers to the products made in a given country and really means the incomes of those who make them.

"Keep the *Australia* in Australian Television," demanded a newspaper advertisement published by local cultural producers' organizations and signed by a long list of their members. "By giving in to this pressure from New Zealand"—which had merely asked that a freely negotiated trade agreement be enforced—"we don't just give away a small part of our power as a nation to define and express our culture through television. We risk losing it entirely. . . . We need a little help. . . . We don't want hand-outs. . . . This problem can be fixed without a tax-payer's cent being spent

[5] SBS Television, 12 Nov 2003.
[6] Channel 9 Television, Melbourne, 3 Dec 2003.

225

on it."[7] In reality the consumer's cent would be diverted to paying for the more expensive local product and consumer choice would be restricted.

The head of the Australian Children's Television Foundation launched an attack on competition from the "xenophobic and parochial" United States.[8] The way to destroy a people, she stated, is to detribalize them by taking away their stories and dreams, replacing them with imported ones. Small cultures had survived through geographical and linguistic isolation, but because of new communications technology, "the old forms of cultural protection and the values inherent in individual cultures are being challenged." The nature and superiority of these "values" went, as usual, unspecified. There followed vituperative remarks about American society and its "sinister" commercial broadcasting. An art director lecturing in the National Gallery, Canberra, turned the beam of hatred on Europe. No more overseas art: "our concerns are not Europe's concerns." There should be a ten-year moratorium on buying imported art.[9]

The power that isolationism, patronage, subsidies, and restricted markets give to cultural bureaucrats is not acknowledged. In the face of this insularity, many of the most talented Australian performers have left the country, in line with the large exodus of native-born young people since about 1990. Only a rare voice points out that trade is by definition a two-way street: Australian performers get a showing overseas, and the electronic revolution enables them to be marketed anywhere. Only a rare voice is raised in favor of

[7] *Australian*, 22 Jun 1998.
[8] *Australian*, 3 Jul 1998.
[9] *Australian*, 31 Mar 2000.

free trade and intellectual openness. The most forceful riposte to the protectionists comes from Imre Salusinszky, who makes a connection between the upsurge of cultural protectionism and the overall climate of opinion about world trade.[10] In the 1990s cultural producers and trades unionists, sensing that the mood was shifting from automatic support for industrial special pleading, switched to arguments based on cultural and national identity.

Salusinszky refers to the children's television bureaucrat cited earlier and says that maybe what she really wants is for the part of Big Bird in *Sesame Street* to be taken by an emu. This should not be shrugged off as a cheap gibe. The move would be consistent with other attempts at de-linking Australia from shared Western culture. Local producers have lobbied to replace the Easter Bunny with the bilby, thus securing the Easter market for newly minted stories about a native animal that few have previously heard of and almost no one has ever seen.

I

Anything said by nationalists in Australia is eclipsed by the French. Conor Cruise O'Brien pictured the French Revolution as a contrivance where "in one end poured a broad and placid stream of universalism, while what came out at the other end, for no visible reason, was a turbulent torrent of militant nationalism."[11] The French have continually campaigned to secure the international prominence of their language, advertise their culture, and keep the competition out

[10] Imre Salusinszky, "The Culture Club Con," *Age*, 24 Jun 1999.
[11] Quoted by Charles Townshend in *Financial Times Magazine*, 17 Jan 2004.

of France. As long ago as 1884 a French diplomat at the Prime Meridian Conference in Washington, which had been convened to consider establishing international time zones, demanded that all motions be translated into French.[12] Failing at that in the face of American concerns about practicality, he demanded a "neutral" prime meridian from which time zones could be calibrated, which was unreasonable because every meridian touches land somewhere. Finally, he declared that if the Anglo-Saxon countries would adopt the "neutral" metric system, France might accept an English meridian, which was voted into existence anyhow (France abstaining). Later, in 1898, French official time was quietly defined as "Paris mean time, retarded by nine minutes, twenty-one seconds."

Similar stubbornness has characterized French interests from that day to this. A French wine maker likened Australian wine to Coca-Cola and called those who buy it philistines.[13] Unluckily for him, Australian wine overtook French wine in the American market in 2002. French chefs produced a manifesto about the loss of culinary identity through the use of alien spices and unfamiliar mixing of foods, which is odd given how many French ingredients originated in the Americas. A colleague tells me that he once heard an Italian start to deliver a paper in English at an international conference, whereupon Fernand Braudel leapt to his feet and exclaimed, "You have a beautiful language, why are you using 'cette langue barbare'?" The speaker reverted to Italian, and most of the audience left the room.

[12] Clark Blaise, *Sir Sandford Fleming and the Creation of Standard Time* (London: Weidenfeld & Nicolson, 2000).
[13] Kym Anderson, "Wine's New World," *Foreign Policy*, May–Jun 2003, p. 47.

Eric Hobsbawm sympathizes with the French: "it is hard to go from global hegemony to regionalism in two generations."[14] He adds that their rearguard action against "the homogenization of an essentially plural humanity by the processes of globalisation" seems doomed but is necessary and not absolutely bound to fail. His is a strangely conservative reading. The world is too varied and dynamic ever to expunge all differences, while it gains innumerable new syntheses from the multiple interactions of globalization. Hobsbawm's own many-sided career is evidence of plurality if anything is. What is now taking place is the extension of opportunities like those he had to many more people. Indeed, he acknowledges this by remarking that what has happened to France "marks the end of the minority cultures in which only the elites needed international communication."

The antiglobalization and anti-American rhetoric that allies France's cultural producers so closely with the country's political establishment is nevertheless contradicted by France's actual integration with the international economy and the internationalized consumption habits of its people. McDonald's has been expanding vigorously in France, despite the highly publicized destruction of one or two of its outlets. And the country is resolutely modern in its separation of church and state. Citizens of whatever ethnic or geographical origin are deemed to be as French as those whose ancestors have lived on French soil for ten or twenty generations. They are expected to absorb French culture in the way that standard-issue Americans or (less speedily) Englishmen were once created out of immigrant families.

[14] Eric Hobsbawm, *Interesting Times: A Twentieth-Century Life* (London: Allen Lane/Penguin Press, 2002), pp. 336–37.

▐▐

Subsidizing the arts is one of cultural protectionism's main purposes. Among the thousands of demands on the British taxpayer, one was made by Gerald Kaufman, chairman of the House of Commons' Culture Committee, when he insisted that to make the "right kind" of British films a great deal of taxpayers' money should be spent.[15] A figure had been suggested by Lord Gowrie, who thought the arts should receive 1 percent of total public funding, to be indexed at 2 percent per year.[16] Olson was right that special interests accept no limitation on what they take out of the common pot.

A shrewd observation about the chorus of demands was made by Ivan Hewett, a BBC music presenter.[17] He remarked that the premier British funding body, the Arts Council, had been founded at a time when the eternal verities of art and the personal taste of the elite coincided, and art was then defined so broadly that it must always want more subsidy. Philip Hensher, too, commented that the system of official intervention reflects an elitist society that no longer exists and only the arbitrary means of funding prevents us from recognizing the fact.[18] Formerly the radio or concert hall was the most convenient way of hearing classical music. Today twenty or thirty versions of any piece can be downloaded or bought in a music shop, and "it serves no end to pretend that the means by which culture is conveyed must be preserved at any cost." No one considers that there may be too many live orchestras for current demand.

[15] BBC 4, 18 Sep 2003.
[16] *Spectator*, 12 Jun 1999.
[17] *Prospect Magazine*, May 1999.
[18] *Spectator*, 12 Jun 1999.

State-sponsored art runs the gamut of political ideo-
logues. At the totalitarian end of the spectrum, murals of
tractors denote Soviet realism, and the most bland and in-
sidious conformity denotes Nazi taste. Bland? Goebbels decreed literary criticism to be a Jewish perversion and that re-
views must be friendly or bland! At the other end of the
spectrum are the subsidies that bestow competitive advantage on favored artists and favored nationals, supporting tens
of thousands of seemingly innocuous galleries, concerts, and
books. The results may sometimes be excellent, but without
open competition there is no good way of telling this or en-
suring it will happen. The longer subsidies and quotas on foreign products persist, the more likely taste will come to rest
within approved bureaucratic parameters. Artistic composition will increasingly have its eye on grant getting.

Every so often a writer does stand up to challenge
these arrangements. One is Richard Pells, who argues that
"the hunger for a hit and the fear of commercial failure are
precisely what give American film, television, books and
magazines their vitality, their emotional connection with
audiences and their immense global popularity."[19] While
part of the success of American cultural exports is no doubt
due to the scale of their distribution network (built on the
back of earlier successes), their box-office appeal must contain an element of what Pells calls "their emotional connection with audiences." This is resented by cultural producers and intellectuals in other countries who are insulated
from the marketplace and have a tendency to create "works
that are neither entertaining nor provocative, just self-
indulgent."

[19] *International Herald Tribune*, 16 Dec 1997.

Cultural protection is conservative. The creativity it fosters is the devising of ever more arcane, emotive, and improbable elaborations of the status quo. Films made with European subsidies are known as "Europuddings," since the ingredients are influenced by the requirement that a mixture of nationalities be employed. The European Union ensures that there is a media desk for each member country and two for Belgium (one for the Flemings, one for the Walloons).[20] The cost of promoting EU film production between 1996 and 2000 was U.S.$333 million. Many films were made, but most were unwatchable or at any rate unwatched. Several crashed at the box office.[21] Europe's most creative directors, writers, actors, and production specialists did not wait to share the largesse; they moved to Hollywood where over one hundred worked on *Titanic* alone. The EU wound up with an audiovisual trade deficit of U.S.$6 billion per annum.

U.K. Lottery money (from a tax on betting that primarily transfers wealth from working-class punters to middle-class cultural producers and consumers) scarcely ever produced a winning film. Of nearly two hundred films, none made a profit or had much critical success. They burned up £70 million on an industry advertised as brimming with talent but which did not conspicuously exercise it.[22] One-half of the films were never shown in a cinema![23] The Film Council accordingly proposed quota schemes and tax deals to encourage American distribution companies to show more British films—any strategy, in fact, other than freeing

---

[20] *European*, 13 Apr 1998.
[21] *Financial Times*, 8 Nov 2002.
[22] *Economist*, 18 Nov 2000.
[23] *Financial Times*, 15 Nov 2002.

producers to make movies that people might go to see of their own free will. If people do not want to watch officially approved productions, the dice must be loaded by hampering competitors. With limited audiences for local products, panic about foreign competition is obvious among cultural producers in country after country. For example, in South Korea Han Jin of the "Emergency Committee to Protect the Screen Quota System" admitted that abolishing quotas would end Korean film production, "because it would be almost impossible to find cinemas to show Korean films."[24]

In Australia the major performing arts companies lost a total of A$13 million in four years at the end of the 1990s, A$11.4 million of this being swallowed up by music and opera companies.[25] This could hardly be ignored even in that prodigal climate, and it is not surprising that a defense of the funding of orchestras was speedily elicited from Richard Mills of the West Australian Opera.[26] His arguments were as follows: Australian musicians are cheap by international standards; orchestras have curatorial and teaching functions and can ward off depression among audience members (depression being billed as the fourth most expensive medical condition); and Australians are becoming less civilized (sic) as a result of prepackaged entertainment crowding their mental space for dreaming, so they should (be obliged to) participate in classical music.

Protectionist arguments are seldom more persuasive or less ad hoc than those put forward by Mills. From the point of view of economics, they constitute no technical case to

[24] *Financial Times*, 3 Apr 1998.

[25] *Australian*, 3 Apr 2000.

[26] *Australian Financial Review*, 7 Apr 2000.

233

answer, but this does not make them insignificant. Their feeble reiteration succeeds in causing economists to lose interest, with the result that the ideas are not vigorously challenged. There is a large literature on the economics of subsidizing the arts, but the worlds of practical politics and advocacy seldom draw on it. In country after country, lobby groups milk taxpayers and cause their choices to be restricted, thereby distorting the pattern of economic activity and—it is important to note—removing the incentive to improve the lobbyists' own products. As Salusinszky concludes for Australia, cultural protectionists "debilitate the very activities that they are meant to promote."[27] When things go badly, protectionists look to the government for cash, compulsion, and intervention, "not to their own performance (hardly surprising, given that they have never functioned in a fully competitive environment . . .) . . . it is never the fact that the music, the drama, the fiction, or the films may not be of sufficient quality."

Moreover, conflicts of interest follow protection as night follows day, to be decided, if they are decided at all, on the basis of politicking. The *Financial Times* reported (20 February 2002) that the Film Council in Britain had awarded grants totalling £23 million to films in which six of its directors had interests. Should further testimony be needed of the sleaze associated with the public funding of the arts, Norman Lebrecht's *Covent Garden* is a scarifying account of the backstabbers, lechers, and so forth involved in running a protected cultural institution via the English Old Boys' Net.[28]

[27] Imre Salusinszky, "A Critique of Cultural Protectionism," Bert Kelly Lecture, Centre for Independent Study, 1999.
[28] Norman Lebrecht, *Covent Garden: The Untold Story. Dispatches from the English Culture War, 1945–2000* (London: Simon & Schuster UK, 2000).

Covent Garden, he says, "embodies few values beyond its own survival." Lebrecht goes on to note (p. 480) that there are people in Britain who are effectively condemned to death because they cannot get timely medical treatment, yet seats at the Royal Opera House and Sadler's Wells are lavishly subsidized. We do indeed live in a world of multiple distortions, and this is one of them.

III

When governments fail to support the arts sufficiently, the alternative is applying moral suasion, sometimes amounting to moral blackmail, to private business. This is not always as far removed from government funding as it may seem, because the pain may be reduced by tax breaks that push some of the cost onto the taxpayer. There was a surge of approaches to businesses from the late 1990s on. CEOs, company directors, and senior managers are not typically aesthetic or reflective people; as managers, business disproportionately hires number-crunchers, with backgrounds in technologies like engineering or accounting. The executives say they have too little time to read. They contribute little to cultural and intellectual life; it is rare for them to do what George Soros has done and write books about world affairs. But they, or their wives, are not immune to the attractions of being seen at the theatre, concerts, or gallery openings, and letting it be known that their companies sponsor such events. This opens the way for a class of intermediaries and impresarios, such as gallery owners, who likewise are seldom cultural producers themselves. There is less attention to activities that do not lend themselves so readily to public gatherings, like research on literary subjects or the writing of poetry.

Subsiding the arts from company funds is ethically dubious. I am not speaking of bequests and donations from the great foundations whose originally commercial wealth supports so many museums, concert halls, galleries, and libraries in the United States (helped, it must be said, by an especially favorable tax regime). That funding comes from the private fortunes of great entrepreneurs and represents capital being recycled into the community by the individuals or families whose energy accumulated it in the first place. Arts funding out of the current profits of listed companies is another matter. It means siphoning off shareholders' money for purposes that ordinary shareholders might not choose and against which they have little or no effective recourse. Institutional investors too often acquiesce, perhaps under some feel-good rubric of the type to which business people are so prone, such as the fad for corporate social responsibility.[29] Refusing to fund the arts would seem like rejecting motherhood and apple pie.

IV

The classic historical case of cultural protection relates to Korea. The fifteenth-century King Sejong required his scholars to devise an alphabet and writing system that would be easy for the populace to learn, something more accessible than the Chinese script in use among the literati.[30] They in-

---

[29] For a critique, see David Henderson, *Misguided Virtue: False Notions of Corporate Social Responsibility* (London: Institute of Economic Affairs, 2001).

[30] Eric Jones, Lionel Frost, and Colin White, *Coming Full Circle: An Economic History of the Pacific Rim* (Boulder, Colo.: Westview Press, 1993), p. 22; John Man, *Alpha Beta: How Our Alphabet Shaped the Western World* (London: Headline, 2000), pp. 108–16.

vented a twenty-nine-character syllabary called Han'gul, which linguists agree was one of the greatest inventions ever in the field of literacy. Together with movable metal type, which the Koreans also possessed, the stage was set for an explosion in popular literacy and a dramatic increase in the availability of printed books. However, Sejong died and the literati were quick to defend the investment each of them had made in learning Chinese characters. They squeezed Han-gul into an almost trivial role.

Language is a prime instrument for protectionists.[31] Many nations seek to preserve and extend the use of their own languages because this defends or increases their soft power, both in the political sense and with respect to markets, where it binds foreigners to them for services and purchases. Language and political influence have always been related, so that it is, for instance, no surprise that Britain continues to support the Commonwealth, which is the ghost of her far-flung empire. What can such a motley collection of countries around the world have in common other than that they were once colored red on the map? The answer is the tradition of British law, higher education, accounting methods, and use of the English language, at least by their elites. Expenditures on maintaining these things are not trivial; the Commonwealth is the largest international organization after the United Nations. Losing the influence that a shared language brings can be costly, as Russia is finding now that several countries once within the USSR are asserting

---

[31] Eric L. Jones, "The Case for a Shared World Language," in Mark Casson and Andrew Godley, eds., *Cultural Factors in Economic Growth* (Berlin: Springer-Verlag, 2000), chapter 9; and Eric L. Jones, "The Costs of Language Diversity," chapter 6 of *The Record*.

their independence and dropping the teaching of Russian in schools in favor of German or English.[32]

A great deal of language protection is obvious rent seeking. How else to explain the campaign, one among many, to have Ulster Scots accepted as a language? (A job advertisement appeared in it in 1999.)[33] An Ulsterman interviewed about this did have the grace to say that the move has a touch of ethnocentricity about it. He noted that the people of Ulster have access to English, the world language, which is a real asset and that the aim of language policy ought to be intelligibility. Does the world really need yet more intraspecific barriers?

The justification of protection is usually a flat assertion that something vital—myths, stories, identity—is lost when a language is lost. All this is presented in terms that imply all right-thinking people must agree. On a second glance, the case is seldom persuasive. The leading British defender of existing languages, David Crystal, has eventually to concede that research has hardly begun to elucidate what is lost from a cultural point of view when language shift occurs.[34] In that case, one might have hoped for fewer premature assertions that so much will indeed be lost. In fairness, I must quote Sybil Marshall, a small-farmer's daughter from the Fens, whose defense of dialect is the most eloquent I have come across: "With dialect," she writes, "goes idiom, with idiom goes natural metaphor, with metaphor goes symbolism, and in symbolism is reflected a philosophy of life and an

---

[32] Marshall R. Singer, "Language Follows Power: The Linguistic Free Market in the Old Soviet Bloc," *Foreign Affairs* 77/1 (Jan–Feb 1998): 19–24.

[33] BBC World Service, 11 Dec 1999.

[34] David Crystal, *Language Death* (Cambridge: Cambridge University Press, 2000), p. 122.

attitude towards death not easy to find among the young today."[35]

Sybil Marshall may be granted the fact that the mass of young English people lack much by way of metaphor that does not come from television or the soccer pitch. The power of language among their ancestors came from the Bible. But it also came from two further facts: that their ancestors originally lived and worked on the land and that until recent decades linguistically able people were trapped in humble jobs in local communities. The semantic somersaults that Kingsley Amis admired in World War II soldiers were, he observed, "the property and product of a kind of person rarely met with by most of those who read books, a very intelligent, humorous man with only rudimentary education."[36] The sons and grandchildren of these men have since escaped into university education and wider opportunities.

Why, indeed, should anyone be encouraged, let alone obliged, to retain the dialects that these men spoke? Why should anyone be pressed into remaining in a subordinate position in provincial society? Dialects and entire languages are the result of linguistic isolation. When markets are conjoined, dialects and languages tend to merge or be sidelined in favour of a lingua franca, suggesting that their aesthetic attractions are not enough to trump considerations of utility. Remember too that most old speakers of dialect lacked in wider vocabulary what they may have possessed in pithiness. The people who wish to see minority languages and local dialects restored are usually privileged members of the larger culture. Who else gains from linguistic restorations except

[35] Sybil Marshall, *A Pride of Tigers* (London: Penguin, 1995), p. 103.
[36] Kingsley Amis, *Memoirs* (London: Penguin, 1992), p. 96.

bureaucrats and specialists in bilingual education? What does it benefit children to be taught a rare local language, with no literature or scientific terminology of its own, as happens in some indigenous groups in Australia and Canada? The energies of these unfortunates are wasted on the desert air and their gateway to the world's store of literature and science is narrowed. Luckily, the mass of most populations ignores the strictures.

Very, very occasionally someone will join this debate on the counterprotectionist side. Here I will quote Russell Hardin, who gives it as his opinion that a majority of languages are culturally poor and give access only to small communities.[37] Hardin refers to the coercion employed to institutionalize minor languages for official transactions, especially in Canada. He notes that defenders of communal "rights" are actually opposed to opportunities for individuals, while children and future generations have no voice for opposing policies of linguistic isolationism.

As it is, language diversity results in conspicuous waste. If fewer languages were in use, heavy expenditures on translation could be cut. The EU spends perhaps one-third of its income on translation. In defense of this, Neil Kinnock, vice president of the European Commission, argues that the cost is only two euros per citizen, a sleight of hand on his part that overlooks both the aggregate cost and the opportunity cost.[38] With the EU's enlargement the number of pages to be translated each year will grow from the present 1.3 million to 2.4 million. Malta has insisted that its na-

[37] Russell Hardin, *One for All: The Logic of Group Conflict* (Princeton: Princeton University Press, 1995), pp. 219–20.
[38] *Financial Times*, 16 Dec 2002.

tional language (an amalgam of Arabic, Italian, and English) become an official EU language.[39] Every document will have to be translated into a language spoken by just 400,000 people. The irony is that 135 posts for translators into Maltese were advertised but only forty people turned up for the preselection tests, and all of them failed. Worse than this, the EU breached its own requirement that the ten enlargement countries must translate the 85,000-page rulebook before joining: Malta was given several months' grace before complying.[40]

Genuine linguistic creativity is shown by the rise of postcolonial literatures in English that are returning to make such a showing in the literary competitions of the homeland. Gains are to be had by standardizing language in order to ease communication among the largest possible number of people. To judge from the emergence of international languages like Airspeak and the enormous growth of World Standard English, the market believes there are such gains. "Market" is a synonym for people who have a living to get.

V

A prominent theme of cultural protectionist demands is the appeal to nationalism. Historically speaking, nations are artificial groupings like teams, some of them extremely recent in origin. Many people, however, enjoy belonging to teams and seem to need them as props of their personal identity. A well-known feature of immigrant life is throwing one's lot in with the adopted nation, denigrating the one left behind, and becoming, as it were, more royalist than the king. This

[39] *Financial Times*, 23 Jan 2004.
[40] *Financial Times*, 6 Mar 2004.

can exacerbate existing xenophobia, with results all too plain in the world's trouble spots. Moreover, the key feature of nationhood is not who is included, since some countries have succeeded in absorbing large immigrant minorities. The key feature is who is excluded. At its worst, exclusion can lead to massacres and expulsions on the grounds of supposed incompatibility. Hitler and Stalin were aces at this game. It is no surprise that many communists and communist parties have mutated into nationalistic fascists.

The concept of national identity, as Charles Townshend comments, holds that nations were primal, natural communities that may embrace a purported historic destiny.[41] The book that Townshend happens to be reviewing, Anthony Smith's *Chosen Peoples*, claims that, syncretic though nations may sometimes be, they were not simply conjured into being during the nineteenth century. Smith's argument appears to be that modern nations are projections and magnifications of old religious identities. This seems to endow them with a powerful history, however much picking and choosing among myths and legends may have been involved in constructing anomalies such as neighboring nations with the same religion, for example, Spain and Portugal. The national project ends by fabricating barriers among peoples, segmenting the world market and raising transaction costs.

The present importance of nationalism lies in its giv-

[41] *Financial Times Magazine*, 17 Jan 2004. For an extreme defense of nations in the context of Australian culture, see the contribution by Robyn Spencer, a founding member of Australians Against Further Immigration, in Steve Vizard et al. eds., *Australia's Population Challenge* (Camberwell, Australia: Penguin, 2003), pp. 202–5.

ing cultural producers teams to cheer and pretexts for subsidizing national art. In reality, the exchanges and cross-
currents of cultural ideas, however suppressed and deferred
by protectionist walls, have been and continue to be so significant that the very concept of exclusively national art is
absurd. Just as outward-looking East Asians argue that there
are no Asian Values—only values—so we may contend that
there is no national art, only art.

Nations do differ in the coherence of their cultures,
but this is mainly because some are open societies while others remain locked in by provincial languages and poor communications. The American poet laureate has remarked that
people in Iran or Eastern Europe or Latin America have fairly
unified cultures and their politicians must at least pretend to
love the national poets.[42] But the United States has an im-
provising culture that makes up in dynamism what it lacks
in shared heritage. Cultural wars are inspired today by the
fear that international economic integration, led by the U.S.
and spread by Global English, will undermine the local monopolies of cultural producers in other countries and oblige
them to compete in an open market for talent and ideas. Any
failure on their part to enter the competition, it must be said,
robs the world of potential syntheses and perpetuates the re-
cycling of hoary tales. Insistence on the nation as the cultural unit leads to intemperate outbursts like the following
by Philip Hensher: "The Duke and Duchess of Northumber-
land, two of the most preposterous vulgarians known to
mankind, seemed to be under the impression that their
Raphael was theirs to dispose of as they saw fit, as if *the na-*

[42] *Financial Times*, 4 Apr 2000.

tion would benefit just as much from the sum of money they had been offered by Americans as from the presence of the painting itself."[43]

An analysis of national identity and the fascist dangers that "remain locked within it" was presented in Australia by Salusinszky in his 1999 Bert Kelly Lecture.[44] He observed that the concept is not fixed in the Jungian collective unconscious but is ideological and as a result contestable. Only in the Marxist mind must art serve ideology. Marxism pushed aside the liberal-humanist notion that connections between the myths of peoples, transcending ideology and nationalism, may legitimately be explored. Arguments for cultural protection based on national identity override the individual's choice and tax him or her for the privilege. Those who can invent national symbols can hope to get them subsidized and have the alternatives penalized or excluded. As Salusinszky says, individuals do not need regulation like this to tell them what their identity is. He is writing for Australians, and by and large they have already voted with their wallets. If they do possess "something called a cultural identity," he states, "then one aspect of that identity is a fierce enjoyment of films, music and television originating from the United States. If this discountenances their cultural betters, then so be it."

VI

The most outstanding contributions to the debate about culture, in the sense of the arts, that have appeared in recent years are Tyler Cowen's *In Praise of Commercial Culture*

[43] *Spectator*, 25 Jan 2003.
[44] Salusinszky, "Cultural Protechonism."

(1998) and *Creative Destruction: How Globalisation Is Changing the World's Cultures* (2002).[45] The first of these volumes, partly because it was the first, came as a shock to conventional antimarket wisdom. Cowen demonstrates that government agencies and public monies are not essential to creating an active and original world of the arts. Some of his most intriguing observations are directed at the way individuals form their taste, devise their judgments, and erect their (mis)perceptions about cultural products. These are insights that strip away the veil of common assumptions, especially the recurrent opinion that all the greatest artists, musicians, and writers are already dead and that the latest art forms are always degenerate. This assumption persists because it is the way successive cohorts of the middle-aged come to see things.

I once studied the manuscript diary of an English banker called John Biddulph. In 1837 he went to a ball, where he was scandalized by couples dancing the newfangled waltz. He wrote, "I am most decidedly of opinion that no woman ever became a practised Voltzer that retained her original purity of mind." Incongruous though this may now seem, the deadly part of it is that the same carping runs through every age's commentary on the latest fashion. The sternest rebukes are aimed at anything smacking of sensuality, at least by those too old to partake of it any longer. Lasciviousness is discovered in anything new—often correctly, because young artists are naturally interested in sex. The best

[45] Tyler Cowen, *In Praise of Commercial Culture* (Cambridge, Mass.: Harvard University Press, 1998); and Tyler Cowen, *Creative Destruction: How Globalization Is Changing the World's Cultures* (Princeton: Princeton University Press, 2002).

days of an admired culture are almost always located in the past, but we should realize that in their own day similar abuse was directed at those who are now seen as great masters. Chopin's contemporaries described his music as "ranting hyperbole and excruciating cacophony," "ear-rending, torturous, and repugnant," as well as "trivial and incoherent." Bruckner was charged with being "the greatest living musical peril, a tonal Antichrist." The very recurrence of such language should alert us to look for the motives beneath its abusive surface.

Cowen urges that capitalism and competition are good for the arts. He has no difficulty in demonstrating, mainly for the United States, that we revel in the largest range, the cheapest and the most accessible products of any age, and these things may be expected to grow in variety and fall further in price. The cost of materials and equipment has come right down. The list of modern offerings is endless and has expanded even in the few years since Cowen wrote: videotapes, compact discs, DVDs, iPods, vast libraries, Internet search engines giving access to whatever information one wants, definitive and better-translated editions of literary works, "better access to Shakespeare than the Elizabethans had," catalogues of paintings full of superb colored plates, and collections of artworks "comparable to or better than those of earlier kings" made for American businessmen.

Between 1965 and 1990 the number of symphony orchestras in the United States increased from 58 to nearly 300, opera companies from 27 to over 150, and nonprofit regional theatres from 22 to 500. In 1947 there were only 357 publishers in the United States; today there are over 49,000, many of them small operators but most of them on the lookout for innovative works. There is no domination by either elitism or mass-market trash. Whereas the blockbusters of history, Foxe's *Book of Martyrs* or Bunyan's *Pilgrim's Progress*, utterly dominated sales in their day, during the 1980s the top fifteen bestsellers in the U.S. accounted for less than 1 percent of total sales. Even in the superstores, bestsellers represent only 3 percent of sales. This is a country where artists' incomes do not depend on political connections or acceptability but on pushing concepts to the limit.

Twentieth-century culture was more of a "festive bazaar" than all previous centuries. It melded together more styles. The dam walls between genres burst. Scott Joplin took classical piano lessons from a German teacher but infused the music with the syncopated rhythms used by black banjo players; he combined high and low culture by echoing Chopin, Debussy, and barroom entertainers. Syntheses of art forms from around the world are still taking place, just as they are in cuisine, as benign but underrated features of globalization. The logical extension of this is more, not less, novelty. But most people's eyes are averted from this.

Cowen shows that cultural pessimism is unwarranted or at most unreliable. The masterpieces of the past have survived a prolonged process of winnowing that contemporary products have not yet undergone. It is too early to take pot shots at contemporary art, music, or literature. The sociology of acts of vandalism against modern works, which are extreme forms of contempt for the new, is revealing in this respect.[46] Rather than being the work of psychotics, such acts are social protests by people who see themselves outside an art world that foists on them objects they cannot understand, making them feel socially inferior and culturally disadvan-

[46] John E. Conklin, *Art Crime* (Westport, Conn.: Praeger, 1994), p. 243.

247

taged. Their protests are unlikely to represent the judgment of history. In the long run, public opinion (a.k.a. the market, in its widest sense) can be left to judge the works.

Markets relax the constraints on internal creativity. The great thing is to evade single buyers—patrons or Arts Councils—since these are likely to cramp one's style, like that of poor Velasquez, who had to paint eighty-one portraits of Philip IV. Escaping from one's family also helps to free the spirit. Many past artists and performers were taught within their families. This probably ensured high accomplishments, since the children could be compelled to spend long hours on practice, but their experimentation was likely to be subsumed in the established ways of their parents. Mozart's father, for instance, steered him away from distributing his compositions in the form of sheet music, which had not been the mode in the father's day.

To round out this account of Cowen's work, corroboration may be found in an article by Lester Thurow.[47] Culture has always consisted of older people telling young ones what to believe and how to act, he observes. By contrast, the new electronic culture jumps directly to the young, has no desire to inculcate any special values, and seeks only to make profits; its amorality has produced a backlash from religious fundamentalists in the United States as great as that unleashed anywhere else. The U.S. creates so much of the electronic culture because it is an immigrant society that lacks a unified idea of what culture is or should be. It is good at bringing in talented foreign performers from anywhere and every-

[47] Lester C. Thurow, "Globalization: The Product of a Knowledge-Based Economy," *Annals of the American Academy of Political and Social Science* 570 (Jul 2000): 19–31.

where, and making them feel like first-class participants in things American.

The analyses by Cowen and Thurow demonstrate the fertility of market culture and explain the fear and outrage it provokes among people concerned to defend their own special interests. Compared with the competitive American market, government-sponsored art tends to be lifeless. Money that could be better spent goes on administration: France has twelve thousand cultural bureaucrats who certainly do have reason to fear the market. Actual cultural producers need not do so. As Frances Cairncross says of the cinema in France and Italy, if those countries were once again to become centers of artistic excellence, the pressure for protection would probably fade away.[48]

In his second book, *Creative Destruction*, Cowen remarks that antiglobalization polemicists are not really concerned with creative diversity but with particular desires of their own. His volume is a sensitive exposition of the merits of cosmopolitan diversity that does admit there are some philosophical difficulties in defending the position. Economic development creates homogeneity and heterogeneity at the same time, and there are problems in reconciling what may be the final outcome. For the moment, I am sufficiently concerned with the wastefulness, suppression of originality, and self-serving rhetoric of cultural protectionism to think that one can scarcely expose these faults enough. Political power trumps economic analysis. Distortions in the world market will continue, because rent seeking is endemic. All that can be hoped for is to minimize it.

[48] Frances Cairncross, *The Death of Distance* (Boston: Harvard Business School Press, 1997), p. 251.

Cowen counters the anxiety that globalization may make all regions culturally uniform by noting that individuals will have more choice, since trade heightens the pace of change and raises the level of diversity per unit of time. "Critics of cross-cultural exchange face an awkward question. If diversity at any point in time is desirable, why is intertemporal diversity not desirable as well?"[49] And he shows that native cultures are usually themselves the result of earlier processes of creative destruction and remixing, since the past has been dynamic, not static: "most cultural innovations are [and have been] far more syncretic than most individuals realize."[50]

VII

Cultural protection consists disproportionately of demands to keep out competition from the United States or, more broadly, from the so-called Anglo-Saxon world and its instrument, the English language. If we can find a non-Anglo-Saxon author who dissents from this campaign, his or her words should carry special weight. Why, though, should anyone abandon calls for protection if these would bring him or her personal advantage? Only those confident of the quality of their own work are likely to scorn the crutches of state aid and the shelter of nationalism's walls.

The individual who most fits the bill is the Peruvian writer Mario Vargas Llosa.[51] He makes the essential points,

[49] Cowen, *Creative Destruction*, p. 137.
[50] Ibid., p. 145.
[51] "Vargas Llosa on Culture and the New International Order," *La Trobe University Bulletin*, Sep–Oct 2002, p. 7; Mario Vargas Llosa, "The Culture of Liberty," *Foreign Policy*, Jan–Feb 2001 (Internet version).

viz., that globalization has expanded rather than curtailed individual liberty and that cultures do not need to be shielded by commissars to remain lively and adaptable. It is not globalization per se that is bringing about change, he says, but modernization, which will unavoidably cause some of the world's folkloric variety to disappear. To this I would add that much of that variety, while colorful in the eyes of tourists from the industrialized world, derives in fact from rural poverty; its loss could not compare with losing the works of Montaigne, Descartes, Racine, and Baudelaire that French intellectuals think are so threatened by Hollywood and the English language. Vargas Llosa dissents from the very notion of cultural identity, which he sees as a collectivist and ideological abstraction of all that is original to free spirits. True identity springs from individual creativity, not geographical affiliation. There will be new syntheses; local cultures that were silenced by domineering nation-states and empires like the USSR will be reborn. Modernization may demolish some anthropological oddities, but it will lead to a more varied future.

PART III

CONCLUSION

Chapter 10

Culture as Reciprocity

Within a generation or so after the Second World War mainstream economists had abandoned serious attempts at cultural explanation. This was partly because culture was hard to isolate and partly because other variables seemed more tractable and more significant. A surprising number did continue to allude to the value systems underlying economic growth and stagnation, but only in passing. Yet a matter assumed, however informally, to be fundamental should have been easier to elucidate. The fact that culture went on receiving casual mention in technical analysis may have testified to unease about the simplifications of formal modeling, together with memories of Max Weber from classes on the history of economic thought.

The minority of economists and area specialists who continued to assert a major cultural effect seldom avoided the charge that they were arguing *post hoc ergo propter hoc*.

Development economics as a whole went into decline. One of the reasons for waning interest in what, during the immediate postwar period, had typically been a prescriptive and interventionist subject was the rise of East Asia. The region's achievement indicated the power of specific sets of growth-promoting policies, at least under the system of world trade then prevailing, so that the search for other keys to economic growth lost its attraction. The East Asian case also showed how thoroughly growth was able to transform cultural life, although this was masked by surface continuities that writers in the Weberian mold seized on to make precisely the opposite claim.

An interest in culture has resurfaced, ironically enough, among scholars who are concerned with the second-order reasons why East Asia has been so specially willing to enact growth-promoting policies. The enthusiasm with which the revival of cultural explanation has been greeted has, in my opinion, more to do with the prominence of those involved and dissatisfaction with standard models of growth than with the success of the mission thus far. In trying to establish that culture is a powerful exogenous variable, the wheel is being reinvented. One cause of this is the neglect of intellectual history; the debates in which David Hume, Adam Smith, Alfred Marshall, and others engaged still have much to say that bears on the analysis of culture, but they are no longer brought routinely to the attention of economics students.

In history, journalism, and throughout the social sciences other than economics, culture is less cautiously, or even sometimes enthusiastically, cited as the basic explanation of all sorts of phenomena—the point at which inquiry may be broken off because social bedrock has supposedly been reached. The obscurity of the subject licenses dogmatism about culture as something inalienable, a belief that slides neatly into the attitude that it is vital to protect national cultures against foreign competition. The fact that national cultures are never pure and all modern cultures include large amounts of borrowing is conveniently forgotten. On occasion culture remains distinct enough to spur or constrain economic action, but there are more occasions when it silently adjusts. There is reciprocity between economies and cultures, but it is asymmetrical: economics dominates, though without always exhausting every other possible influence.

If the aim is to discover general principles by which culture operates, it is unhelpful to have in mind merely one or two faiths, one or two countries, or one or two centuries. Only a wide range of examples and broad and long comparisons will suffice, although poor documentation, as well as conceptual problems, makes systematic inquiry difficult. As Rodney Stark points out, historians may be ill at ease with even the rather limited level of abstraction needed to guard against taking cultural appearances at face value.[1] Together with many in the social sciences, they permit the descriptive profusion that can be observed to lure them into the depths of cultural fixity, oddly neglecting the fact that while cultures differ across space at any one time, they also differ *through* time. The bulk of the economics profession, on the other hand, is even today drawn toward cultural nullity, that is, toward dismissing culture as derivative or insignificant. Neither approach is satisfactory; together they remind me of the authority cited by Robert Ellickson, who found law-

---

[1] Rodney Stark, *The Rise of Christianity* (Princeton: Princeton University Press, 1996), p. 22.

and-society to be a swamp but law-and-economics to be a desert.[2]

Much of the literature about culture, especially that relating to business cultures, consists of snapshots of social behavior and attitudes. The cultures under consideration do differ visibly at a given moment, but this observation is not very helpful. Culture is a process, and processes are not best illustrated by sets of stills. It is not surprising that the mixtures of attributes called behavior (and more superficial matters, like deportment) differ among societies. The deeper questions are why is this so, is it significant, and what may change it?

Every culture represents an equilibrium among current economic and social forces. Such equilibria are unlikely to be permanent; they will very slowly change their positions in the gradual way geological strata shift, or they may lurch to new positions as strata do during earthquakes. It has to be admitted that our understanding of the timing of cultural change is no better than that of geologists struggling to predict earthquakes and tsunamis. Where cultural equilibria do seem to persist over long periods, the chances are that market competition is weak and thus there is no special reason why old practices should be abandoned for new ones. Alternatively, the equilibria may be perpetuated by formal institutions supported by political interests, though even so the sluggishness of change in institutional terminology can create false impressions of stasis. (Informal institutions are better relabeled as culture if they do not derive from explicit choices on the part of those in power). Only if it can be

---

[2] Robert C. Ellickson, *Order without Law* (Cambridge, Mass.: Harvard University Press, 1991), p. 147, referring to the late Arthur Leff.

shown that culture is persistently greater than the sum of its parts will the topic be worth pursuing. The underlying forces are what should be sought first, as most of the economics profession has intuitively grasped.

Undoubtedly culture, in the form of preferences and behavioral routines, can hold implications for the economy. It can affect transaction costs. In many instances the effects are likely to be small and will wash out over time, but we should not start by assuming that this will be the case or that the effects are certain to be trivial.[3] Much depends on the length of time that interests us, since it has to be conceded that, although culture can change with astonishing rapidity, it usually alters rather slowly. Nevertheless, cultural sluggishness is probably more a pointer to weak stimuli than evidence of genuine stasis.[4] Since few studies of culture specify all of the relevant components in advance, it is rarely clear in which respects change should have been anticipated. It is also doubtful how often we can separate the role of blind culture from that of social institutions. As has been indicated, the conflation of culture and institutions is a ready source of confusion.

[3] As shown by Andrew Godley, *Jewish Immigrant Entrepreneurship in New York and London 1880–1914: Enterprise and Culture* (Basingstoke, U.K.: Palgrave, 2001).

[4] I cite once more the remark by Wilhelm about the persistence of folkways in China, which he attributes to adaptation to conditions that have "remained unchanged for thousands of years" (Richard Wilhelm, *Chinese Economic Psychology* (New York: Garland, 1982), p. 45; this is not to be taken literally as history, but it is highly suggestive. For an explicit historical account of the propensity of the Chinese economy, society, and polity to return to an equilibrium, see Gang Deng, *The Premodern Chinese Economy: Structural Equilibrium and Capitalist Sterility* (London: Routledge, 1999).

Is all effort at cultural explanation, then, forlorn? Not necessarily, but it is easy to expect too much. A small advance may be made by acknowledging that culture is contingent as well as intrinsically labile and by observing how fast its shape may change when markets merge and offer wider opportunities for cultural exchange. Markets act by spreading information about alternatives and bringing established ways into contact with new ones. An analysis of custom in economics by the nineteenth-century English economist Alfred Marshall, in his *Principles* and elsewhere, as glossed by Ekkehart Schlicht, is a useful summary of the issues.[5] Historians and social scientists tend to be uncomfortable with the abstract approach taken by Marshall, although he was the most historically minded of economists. On the other hand, many modern economists do not demonstrate Marshall's facility at envisaging historical examples while building their models. But understanding Marshall and Schlicht is worth an effort. They employ the term custom as a partial synonym for culture. The customs or habits prevailing at any one time bear on the relative cost of transactions. Custom tends to preserve the existing state of affairs, though it is important to grasp that in Marshallian analysis it is not a mystical "given" but the sluggish residue of past decisions. If we knew more economic history, we could make a better start at disaggregating those decisions.

Traditional societies are the ones where custom is writ

[5] Ekkehart Schlicht, "Custom and Competition," in Tiziano Raffaelli et al., eds., *The Elgar Companion to Alfred Marshall* (Cheltenham, U.K.: Edward Elgar, forthcoming). I am grateful to Professor Schlicht for an early copy of this piece; needless to say, he is not responsible for my further gloss. See also Ekkehart Schlicht, *On Custom in the Economy* (Oxford: Clarendon Press, 1998).

largest: they are habitual in their ways, the elements of the customary in them being so prominent that choice is crowded into corners. Over any given length of time, deviations from established practice are fewer than in modern societies. A defining characteristic of the modern is that it permits continual choice over a wide range. This tends to bring the modern world and its presentation by the Western media into conflict with the elders and patriarchs of other societies, who sense the challenge to their influence and the ideologies that rationalize it. The elders and elites cannot be expected to think favorably of Western culture when a major, perhaps the main, private use of the Internet is looking up pornography. Their resistance, and the resistance of younger men who have imbibed their ideological teaching without considering the options dispassionately, is of obvious significance in foreign affairs as well as commerce.

The mixing of custom and choice at any one time produces, almost tautologically, the existing culture. Customs are never absolutely settled, and slight deviations in behavior will continually shift the equilibria a little. Deviations may be brought about by real-world phenomena, such as a very good or very bad harvest or a military victory or defeat. There were plenty of such shocks in history. This Marshallian reading is not very different—though more cautiously expressed—from that of Julian Simon, who made cultural values depend entirely on the economy. Marshall stresses how hard it is to detect minor shifts, and Simon admits there will be adjustment lags. Small adjustments may nevertheless be reiterated and produce a mildly altered culture that is unlikely to advertise the extent to which it differs from what went before. People adopt fashionable new terms from time to time but seem to be comfortable retaining old ones as well.

Where translation is involved, the translators are likely to choose words that clothe novel practices in familiar guise. This will once again conceal the fact of gradual evolution, something which is further compounded by the poor historical sources available for much of the non-Western world and the derisory proportion of scholarly resources we devote to interpreting them. In any case, some cultures may not change substantially over quite long periods and may therefore seem unexciting. The slightly new menu of habits that is always emerging will nevertheless affect relative costs and continually weight the scales in favor of still more small deviations.

Marshall was keen to demonstrate how culture had been refashioned over the generations by the "almost unconscious balancing" of the incentives for and against certain practices. He quoted the tag *natura non facit saltum*: nature does not make leaps. He was especially interested in the possibility of an economic explanation of Asian economic behavior, which in his day was interpreted as ruled by ancient custom. The prevailing culturally relativist view was that Asian culture was an antique, undifferentiated complex that could be taken as given and would not repay analysis in economic terms. The East Asian Miracle has blown the fantasy of a timeless East out of the water, though Marshall himself did not have the advantage of observing this. He was happy to accept the rider that in "backward countries" some habits might outlive the circumstances that had created them: change thus takes place at different rates, further blurring what we are trying to observe and contributing to the illusion of cultural stability. For "backward country" we can read "traditional society," though either label may mean only that economic stimuli are weak.

Marshall deduced that the apparently static economies of Asia had been produced by prolonged rebalancings of economic forces. This was astute of him, but it was an economist's astuteness, which implicitly assumed the central importance of even a little competition. As we have seen, this insight, though correct, can be over- as well as underemphasised. In traditional societies there was too little competition to eliminate all mediocre practices quickly. Because the selection environment was weak, the strangest varieties of behavior continued to flower unchecked. The world would have to wait for communications and the markets for ideas to expand and interconnect before local variety collapsed into a distinctly smaller number of prominent strands—into groupings dominated by a few major languages, religions, and civilizations.

Deepak Lal has urged that the "murky concept" of culture should be subdivided into material culture (ways to make a living) and cosmology (ways of understanding the world).[6] Material culture is more malleable than the cosmological variety and, as he says, can alter rapidly in response to changes in the environment. Cosmology, which he traces back to humanity's early evolution, does not change so fast: it drags. The effect of cosmology is to reduce that part of transaction costs attributable to the cost of policing exchanges, especially exchanges between individuals who never come face to face. But one must ask just how sticky cosmologies really are and how useful is it to think of humanity as divided into cultures with mutually exclusive atti-

[6] Deepak Lal, "India," in Peter Bernholz and Roland Vaubel, eds., *Political Competition, Innovation and Growth in the History of Asian Civilizations* (Cheltenham, U.K.: Edward Elgar, 2004), pp. 136–37.

tudes toward the issue that Plato called "how one should live."

Cosmological features are prima facie important but it is easy to take too static a view of them and hence to fall away from a Marshallian view toward cultural fixity. The cosmologies we see today are themselves the results of historical evolution and are not intrinsically beyond the scope of further human choice. History has long been fraught with struggles and exchanges between the largest groupings, the civilizations. A look at history shows that worldviews have long been influencing one another, while a glance at modern international economic integration suggests that the world really is being suffused by international (less pertinently, Western or American) notions, lamented or extolled according to taste. The cognitive dissonance set up by the accompanying economic growth is capable of altering deep as well as superficial forms of behavior. Certainly, friction accompanies change, and the events of history take place in the lag times, but the sound and fury of resistance too easily distract us into believing that modern norms will be slow to catch on or may in the long run be frustrated by incompatible localisms.

Debate about these matters can rather readily descend into arguments about whether the glass is half-full or half-empty. Much depends on how long we are prepared to allow for convergence to work itself out and on what we regard as valid indicators of the process. We may have to allow decades or generations for coalescence into larger and larger markets to have a profound effect on attitudes toward "how one should live" as well as on material outcomes. To grasp the underlying processes and avoid being deflected by current affairs, a historical perspective is needed. Such a prospect should not faze us; not only is it essential for grasping the basic process and the direction of change, but change has often been quicker than expected (consider East Asia). Now that comparable information is swirling through most of the existing economic systems, we need no longer anticipate only the glacial rate of change typical of past epochs. To my mind, the rapid spread of international law and impersonal corporations in place of negotiations and relationship business signals the contemporary pace of change.

Agreed, there is enough silliness in the Western world to cast doubt on the idea that larger markets and access to more and better information are ipso facto sufficient to eliminate lunatic beliefs and untested therapies. Far from it. Cultural history may have passed through four phases. First, for untold ages, mediocrity could persist unchallenged in tiny communities under the arbitrary sway of some chief or shaman. For millennia, then, humanity was too poor and dispersed for ideas to come into vigorous competition. Secondly, as societies grew larger, many local idiosyncrasies were subsumed in others. Animist religions that worshiped purely local features of topography and so forth gave way to better-organized churches founded on cosmologies with a wider embrace. When societies grew large and interconnected enough for great intellectual struggles to take place, these tended to take place between alternative organized ideologies, claimants to universal truth, like the Roman Catholic and Protestant churches. Both of these were eager to debar open inquiry and prepared to burn dissidents alive. "E pur si muove," as Galileo is said to have whispered.

Then, thirdly, over a few centuries intellectual competition beat out of the public sphere the more unreasonable opinions (for instance, hapless old women were no longer

burned as witches). Rapid economic growth and a number
of more or less related intellectual changes left the worst in-
tolerances and least defensible notions to one side.[7] Scientific
modes of thought became de rigueur in educated circles and
respected throughout society. Scholarly knowledge became
well enough thought of to beat untested beliefs back to holes
and corners, such as the horoscope columns in newspapers.

Almost simultaneously, economic growth created
higher incomes that were distributed and redistributed in
more egalitarian ways by progressive taxation and the welfare state. Despite the inequalities of wealth that remain, the
benefits of relatively more equal income have been so great
as to be beyond dispute. But it is possible that wider prosperity has drawn part of society into a fourth phase, the antithesis of the order that brought it about. This antithesis is
the cultural and intellectual mediocrity that pockmarks the
face of reason today. The West has grown rich and afforded
a measure of tertiary education for larger and larger numbers
of people. Not all of them are uncritical, and some are inclined to turn the glare of their various personal disquiets
onto the status quo, exaggerating the failings of (for instance) conventional medicine, thinking that creationism is
on a par with the theory of evolution, and automatically dis-
believing government reports even about phenomena such
as UFOs. Not surprisingly, the most trumpeted manifesta-
tions of pseudorationality occur in the largest rich society,
the United States. There is enough error, arrogance, and dis-

[7] Cf. Eric L. Jones, "Technology, the Human Niche and Darwinian Explanation," in Eric Jones and Vernon Reynolds, eds., *Survival and Religion:
Biological Evolution and Cultural Change* (Chichester, U.K.: John Wiley,
1995), pp. 163–86; Alexander Broadie, *The Scottish Enlightenment* (Edinburgh: Birlinn, 2001).

simulation by medics, natural scientists, politicians, and civil servants to stoke the fires of skepticism, but surely not enough to justify a new age of unreason.

Western society has thus become more democratic without, on the face of it, public discourse becoming more profound. Perhaps one should say that society has become more democratic and at the same time more populist. An astonishing range of beliefs can be entertained that authority figures had previously managed to quash. Fifty years of vigorous market competition has curbed much paternalism (which is to say, the elite dictating taste for everybody else), put youth culture at center stage, and relegated former high culture to specialist audiences. On the other hand, Cowen's evidence about the larger and larger provision in the United States of the apparatus of high culture—libraries, museums, galleries, orchestras—suggests that it is not all loss and what has really happened is a widening of opportunities and concomitant fragmenting of responses. It so happens that the power of mass communications has made pop culture easily available to the young, and they prefer it to offerings more associated with schoolteachers than celebrities. Prosperity means they can afford much of what they want. Affluence and information technology, then, have relaxed the selection environment, and one result has been to permit the flowering again of mediocre beliefs as they once flowered in poor, isolated ancestral villages. It is possible, as Ekkehart Schlicht reminds me, that because competition among systems of belief creates uncertainty, it may actually increase rather than abate superstition. David Hume thought so. High culture nevertheless remains on offer; a taste for it may be substantially age related, and successive birth cohorts may come to it in good time.

As an explanation of how custom and competition interacted to produce the slow-moving equilibria of traditional societies, Marshall's concept of continual rebalancing is enlightening. Gradualism does warrant more attention than it usually receives, but it is only one aspect of the story. Recounting that part may not even be the most persuasive way of demonstrating just how contingent culture is. To gradualism I would therefore add the known adjustments of culture at times of historical trauma—rapid responses to abrupt shifts in the balance of incentives. The discontinuities reveal just how plastic culture can be. The speed with which behavior and values can alter if the previous balance of incentives is overthrown exposes their shallowness, especially among the young, who have had little time in which to put down roots. Cases in point are the astonishing volte-faces in rigidly conservative sexual mores during wartime, to which we can refer as a final illustration of culture's essentially unstable quality.

Most people know of the standard version of late Victorian morality and the repressive attitude of the Christian churches. They will probably also be aware that moral and sexual conservatism was not the whole story and will have heard about the Victorian underworld, the extent of child prostitution, and the hypocritical behavior among the rich (there were secret staircases in certain big houses giving access to the servants' quarters for sexual purposes).[8] Despite plentiful evidence of covert indulgence by the rich, there will be little dissent from the received opinion that as far as

---

[8] See, for instance, Pamela Horn, *High Society: The English Social Elite, 1880–1914* (Stroud: Alan Sutton, 1992). The then duke of Westminster recommended walking on the outside of the staircase when engaging in nocturnal adventures, because it creaks less (p. 137).

most people were concerned, society before 1914 was sexually repressive. The majority had apparently internalized the norms preached in church and chapel, which was the best accommodation they could make, especially women, who would bear the costs of an illicit pregnancy and who could secure a home and a share of a weekly wage only within traditional marriage.

Even this does not quite capture the whole situation. Social changes associated with industrialization and urbanization, especially relating to the employment of single women, were stirring a premonitory reaction against bourgeois convention before the First World War. In the 1930s Magnus Hirschfield looked back and noted this. He saw that morality had been starting to loosen and remarked in an unconsciously Marshallian way that nature does not make leaps. He demonstrated, however, that war conditions raised this development to "the realm of the fantastic."[9] In terms of prevailing morality the change *was* fantastic. After the briefest initial pause, traditional values went out of the window. Within weeks, according to two other authorities writing in the 1930s, Fischer and Dubois, "an almost universal orgy of sexual licence and debauchery" spread across Europe.[10] Millions of men resorted to prostitutes, with official sanction and supervision. Women at home turned, in what were clearly unprecedented numbers, to adultery and prostitution. As the war continued, such behavior became more flagrant. Venereal disease became epidemic.

All this was astonishing in view of previous attitudes

[9] Magnus Hirschfield, *The Sexual History of the World War* (New York: Panurge Press, 1934), p. 11. See also H. C. Fischer and E. X. Dubois, *Sexual Life during the World War* (London: Francis Aldor, 1937).
[10] Fischer and Dubois, *Sexual Life*, p. 7.

and practices. Whether it astonishes as a feature of human behavior depends on what one expects on the part of vast numbers of young men suddenly uprooted from their communities and exposed not only to the licentious chatter of the barrack room but to the imminent prospect of being maimed or slaughtered. With this an all-too-likely fate, even the high risk of venereal disease was not enough to ensure restraint. From a conventional point of view, the willingness of women to follow suit is more surprising, but however much individuals declined to admit it in their later years, it is well recorded. A mood of abandon, which according to circumstances was either selfless sacrifice to one's doomed lover or outright promiscuity, swept across Europe behind the lines of the trenches. Admittedly, not everything from the past was swept away. There was an outbreak of bigamy that can be attributed to women's residual reluctance to engage in sexual relations without a wedding ring. Yet altogether the change amounted to an alteration in European culture that was nothing short of spectacular.

Marshall and Hirschfield were overinsistent on the analogy that nature never makes leaps. Nature may refrain, but culture comes close to leaping at times. The long and short of it is that, while culture usually creeps from one equilibrium to the next, as minor changes in costs and rewards take effect, and so is never genuinely the same thing from one generation to the next, a shock will every so often quickly move it a great distance from the point of origin. A reversal of the new influences may return behavior some way toward the old norms, though not the whole way, as may be seen from the social history of the interwar period. The forces at work lie outside culture itself. As to economic development, culture may act as a brake or filter but is seldom likely to be the original source of change, and treating it as the active ingredient should be done only with caution.[11] To borrow once again Walter Bagehot's celebrated remark about Lombard Street, cultures are usually dull but sometimes very agitated.

[11] Cf. Eric L. Jones, *Growth Recurring: Economic Change in World History*, 2d ed. (Ann Arbor: University of Michigan Press, 2000), p. 106.

Bibliography

Abramson, Paul R., and Ronald Inglehart. *Value Change in Global Perspective*. Ann Arbor: University of Michigan Press, 1995.

Allen, Robert C. "Agricultural Productivity and Rural Incomes in England and the Yangtze Delta, c. 1620–c. 1820." 2003. www.econ.ku.dk/Zeuthen.

Altman, Morris. "Culture, Human Agency, and Economic Theory: Culture as a Determinant of Material Welfare." *Journal of Socio-Economics* 30 (2001): 379–91.

Amis, Kingsley. *Memoirs*. London: Penguin, 1992.

Anderson, Kym. "Wine's New World." *Foreign Policy* 136 (May–Jun 2003): 47–54.

Basu, Kaushik, et al. "The Growth and Decay of Custom." *Explorations in Economic History* 24 (1987): 1–21.

Bauer, Peter. *From Subsistence to Exchange*. Princeton: Princeton University Press, 2000.

Bellin, Eva. "The Political-Economic Conundrum: The Affinity of Economic and Political Reform in the Middle East and North Africa." *Carnegie Papers* 53 (Nov 2004).

Bian, Wen-Qiang, and L. Robin Keller. "Chinese and Americans Agree on What Is Fair, but Disagree on What Is Best in Societal

Decisions Affecting Health and Safety Risks." *Risk Analysis* 19 (1999): 439–52.

Blaise, Clark. *Sir Sandford Fleming and the Creation of Standard Time.* London: Weidenfeld & Nicolson, 2000.

Blum, Ulrich, and Leonard Dudley. "Standardised Latin and Medieval Economic Growth." *European Review of Economic History* 7 (2003): 213–38.

Broadie, Alexander. *The Scottish Enlightenment.* Edinburgh: Birlinn, 2001.

Brown, Rajeswary Ampalavanar. *Capital and Entrepreneurship in South-East Asia.* New York: St. Martin's Press, 1994.

Bud-Frierman, Lisa, ed. *Information Acumen: The Understanding and Use of Knowledge in Business.* London: Routledge, 1994.

Burke, Jason. *Al-Qaeda: Casting a Shadow of Terror.* London: I. B. Tauris, 2003.

Burne, Jerome. "Highly Selective Sex." *Financial Times Magazine,* 13 Sep 2003.

Byas, Hugh. *The Japanese Enemy.* London: Hodder & Stoughton, 1942.

Cairncross, Frances. *The Death of Distance: How the Communications Revolution Will Change Our Lives.* Boston: Harvard Business School Press, 1997.

Casson, Mark C. *Economics of Business Culture: Game Theory, Transaction Costs and Economic Performance.* Oxford: Clarendon Press, 1991.

———. "The Historical Significance of Information Costs." Mimeo, Reading University, 1995.

Caute, David. *The Dancer Defects: The Struggle for Cultural Supremacy during the Cold War.* New York: Oxford University Press, 2003.

Chabal, Patrick, and Jean-Pascal Daloz. *Africa Works: Disorder as*

Political Instrument. Oxford: International African Institute/James Currey, 1999.

Chang, Jung. *Wild Swans.* London: Flamingo, 1993.

Child, M.T.H. *Farms, Fairs and Felonies: Life on the Hampshire-Wiltshire Border 1769–1830.* Andover, U.K.: privately printed, 1967.

Chow, Gregory C. "Challenges of China's Economic System for Economic Theory." In Ross Garnaut and Yiping Huang, eds., *Growth without Miracles.* Oxford: Oxford University Press, 2001.

Christman, Henry. *Tin Horns and Calico: An Episode in the Emergence of American Democracy.* New York: Collier Books, 1961.

Cipolla, Carlo. *Literacy and Development in the West.* (Harmondsworth, U.K.: Penguin, 1969.

Clare, George. *Berlin Days, 1946–47.* London: Pan, 1990.

Clark, Gregory. "Economists in Search of Culture: The Unspeakable in Pursuit of the Inedible?" *Historical Methods* 21 (Fall 1988): 161–64.

Coble, Parks M. *Chinese Capitalists in Japan's New Order: The Occupied Lower Yangzi, 1937–1945.* Berkeley: University of California Press, 2003.

Coleman, William Oliver. *Economics and Its Enemies.* Basingstoke, U.K.: Palgrave, 2002.

Colson, A. M. "The Revolt of the Hampshire Agricultural Labourers and Its Causes, 1812–1831." M.A. thesis, London University, n.d. (1936).

Conklin, John E. *Art Crime.* Westport, Conn.: Praeger, 1994.

Conrad, Peter. *Where I Fell to Earth.* London: Chatto & Windus, 1990.

Cowen, Tyler. *In Praise of Commercial Culture.* Cambridge, Mass.: Harvard University Press, 1998.

———. *Creative Destruction: How Globalization Is Changing the World's Cultures.* Princeton: Princeton University Press, 2002.

Crenson, Matthew A. *The Un-Politics of Air Pollution.* Baltimore: Johns Hopkins University Press, 1971.

Crichton, Michael. *Travels.* London: Macmillan, 1988.

Crystal, David. *Language Death.* Cambridge: Cambridge University Press, 2000.

Dasgupta, Ajit. "India's Cultural Values and Economic Development: A Comment." *Economic Development and Cultural Change* 13 (1964): 100–102.

David, Paul A. "Understanding the Economics of QWERTY: The Necessity of History." In William N. Parker, ed., *Economic History and the Modern Economist.* Oxford: Blackwell, 1986.

Davie, Grace. *Europe: The Exceptional Case.* London: Darton, Longman & Todd, 2002.

Dawson, Doyne. "The Assault on Eurocentric History." *Journal of the Historical Society* 3 (2003): 403–27.

Deane, John Bathurst. *The Worship of the Serpent Traced throughout the World.* London: J. G. & F. Rivington, 1833.

Deng, Gang. *Development versus Stagnation.* Westport, Conn.: Greenwood Press, 1993.

———. *The Premodern Chinese Economy: Structural Equilibrium and Capitalist Sterility.* London: Routledge, 1999.

Diamond, Jared. *The Rise and Fall of the Third Chimpanzee.* London: Vintage, 1992.

Dixon, R.M.W. *The Rise and Fall of Languages.* Cambridge: Cambridge University Press, 1997.

Eagleton, Terry. *The Gatekeeper: A Memoir.* London: Allen Lane/ Penguin, 2001.

Eberhart, Nicholas. "Some Strategic Implications of Asian/Eurasian Demographic Trends." Harvard Center for Population and Development Studies Working Paper 14 # 8, Nov 2004.

Edgerton, Robert B. *Sick Societies: Challenging the Myth of Primitive Harmony.* New York: Free Press, 1992.

Ellickson, Robert C. *Order without Law*. Cambridge, Mass.: Harvard University Press, 1991.

Faulk, Henry. *Group Captives: The Re-Education of German Prisoners-of-War in Britain, 1945–48*. London: Chatto & Windus, 1977.

Feuerwerker, Albert. *China's Early Industrialization: Sheng Hsuan-Huai (1844–1916) and Mandarin Enterprise*. New York: Atheneum, 1970.

Field, Frank. *Neighbours from Hell*. London: Politico, 2003.

Finn, James, ed. *Global Economics and Religion*. New Brunswick, N.J.: Transaction Books, 1982.

Fischer, David Hackett. *Albion's Seed: Four British Folkways in America*. New York: Oxford University Press, 1989.

Fischer, H. C., and E. X. Dubois. *Sexual Life during the World War*. London: Francis Aldor, 1937.

Fletcher, Richard. *The Barbarian Conversion: From Paganism to Christianity*. New York: Holt, 1998.

Frank, Robert H. *Passions within Reasons: The Strategic Role of the Emotions*. New York: W. W. Norton, 1988.

Frank, Robert, and Philip Cook. *The Winner-Take-All Society*. New York: Free Press, 1995.

Frater, Alexander. *Chasing the Monsoon*. London: Penguin, 1991.

Gatty, Harold. *Nature Is Your Guide*. London: Collins, 1958.

Geertz, Clifford. *The Interpretation of Culture*. New York: Basic Books, 1973.

Gifford, Don. *The Farthest Shore: A Natural History of Perception*. London: Faber & Faber, 1990.

Godley, Andrew. *Jewish Immigrant Entrepreneurship in New York and London 1880–1914: Enterprise and Culture*. Basingstoke, U.K.: Palgrave, 2001.

Goldsmith, Raymond W. *Premodern Financial Systems: A Historical Comparative Study*. Cambridge: Cambridge University Press, 1987.

Goodkind, Daniel M. "Creating New Traditions in Modern Chinese Populations: Aiming for Birth in the Year of the Dragon." *Population & Development Review* 17/4 (1991): 663–86.

Goodwin, Godfrey. *The Private World of Ottoman Women*. London: Saqi Books, 1997.

Goudsblom, Johan, Eric Jones, and Stephen Mennell. *The Course of Human History: Economic Growth, Social Process, and Civilization*. Armonk, N.Y.: M. E. Sharpe, 1996.

Green, Michael. *Nobody Hurt in Small Earthquake*. London: Bantam Books, 1991.

Greif, Avner. "Cultural Beliefs and the Organization of Society: A Historical and Theoretical Reflection on Collectivist and Individualist Societies." *Journal of Political Economy* 102 (1994): 912–50.

Gunderson, Gerald A. *A New Economic History of America*. New York: McGraw-Hill, 1976.

Gurr, T. R. "Historical Trends in Violent Crime: A Critical Review of Evidence." *Crime and Justice* 3 (1981): 295–355.

Hallpike, C. R. *The Principles of Social Evolution*. Oxford: Clarendon Press, 1986.

Hardin, Russell. *One for All: The Logic of Group Conflict*. Princeton: Princeton University Press, 1995.

Harding, Mike. *A Little Book of the Green Man*. London: Aurum Press, 1998.

Harrison, Lawrence, and Samuel Huntington, eds. *Culture Matters: How Values Shape Human Progress*. New York: Basic Books, 2000.

Harrisson, Tom. *World Within: A Borneo Story*. Singapore: Oxford University Press, 1984.

Hartwell, R. M. *The Industrial Revolution and Economic Growth*. London: Methuen, 1971.

Hartz, Louis, ed. *The Founding of New Societies.* New York: Harcourt, Brace & World, 1964.

Headrick, Daniel R. *When Information Comes of Age: Technologies of Knowledge in the Age of Reason and Revolution, 1700–1850.* New York: Oxford University Press, 2000.

Henderson, David. *Misguided Virtue: False Notions of Corporate Social Responsibility.* London: Institute of Economic Affairs, 2001.

Herskovits, M. J. *Economic Anthropology.* New York: W. W. Norton, 1963.

Hirschfield, Magnus. *The Sexual History of the World War.* New York: Panurge Press, 1934.

Hobsbawm, Eric. *Interesting Times: A Twentieth-Century Life.* London: Allen Lane/Penguin, 2002.

Hobson, John. *The Eastern Origins of Western Civilisation.* Cambridge: Cambridge University Press, 2004.

Horioka, Charles Yuji. "Why Is Japan's Household Saving Rate So High?" *Journal of the Japanese and International Economies* 4 (1990): 49–92.

Horn, Pamela. *High Society: The English Social Elite, 1880–1914.* Stroud, U.K.: Alan Sutton, 1992.

Hostetler, John A. *Amish Society.* Baltimore: Johns Hopkins University Press, 1980.

Howarth, David. *Tahiti: A Paradise Lost.* New York: Viking, 1984.

Howell, David. "Don't Blame Asian Values." *Prospect*, Oct 1998, pp. 14–15.

Hughes, Barry B. *World Futures.* Baltimore: Johns Hopkins University Press, 1987.

Hughes, Jonathan. "A World Elsewhere: The Importance of Starting English." Mimeo, Northwestern University, 1985.

Huntington, Samuel. *The Clash of Civilizations and the Remaking of World Order.* New York: Simon & Schuster, 1996.

———. "The Hispanic Challenge." *Foreign Policy*, Mar–Apr 2004 (Internet version).

Hutton, Ronald. *The Pagan Religions of the Ancient British Isles*. Oxford: Blackwell, 1991.

———. *The Stations of the Sun: A History of Ritual in Britain*. Oxford: Oxford University Press, 1996.

Huxley, Elspeth. *Love among the Daughters*. London: Quality Book Club, 1968.

Hwang, Alvin, et al. "The Silent Chinese: The Influence of Face and *Kiasuism* on Student Feedback-Seeking Behaviors." *Journal of Management Education* 28 (Feb 2002): 70–98.

Innis, H. A. *Empire and Communications*. Oxford: Clarendon Press, 1950.

Islamoglu, Huri, and Peter C. Perdue. "Introduction." *Journal of Early Modern History* 5 (2001): 271–81.

Jefferies, Richard. *The Amateur Poacher*. Oxford: Oxford University Press, 1978.

Johnston, Douglas, and Cynthia Sampson, eds. *Religion, the Missing Dimension of Statecraft*. New York: Oxford University Press, 1994.

Jones, David M. *Political Development in Pacific Asia*. Cambridge: Polity Press, 1997.

———. "Out of Bali: Cybercaliphate Rising." *National Interest*, Spring 2003, pp. 75–85.

Jones David M., and David Brown. "Singapore and the Myth of the Liberalizing Middle Class." *Pacific Review* 7 (1994): 79–87.

Jones, Eric L. "Subculture and Market." *Economic Development and Cultural Change* 32/4 (1984): 873–79.

———. "The History of Natural Resource Exploitation in the Western World." *Research in Economic History*, Suppl. 6 (1991): 235–52.

———. "Asia's Fate: A Response to the Singapore School." *National Interest*, Spring 1994, pp. 18–28.

———. "Culture and Its Relationship to Economic Change." *Journal of Institutional and Theoretical Economics* 151/2 (1995): 269–85.

———. "Technology, the Human Niche and Darwinian Explanation." In Eric Jones and Vernon Reynolds, eds., *Survival and Religion: Biological Evolution and Cultural Change*. Chichester, U.K.: John Wiley, 1995.

———. "Through the Garbage Can, Darkly." *National Interest*, Fall 1996, pp. 97–101.

———. "The European Background." In S. L. Engerman and Robert E. Gallman, eds., *The Cambridge Economic History of the United States*. Cambridge: Cambridge University Press, 1996.

———. "Cultural Nostalgia." *International Studies Review* 1/3 (1999): 131–34.

———. *Growth Recurring*. 2d ed. Ann Arbor: University of Michigan Press, 2000.

———. "The Case for a Shared World Language." In Mark Casson and Andrew Godley, eds., *Cultural Factors in Economic Growth*. Berlin: Springer-Verlag, 2000.

———. "A Long-Term Appraisal of Country Risk." In Ross Garnaut and Yiping Huang, eds., *Growth without Miracles: Readings on the Chinese Economy in the Age of Reform*. Oxford: Oxford University Press, 2001.

———. *The Record of Global Economic Development*. Cheltenham, U.K.: Edward Elgar, 2002.

———. *The European Miracle*. 3d ed. Cambridge: Cambridge University Press, 2003.

———. "The East Asian Miracle." *Business History* 45 (2003): 119–24.

————. "Environment: Historical Overview." In Joel Mokyr, ed., *The Oxford Encyclopedia of Economic History*, vol. 2. New York: Oxford University Press, 2003.

————. "China: A Cautionary Note from Development History." In Loren Brandt and Tom Rawski, eds., *China's Economic Transition*. Forthcoming.

————, ed. *Agriculture and Economic Growth in England 1650–1815*. London: Methuen, 1967.

Jones, Eric, Lionel Frost, and Colin White. *Coming Full Circle: An Economic History of the Pacific Rim*. Boulder, Colo.: Westview Press, 1993.

Jones, Eric L., and Sylvia B. Jones. "The Book Industry." In *The Oxford Encyclopedia of Economic History*, vol. 1. New York: Oxford University Press, 2003.

Kacelnik, Alex. "The Sciences of Risk." *Wissenschaftskolleg zu Berlin Jahrbuch*, 2001/2002, pp. 363–64.

Karsten, Peter. "'Bottomed on Justice': A Reappraisal of Critical Legal Studies Scholarship Concerning Breaches of Labor Contracts by Quitting or Firing in Britain and the U.S., 1630–1889." *American Journal of Legal History* 34 (1990): 213–61.

Kavanagh, P. J. *The Perfect Stranger*. London: HarperCollins, 1991.

Keeley, Lawrence H. *War before Civilization: The Myth of the Peaceful Savage*. New York: Oxford University Press, 1996.

Kerr, Alex. *Dogs and Demons: The Fall of Modern Japan*. London: Penguin, 2001.

Killick, Tony, ed. *The Flexible Economy*. London: Routledge, 1995.

Kim, Dae Jung. "Is Culture Destiny? The Myth of Asia's Anti-Democratic Values." *Foreign Affairs* 73 (2004): 189–94.

Kirwen, Michael C. *African Widows*. Maryknoll, N.Y.: Orbis Books, 1979.

Knight, Jack. *Institutions and Social Conflict*. Cambridge: Cambridge University Press, 1992.

Krugman, Paul. "The Myth of Asia's Miracle." *Foreign Affairs* 73 (Nov–Dec 1994): 62–78.

Kuran, Timur. "The Unthinkable and the Unthought." *Rationality and Society* 5 (1993): 473–505.

———. *Private Truths, Public Lies.* Cambridge, Mass.: Harvard University Press, 1995.

———. "Islam and Underdevelopment: An Old Puzzle Revisited." *Journal of Institutional and Theoretical Economics* 153 (1997): 41–71.

Lal, Deepak. *Unintended Consequences: The Impact of Factor Endowments, Culture, and Politics on Long-Run Economic Performance.* Cambridge, Mass.: MIT Press, 1998.

———. "India." In Peter Bernholz and Roland Vaubel, eds., *Political Competition, Innovation and Growth in the History of Asian Civilizations.* Cheltenham, U.K.: Edward Elgar, 2004.

Landes, David. *The Wealth and Poverty of Nations.* New York: W. W. Norton, 1998.

Lebrecht, Norman. *Covent Garden: The Untold Story. Dispatches from the English Culture War, 1945–2000.* London: Simon & Schuster UK, 2000.

Lee, Kuan Yew. "The East Asian Way." *New Perspectives Quarterly* 9 (1992): 4–13.

Lewthwaite, G. R. "Man and the Sea in Early Tahiti: A Maritime Economy through European Eyes." *Pacific Viewpoint* 7 (1966): 28–53.

Li, Xiaorong. "'Asian Values' and the Universality of Human Rights." *Business and Society Review*, nos. 102/103 (1998): 81–87.

Liebowitz, S. J., and Stephen E. Margolis. "The Fable of the Keys." *Journal of Law and Economics* 33 (1990): 1–25.

Lindert, Peter. "Voice and Growth: Was Churchill Right?" *Journal of Economic History* 63 (2003): 315–50.

Little, Reg., and Warren Reed. *The Confucian Renaissance*. Annandale, Australia: Federation Press, 1989.

Lomax, Eric. *The Railway Man*. London: Vintage, 1996.

Lorenz, Dagmar. "How the World Became Smaller." *History Today*, Nov 1996, pp. 45–50.

Macdonell, A. G. *England, Their England*. London: Macmillan, 1933.

MacSwan, Norman. *The Man Who Read the East Wind: A Biography of Richard Hughes*. Kenthurst, Australia: Kangaroo Press, 1982.

Maddison, Angus. "Economic Progress: The Last Half Century in Historical Perspective." In Ian Castles, ed., *Facts and Fancies of Human Development*. Academy of the Social Sciences in Australia, Occasional Papers 1. Canberra: ASSA, 2000.

Magee, Gary. "A Study of the Abandonment of Superior Technologies and the Reversibility of Technological Change." B.Ec. honors dissertation, Department of Economic History, La Trobe University, 1990.

Maine, Henry. *Dissertations on Early Law and Custom*. London: John Murray, 1883.

Mamdani, Mahmood. "Whither Political Islam? Understanding the Modern Jihad." *Foreign Affairs*, Jan–Feb 2005, pp. 148–55.

Man, John. *Alpha Beta: How Our Alphabet Shaped the Western World*. London: Headline, 2000.

Manning, Patrick, et al. "American Historical Review Forum: Asia and Europe in the World Economy." *American Historical Review* 107 (2002): 419–80.

Marriott, Edward. *The Lost Tribe: A Search through the Jungles of Papua New Guinea*. London: Picador, 1997.

Marshall, Alfred. *Principles of Economics*. London: Macmillan, 1961.

Marshall, Sybil. *A Pride of Tigers*. London: Penguin, 1995.

Mayhew, Anne. "Culture: Core Concept under Attack." *Journal of Economic Issues* 21 (1987): 587–603.

McCulloch, J. R. *McCulloch's Universal Gazetteer*. New York: Harper & Bros., 1844–45.

Moisy, Claude. "Myths of the Global Information Village." *Foreign Policy* 107 (Summer 1997): 78–87.

Mokyr, Joel. "Disparities, Gaps, and Abysses." *Economic Development and Cultural Change* 33 (1984): 173–77.

———. "The Enduring Riddle of the *European Miracle:* The Enlightenment and the Industrial Revolution." Mimeo, Northwestern University, 2002.

Morishima, Michio. *Why Has Japan "Succeeded"? Western Technology and the Japanese Ethos*. Cambridge: Cambridge University Press, 1982.

Morris, Jan. *Fifty Years of Europe*. London: Penguin, 1997.

Morris, Richard. *Churches in the Landscape*. London: J. M. Dent, 1989.

Mortimer, John. *Clinging to the Wreckage*. Harmondsworth, U.K.: Penguin, 1982.

Muhlberger, Steven, and Phil Paine. "Democracy's Place in World History." *Journal of World History* 4 (1993): 23–45.

Munz, Peter. "The Two Worlds of Anne Salmond in Postmodern Fancy Dress." *New Zealand Journal of History* 28/1 (1994): 60–75.

Nathan, Andrew J. "Is Chinese Culture Distinctive? A Review Article." *Journal of Asian Studies* 52 (1993): 923–36.

Noland, Marcus. "Religion, Culture, and Economic Performance." http://www.iie.com/publications/wp/2003/03–8.pdf.

North, Douglass C. *Understanding the Process of Economic Change*. Princeton: Princeton University Press, 2005.

Olson, Mancur. *The Rise and Decline of Nations*. New Haven: Yale University Press, 1982.

Phelps Brown, Henry. *The Origins of Trade Union Power*. Oxford: Clarendon Press, 1983.

Pomeranz, Kenneth. *The Great Divergence*. Princeton: Princeton University Press, 2000.

Porter, Michael, and Victor Millar. "How Information Gives You Competitive Advantage." *Harvard Business Review*, Jul–Aug 1985, pp. 149–60.

Posner, Richard A. *The Economics of Justice*. Cambridge, Mass.: Harvard University Press, 1981.

Price, Charles A. "Ethnic Intermixture in Australia." *People and Place* 1 (1993): 6–8.

Pryce-Jones, David. *The Closed Circle: An Interpretation of the Arabs*. London: Paladin, 1990.

Pun, Ngai. "Becoming Dagongmei [Working Girls]: The Politics of Identity and Difference in Reform China." *China Journal* 42 (1999): 1–18.

Raby, Geoff. *Making Rural Australia*. Melbourne: Oxford University Press, 1996.

Ravault, René-Jean. "Is There a Bin Laden in the Audience? Considering the Events of September 11 as a Possible Boomerang Effect of the Globalization of US Mass Communication." *Prometheus* 20 (2002): 295–300.

Rawski, Thomas G. "Social Capabilities and Chinese Economic Growth." Mimeo, University of Pittsburgh, 2002.

Read, Donald. *The Power of News: The History of Reuters 1849–1989*. Oxford: Oxford University Press, 1992.

Rowse, A. L. *The Case Books of Simon Forman*. London: Picador Pan Books, 1976.

Sachs, Jeffrey, and Andrew Warner. "Natural Resource Abundance and Economic Growth." Harvard Institute for International Development, Discussion Paper 517a, Oct 1995.

Sack, P. L. "The Triumph of Colonialism." In P. L. Sack, ed., *Prob-*

lems of Choice: Land in Papua New Guinea's Future. Canberra, Australia: ANU Press, 1974.

Samuelson, Robert J. "Seeking Capitalism's Spirit." *Australian Financial Review*, 19 Jan 2001.

Sandall, Roger. *The Culture Cult: Designer Tribalism and Other Essays*. Boulder, Colo.: Westview Press, 2001.

Schlicht, Ekkehart. *On Custom in the Economy*. Oxford: Clarendon Press, 1998.

———. "Custom and Competition." In Tiziano Raffaelli et al., eds., *The Elgar Companion to Alfred Marshall*. Cheltenham U.K.: Edward Elgar, forthcoming.

Schofield, R. S. "Dimensions of Illiteracy, 1750–1850." *Explorations in Economic History* 10 (1973): 437–54.

Schwartz, Peter. *Inevitable Surprises*. London: Simon & Schuster/ Free Press, 2003.

Sen, Amartya. "More than 100 Million Women Are Missing." *New York Review of Books*, 20 Dec 1990.

———. "Asian Values and Economic Growth." In UNESCO, *World Culture Report 1998: Culture, Creativity and Markets*. Paris: UNESCO Publications, 1998.

Sharpe, J. A. *Bewitching of Anne Gunter*. London: Routledge, 2000.

Simon, Julian. *The Effects of Income on Fertility*. Chapel Hill, N.C.: Carolina Population Center, 1974.

Simoons, Frederick J. *Eat Not This Flesh: Food Avoidances from Prehistory to the Present*. 2d ed. Madison: University of Wisconsin Press, 1994.

Singer, Marshall R. "Language Follows Power: The Linguistic Free Market in the Old Soviet Bloc." *Foreign Affairs* 77 (Jan–Feb 1998): 19–24.

Smith, Adam. *The Wealth of Nations*. London: J. M. Dent, 1910.

Snell, K.D.M. "The Culture of Local Xenophobia." *Social History* 28 (2003): 1–30.

Sowell, Thomas. *The Economics and Politics of Race: An International Perspective.* New York: William Morrow, 1983.

Spencer, Robyn. "Australia: Worth Preserving or Past Its Use-by Date?" In Steve Vizard, et al., eds., *Australia's Population Challenge.* Camberwell, Australia: Penguin, 2003.

Spizzica, Maria. "Cultural Differences within 'Western' and 'Eastern' Education." Paper presented to the First National Conference on Tertiary Literacy, Victoria University of Technology, Melbourne, 15–16 Mar 1996.

Stark Rodney. *The Rise of Christianity: A Sociologist Reconsiders History.* Princeton: Princeton University Press, 1996.

Steinberg, Theodore. *Nature Incorporated: Industrialization and the Waters of New England.* Cambridge: Cambridge University Press, 1991.

"Symposium: The New World of the Gothic Fox: Culture and Economy in English and Spanish America." *Partisan Review* 621 2 (1995): 179–233.

Temin, Peter. "Is It Kosher to Talk about Culture?" *Journal of Economic History* 57/2 (1997): 267–87.

Tennant, Kylie. *Australia: Her Story.* London: Pan Books, 1964.

Thompson, E. P. *Whigs and Hunters.* London: Penguin, 1977.

Thurow, Lester C. "Globalization: The Product of a Knowledge-Based Economy." *Annals of the American Academy of Political and Social Science* 570 (Jul 2000): 19–31.

Turner, Frederick Jackson. *The Frontier in American History.* New York: Henry Holt & Co., 1920.

Utley, Garrick. "The Shrinking of Foreign News: From Broadcast to Narrowcast." *Foreign Affairs* 76 (Mar–Apr 1997): 2–10.

Van Zanden, Jan Luiten. "The 'Revolt of the Early Modernists' and the 'First Modern Economy': An Assessment." *Economic History Review* 55 (2002): 619–41.

Vargas Llosa, Mario. "The Culture of Liberty." *Foreign Policy*, Jan–Feb 2001 (Internet version).

"Vargas Llosa on Culture and the New International Order." *La Trobe University Bulletin*, Sep–Oct 2002.

Veliz, Claudio. "A World Made in England." *Quadrant*, Mar 1983, pp. 8–19.

Wallraff, Barbara. "What Global Language?" *Atlantic Monthly*, Nov 2000, pp. 52–66.

Waswo, Ann. *Modern Japanese Society 1868–1944*. Oxford: Oxford University Press, 1996.

Waterhouse, Keith. *City Lights*. London: Hodder & Stoughton, 1994.

Watkins, Susan Cotts. *From Provinces into Nations: Demographic Integration in Western Europe, 1870–1960*. Princeton: Princeton University Press, 1991.

Watson, James L., ed. *McDonald's in East Asia*. Stanford: Stanford University Press, 1997.

Webb, Walter Prescott. *The Great Frontier*. Boston: Houghton Mifflin, 1952.

Wilfrid, Blunt. *The Compleat Naturalist: A Life of Linnaeus*. London: Collins, 1971.

Wilhelm, Richard. *Chinese Economic Psychology*. New York: Garland, 1982.

Williamson, Jeffrey. "Living Standards in Asia before 1940." In A.J.H. Latham and Heita Kawakatsu, eds., *Asia Pacific Dynamism 1550–2000*. London: Routledge, 2000.

Witt, Ulrich. "Evolution and Stability of Cooperation without Enforceable Contracts." *Kyklos* 39 (1986): 245–66.

Wood, Forrest G. *The Arrogance of Faith: Christianity and Race in America from the Colonial Era to the Twentieth Century*. New York: Alfred A. Knopf, 1990.

Woodhead, Linda, and Paul Heelas. *The Spiritual Revolution: Why Religion Is Giving Way to Spirituality.* Oxford: Blackwell, 2004.

Zakaria, Fareed. "Asian Values." *Foreign Policy*, Nov–Dec 2002. (Internet version.)

——. *The Future of Freedom: Illiberal Democracy at Home and Abroad.* New York: W. W. Norton, 2003.

Zuboff, Shosanna. *In the Age of the Smart Machine.* Oxford: Heinemann, 1988.

Index

affluenza, 13, 180
Afghanistan, 87
Africa, 8, 14, 37, 37n6, 38n8,
 59n9, 72, 87, 150n14, 153, 210;
 Nigeria, 18, 125, 209; South
 Africa, 125
African widows' syndrome, 37, 39
Al Jezeera, 213
Allen, Robert, 113–14, 115
Al-Qaeda, 209, 210
Altman, Morris, 82–83
Amis, Kingsley, 239
Amish, 40–43, 153
Amnesty International, 213
Ardeshir, Daraius, xiv
Argentina, 163
Armani, Giorgio, 189
arts and entertainment, 184, 185,
 196, 200, 205–8, chapter 9 pas-
 sim; business funding of, 235–
 36
Asian crisis, 162, 166, 217
Asian values, 12, 13, 162, 164–
 68, 178–82, 188, 217, 243
Ataturk, Kemal, 47

Australia, 65–6, 88, 92, 129n30,
 131, 136, 151, 152, 154–58,
 163, 224–27, 233, 234, 240,
 242n, 244; migration to or
 from, 155–58; Queensland,
 155
avian influenza, 105

Bagehot, Walter, 48, 271
Bauer, Peter, 10, 11, 152
Berger, Brigitte, 5, 6
Biddulph, John, 245
Bloch, Marc, 11–12, 122, 131,
 137n2
book trade, 125–26
Borneo, 57–58
Boylan, Brian, 195–96
Braudel, Fernand, 228
Brazil, 151, 162, 163, 205–6, 208
Brecht, Bertolt, 73
Britain, 135–45, 156, 168n11,
 178, 179, 183, 194, 201, 230,
 232, 234, 237–39. *See also*
 England
Bruckner, Anton, 246